Currency Strategy

Wiley Finance Series

Currency Strategy

The Practitioner's Guide to Currency Investing, Hedging and Forecasting

Callum Henderson

JOHN WILEY & SONS, LTD

Published 2002   John Wiley & Sons Ltd,
The Atrium, Southern Gate, Chichester,
West Sussex PO19 8SQ, England

Telephone   (+44) 1243 779777

Email (for orders and customer service enquiries): cs-books@wiley.co.uk
Visit our Home Page on www.wileyeurope.com or www.wiley.com

Copyright © 2002   Callum Henderson

Reprinted March 2004

This publication is designed to provide accurate and authoritative information in regard to the
subject matter covered. It is sold on the understanding that the Publisher is not engaged in
rendering professional services. If professional advice or other expert assistance is required, the
services of a competent professional should be sought.

Other Wiley Editorial Offices

John Wiley & Sons Inc., 111 River Street, Hoboken, NJ 07030, USA

Jossey-Bass, 989 Market Street, San Francisco, CA 94103-1741, USA

Wiley-VCH Verlag GmbH, Boschstr. 12, D-69469 Weinheim, Germany

John Wiley & Sons Australia Ltd, 33 Park Road, Milton, Queensland 4064, Australia

John Wiley & Sons (Asia) Pte Ltd, 2 Clementi Loop #02-01, Jin Xing Distripark, Singapore 129809

John Wiley & Sons Canada Ltd, 22 Worcester Road, Etobicoke, Ontario, Canada M9W 1L1

Library of Congress Cataloging-in-Publication Data

British Library Cataloguing in Publication Data

A catalogue record for this book is available from the British Library

ISBN 0-470-84684-4

Typeset in 10/12pt Times by TechBooks, New Delhi, India
Printed and bound in Great Britain by Antony Rowe, Chippenham, Wiltshire
This book is printed on acid-free paper responsibly manufactured from sustainable forestry
in which at least two trees are planted for each one used for paper production.

Dedicated to Tamara, Judy and Gus

Contents

Acknowledgements

In getting this book from the first stage of an idea to the printed edition, I am greatly indebted to Sally Smith and Rachael Wilkie of John Wiley & Sons publishing company for the initial invitation to write on this topic and subsequently for their advice, encouragement and diligent editorial work. It is a pleasure to work with people as professional as these.

Greg Edwards and Emmanuel Acar, experts in their respective fields of corporate and investor currency risk management, were kind enough to read Chapters 7–9 and make corrections, suggestions and constructive criticism, without which this work would have undoubtedly been the poorer. TJ Marta provided charts and good advice. Specific thanks must go to Anil Prasad for allowing me the time to complete the book.

My deepest gratitude goes to my wife Tamara, for her patience, love and understanding while I attempted to write this book on top of a full-time job as a currency strategist. I am also as ever indebted to my father and to the memory of my mother, who battled to get me to read at an early age, an effort that successfully unleashed an avalanche of reading, inquiry and travel. What little or otherwise I have become is down to their dedication and love and a very simple rule — to fail is forgivable but to fail to try is not.

More generally, and outside of the specific framework of this book, anyone's knowledge of financial markets is a reflection both of their experience and of their interaction with market participants. Theory is fine but there is nothing like watching and listening how it is done at the sharp end. In my career, I have been fortunate enough to come across a broad spectrum of experts in their respective fields, in central banks, in dealing rooms and within government and international organizations. They in turn have been kind enough to give of their time and their views. Space, consistency and in some cases the respected need for anonymity require that these do not be named individually. Suffice to say they know who they are and it is my pleasure and privilege to know them.

Last but not least, I wish to thank the reader. Having served in many capacities in my career, in journalism, in business, in analysis and finally in banking, an abiding theme of mine has been to keep a clear focus on the most important person in whatever field one is in — the client. Too many forget this most fundamental aspect of commerce. Thus, in this small way, I thank the reader for taking his or her time to examine the ideas I have presented here and trust that in some measurable way they feel they have benefited from the experience.

Biography

Callum Henderson is head of Emerging EMEA Strategy for a leading US investment bank, based in London, responsible for Emerging EMEA research, FX and Fixed Income Strategy. A widely quoted authority on both emerging and currency markets, Mr Henderson has written articles for a number of leading financial journals and given seminars around the world on global currency markets, in particular on currency crises.

Mr. Henderson is the author of three previous books covering the Asian economic story, Asia Falling, China on the Brink (awarded Best Business Book of 1999 by the Library Journal of the U.S.) and Asian Dawn.

Prior to his current position, Mr. Henderson was part of the Citibank FX Strategy team which has been top-ranked by leading publications, and Manager of FX Analysis – Asia for Standard & Poor's MMS, based in Hong Kong and New York.

Mr. Henderson holds a B.A. Honours in Politics, Economics and French and an M.A. in Middle East Politics and Economics.

The views expressed in this book are those of the author and do not necessarily reflect those of his employer.

Introduction

It is the largest and most important financial market in the world. If you are in business or in finance, it affects just about everything you do, whether you like it or not, whether you know it or not. Along with the interest rate, it is the most important price of a free and open economy. It is the fuel of economic trade and liberalization and without it globalization would never have happened. It is also one of the least well understood markets outside of those who choose to follow it in whatever capacity of their profession. It is variously described as the "currency" or "foreign exchange" or "FX" market, and it can be maddening and frustrating, but if you are a senior corporate officer or an institutional investor you are compelled to know what it is, how it works and how it affects you.

It should be stated right at the beginning that this is a book targeted not at the ordinary man or woman on the street but at the currency market practitioners themselves, at those whose "flows" are responsible for moving the market in the first place. The aim of this book is a simple one — to help currency market practitioners, from corporate Treasurers and Chief Executives to hedge funds and "real money" managers, execute more prudent and profitable currency decisions in their daily business.

This is no small aim and it is certainly not taken lightly. There is of course already a rich literature on the subject of exchange rates, as many readers will no doubt be aware. When you took business courses or did an economics degree at whatever level you probably had to wade your way through several of these. Why then the need for yet another book on exchange rates? The frank answer is that I felt there was a gaping hole in that "rich" literature, a massive omission that was intolerable and had to be addressed. Simply put, few if any of these works appeared to be aimed at the actual people who would have to put the theory into practice and actually execute the currency market transaction. It was as if a bank had written a series of books not for its clients or customers but instead for its own private, intellectual interest. The vast majority of the existing literature on exchange rates appeared to have been written from a very academic or theoretical perspective. To be sure, there are notable exceptions and in any case there is absolutely nothing wrong with academic theory. Few of these however went the extra mile and explained how to translate the theory into currency investing or hedging strategies. My aim here therefore is to address this "gaping hole" and try and do a better job of explaining both currency market theory and practice from the perspective of being a market participant myself, albeit in an advisory capacity.

The currency market is not just my job. It is a passion and interest of mine and has been so for many years now. I started covering it in 1991 as a journalist in the run up to the Sterling crisis the subsequent year and "Black Wednesday", September 16, 1992, when the UK currency was forced out of the Exchange Rate Mechanism (ERM) and promptly collapsed in value. The abiding memory of mine to this day is of the sheer power of the currency market in its ability to "defeat" the might and resolve of such a respected central bank as the Bank of England, which gave everything it had in its effort to defend sterling's ERM "floor" against the Deutschmark of 2.7778. It is a memory of currency dealers screaming down the phone, of wave after wave of official intervention to support sterling being swatted aside by the sheer weight of selling pressure. The lesson of this neither is nor should be that financial markets will out in all cases. Rather, it is that the currency market has become so huge that it simply cannot be resisted for any length of time. In the case of "Black Wednesday" — or "White Wednesday" as many would have it subsequently — the UK economy was experiencing a severe recession and thus simply could not tolerate the raising of UK interest rates needed to support sterling and keep it within its ERM band commitment. The economic pain of this interest rate and exchange rate commitment was completely at odds with the economic reality in the UK at that time. Moreover, UK foreign exchange reserves were fast being wiped out in that defensive effort. In 1992, the global currency market's *daily turnover* was the equivalent of USD880 billion, according to the Bank of International Settlements (BIS) tri-annual survey. Thus, the Bank of England's ability to intervene to support sterling, albeit in the billions, was dwarfed by the size of the forces opposing it. As of the 1998 BIS survey, daily turnover had increased to some USD1.5 *trillion*, subsequently falling back to USD1.2 trillion in the 2001 survey in the wake of the creation of the Euro.

Needless to say, the Bank of England has certainly not been alone in its inability to defeat the power of the currency market. The following year, the remaining members of the ERM were forced under truly extraordinary pressure to abandon the narrow 2.25% bands required by the ERM commitment, widening them to 15%. On one day alone, on that Friday, July 30, before the weekend move to capitulate and widen the ERM bands, tens of billions of dollar equivalent were expended in an ultimately futile attempt to support member currencies. Depending on your point of view, even the feared German central bank, the Deutsche Bundesbank had been defeated (though the sceptical maintain that its effort to save the ERM was at best half-hearted). Whatever the case, it was an important lesson; not least that the currency market can act with unparalleled force and ferocity if it is so impelled. There was of course the obvious question — why and how could such extraordinary events happen in the currency market, events that were certainly not predicted by economists and which sometimes did not appear justified by the "fundamentals"?

For me, as for many people in the field, that time was the start of a journey, a journey I suspect without an ultimate destination. One remains forever a student and the capacity for being taken by surprise remains endless. As a senior currency strategist for a global investment bank, the losses that one can incur as a result of making forecasting or recommendation mistakes are not so much financial as reputational, but for that I would argue they are no less painful. As a member of that relatively small group of individuals who for good or ill seek to forecast exchange rates and make currency recommendations, you live or die by your reputation. You do not have the luxury of resorting to vague rhetoric and that is indeed how it should be.

Nonetheless, as anyone who has tried knows, forecasting exchange rates is both an educational and a humbling business. A factor that is deemed a crucial market driver one minute may be spurned the next as irrelevant. Most attempts within economic "fundamental" analysis to analyse exchange rates are based on some form of equilibrium model, which presupposes that there is an ideal or an equilibrium level to which exchange rates will revert. While equilibrium exchange rate models such as those that focus on Purchasing Power Parity (PPP), the monetary and portfolio approaches, and the external balance, real interest rate differentials and the Real Effective Exchange Rate (REER), are extremely useful when trying to predict long-term exchange rate trends, most have a relatively poor track record over a shorter time frame. They provide a framework for currency forecasting and analysis and alert the users of them to important changes in the real economy and how those in turn might affect exchange rates over the medium to long term. For instance, economists would say that an appreciation of a currency's REER value should eventually cause deterioration in a country's external balance, which should lead to a loss of export competitiveness and the eventual need for a REER depreciation of the exchange rate in order to offset that lost competitiveness. The most effective way of achieving this is through a depreciation of the *nominal* exchange rate (as in the one you use when you take a trip to France). For a corporate this may be an invaluable guide as to the long-term exchange rate trend, which they can use to determine the parameters of their budget rates and also to set a strategic hedging policy. What this does not do however is tell the user when these events are likely to happen. It can provide a framework, a corridor, but it is unable to be more specific. In short, such models are limited in their ability to forecast exchange rates over the period on which most currency market practitioners are focused — 1 day to 3 months.

The economics profession usually deals with this inconvenience in one of two ways — either by ignoring it or by dismissing short-term currency moves as "speculative" and therefore not capable of being predicted. It has long been my view that such a response was inadequate and that in order to study currency markets one might therefore have to include other disciplines, albeit within a single analytical framework. Indeed, where economics has for the most part failed to predict such short-term moves, other disciplines such as technical and capital flow analysis have succeeded. Granted, their success is not perfect, but it has been measurably better.

Furthermore, while it has to be stressed that such long-term valuation models are important and useful guides to long-term trends, they are flawed as forecasting tools because the very concept of "equilibrium" is itself flawed. Such a concept is a useful and logical construct, providing a framework around which economic analysis can be built and allowing one to focus on a final outcome. The specifics of that final outcome are likely to remain vague however. While an equilibrium model may be able to tell what the final outcome is likely to be, it will not be able to tell you when that outcome will happen nor what might happen in the getting there, which might change or distort that outcome. Moreover, while the construct of equilibrium may well be close to academic hearts, it seems rarely evident in real life, which remains in a constant state of flux. An equilibrium level relates to a point to which exchange rates, if they are temporarily divergent from it, will revert back. In other words, it relates to an ultimate destination, or a "final outcome" as described above. Markets however are volatile and can fluctuate widely. Yet markets are an expression of economic reality, which means that the economic reality itself fluctuates. In turn, this means that the equilibrium level resulting from that economic reality also fluctuates and instead of being a stationary, single, final outcome is rather a moving target. In economic jargon, the equilibrium level of an exchange rate is both cause and effect of the present level of exchange rates, moving over time, such movement constantly reducing or increasing the present exchange rate's over- or undervaluation relative to that equilibrium. This is not to say that trying to track an equilibrium exchange rate level is not an important exercise. Rather, it is to point out the practical limitations of such equilibrium-based exchange rate models.

As well as examining the limitations of exchange rate models, it is also important to dispose right at the start with a few myths that surround financial markets in general and more specifically the subject of this book, the currency market. Firstly, classical economic theory asserts that market practitioners are "objective", that is they are completely independent of and are not affected by the market conditions in which they operate. Intuitively, we know this to be nonsense. An investor is not only directly affected by present market conditions such as liquidity and volatility but also by past experience. Past successes may make our investor bolder in their future investment decisions, while past losses may make them much more cautious. As John Donne would have it, no man is an island, so the same is true for the market practitioner, who can both be affected by and can affect market conditions. In short, they are both cause and effect. We can see this with that most fundamental of economic principles, supply and demand. Here too, there is no "objectivity". Each is affected by the other — and we know this because if it were not the case price trends could not happen. If they were completely independent of each other, supply would instantly match demand and vice versa, thus stopping a price trend before it had begun. Yet, this is not the case. Price trends across asset and currency markets can last for days, weeks, months or even years.

Another widely held myth is that markets are perfectly "efficient". The suggestion here is that both information availability and distribution are perfect — that all market participants have equal access to available, market-moving information. Furthermore, the assumption of market efficiency is that all market participants are "rational" and are profit-seeking. Like the suggestion of "objectivity", this is also the stuff of nonsense. Information is widely and freely available, but neither its availability nor its distribution is perfect. Indeed, one could argue that the very purpose of currency market practitioners is to get information that others do not have. Equally, the very concept of being "rational" is a subjective one and open to interpretation. Further, currency dealers are "rational" to the extent that they are trying to make a profit. However, cautious investors or corporate Treasurers who are seeking to manage their currency risk are not trying to make a profit. Rather, they are trying to limit any possible loss from their original currency exposure. Central banks and Treasury departments, who also operate within the currency market, are also not for the most part profit-seeking. Trying to impose an all-fits-one approach to explaining exchange rates simply does not work. For this very reason, economics by itself has had mixed results at best in forecasting exchange rates. The dynamics of the currency market are different from other markets and this should be taken into account.

As we have seen, equilibrium exchange rate models help to provide the framework and the direction for long-term exchange rate analysis, but they are for the most part incapable of being more specific or more accurate over a shorter time frame. In trying to forecast short-term exchange rate moves, it may be necessary to use other tools and even other analytical disciplines. Within this book, there are outside of economics four types of analysis that we will look at for this purpose: flow, technical, risk appetite and market psychology. Depending on what kind of currency market practitioner you are, you may view one or more of these analytical disciplines with some scepticism. This is all to the good, for if someone is to use any form of analysis in their daily business they first have to be convinced that it actually works. We will examine these types of analysis in detail in the first four chapters of this book. For instance, market psychology may be thought of as an excessively vague concept incapable of serious analysis or use, yet this is precisely what the field of "behavioural finance" seeks to explain. How else to explain the fact that political events that do not materially affect economic fundamentals can have *lasting* impact on exchange rates, were it not for the fact that such events changed the "psychology" or "sentiment" of the market? In early 1993, the then US Treasury Secretary Lloyd Bentsen was reported as saying that the Japanese yen was undervalued. This statement and others after it led the market to believe that the US was deliberately seeking to devalue the US dollar against the yen in order to reduce the huge US–Japan trade deficit. Whatever the reality, the market convinced itself that this was the case and for two years after that statement the yen rose inexorably against the US dollar. Did economic "fundamentals" play a part? Of course they did. Japan's huge trade and current account surpluses with the US meant that for the dollar–yen exchange rate to remain stable Japan had to export to the US the same amount of capital through its capital account deficit. At times when this was not the case, the yen was bound to appreciate and so it transpired. The trigger, the catalyst for this subsequent yen appreciation was however a change in market sentiment or psychology — and it took another change in market sentiment resulting from the new US Treasury Secretary Robert Rubin's call for an orderly reversal of the dollar weakness for that yen appreciation to reverse.

The subject of technical analysis also draws mixed reactions. While widely followed by currency dealers and the leveraged fund community, many corporate officers and investors appear to regard it with scepticism — and many economists look on it as some form of voodoo or witchcraft. Yet technical analysis or "charting" has a strong following not for any ideological reason, but simply because it "works". Like any other form of analysis, there are technical analysts who are highly regarded by the market for their accuracy in meeting their forecasts, and those that are less successful. The appealing thing however for many market practitioners is that technical analysis has targets at all. While there are important exceptions, too many within the economics profession remain content to talk eloquently if vaguely, attaching a multitude of caveats and in sum coming to no conclusion whatsoever. Needless to say, decisions on whether or not to hedge or invest cannot tolerate such imprecision. Where the strength of equilibrium exchange rate models is in providing a long-term exchange rate view, the strength of technical analysis is in predicting the timing of currency moves. In particular, it can be especially effective in predicting when those fundamentally-based long-term trends may take place.

A more recent addition, at least in its present form, to this group of short-term analytical disciplines is "flow" analysis, which involves the tracking of a bank's client flows, again for the purpose of forecasting short-term exchange rate moves. The benchmark flow analysis product within the industry has been for some time *CitiFX Flows*. The field of behavioural finance has undertaken considerable research into behavioural patterns such as investor herding, which can both be responsible for accelerating short-term trends and also for reversing them. The broad rule of such trends is that the longer they continue the more they become self-fulfilling. This is of course how financial bubbles develop, in whatever kind of market. As the old adage goes, when you find your taxi driver giving you stock tips, it's probably time to get out of the market! We shall look at this recent yet intriguing discipline of flow analysis later in the book.

Most works to date on exchange rates rely purely on "fundamental" analysis, falling back on the traditional exchange rate models. While several of these are notable, most would appear to come up short on two grounds. Firstly, they fail to address the issue of the forecasting inaccuracy of those models. Secondly, few have included other analytical disciplines to try to improve on that forecasting inaccuracy. Crucially, few have tried to see exchange rates from the perspective of the end user of analysis or the currency market practitioner. For those who trade, invest or hedge in the currency market, the bottom line is indeed the bottom line. Fundamental economic analysis is the means, it is not the end. A key aim of this book is to include other analytical disciplines and also to use a more currency-focused form of economic analysis or as I term it "currency economics", both for the purpose of trying to improve currency forecasting and recommendation accuracy. Using these various disciplines, I would recommend that currency market practitioners adopt an integrated approach towards currency forecasting and strategy that is both rigorous and flexible. Equilibrium exchange rate models should still be used as the guide for short-term exchange rate trends, but for short-term moves a combination of currency economics, flows, technical analysis, risk appetite and market psychology should be used. Therefore, at its most ambitious this book, ***Currency Strategy: The Practitioner's Guide to Currency Investing, Hedging and Forecasting*** seeks to provide a new and more focused framework for currency analysis and thereafter to apply it to the decision-making process of the currency market practitioner themselves.

The fact that the currency market affects just about every aspect of our economic life is a relatively recent phenomenon. Before 1971–1973, when the Bretton Woods system of pegged exchange rates, which had lasted since 1944, finally collapsed, you would have been laughed at if you had suggested as much. Currency risk was not a primary consideration. Indeed, the last 30 years have marked the first time in monetary history that all major currencies have been freely floating and completely independent of some commodity peg. You could say as a result that we are living in a time of monetary experiment, an experiment which remains the subject of great controversy and debate as to whether or not it has been beneficial or harmful. For my part, I nail my colours to the mast from the outset. I am an unequivocal, unashamed proponent of free trade and free capital markets. There is little doubt that free and open competition carries with it a harsh discipline. Yet, just as there are flaws with that other experiment, democracy, so it can be measured only on a relative basis; that is, it is the worst option, apart from all the rest. Attempts at subsidizing the economy have clearly failed, thus for now free trade and capital markets reign supreme until such time as better alternatives come along. The currency markets are the fuel within the engine of globalization, an experiment that provides the liquidity for the world's markets.

That experiment began more precisely on August 15, 1971 when US President Richard Nixon announced that the US was abandoning its convertibility commitment between the value of the US dollar and gold at the rate of USD35 per ounce of gold. A diplomatic band-aid was subsequently attempted in December 1971 in the form of the so-called "Smithsonian Agreement", but the attempt to keep major exchange rates pegged and shackled finally collapsed in March 1973. As with the ERM crises of 1992 and 1993, the cost of defending a currency peg that was incapable of responding to economic changes was eventually viewed as intolerable. The 1971–1973 period was unquestionably *the* seminal turning point in the development of the currency markets. Subsequently, there were historical events of varying importance, not least the development of the European Monetary System or the "Snake" which was succeeded by the ERM, the various oil crises, the Plaza and Louvre Accords of 1985 and 1987 respectively, and the coordinated G7 effort to achieve an "orderly reversal" of dollar weakness from 1995 onwards. None of these however carried the same weight as that of the second most important event in the recent life of the currency markets, the break-up of the Soviet Union and the ending of the Cold War. The coming to power in the Soviet Union of Mikhail Gorbachev in 1985 was a momentous event, the effects of which are arguably still being felt to this day. *Glasnost* and *perestroika* were primarily viewed as political doctrines of change, but they also reflected significant economic change and not just for the Soviet Union.

The tearing down of the Berlin Wall and the ending of the Soviet occupation of Eastern Europe marked the end of an era of hostility, conflict and subjugation, but it also marked the beginning of the tearing down of global trade and capital barriers. The competition of the future would not be with arms, but instead with trade and economic competitiveness. This most recent phase of globalization is widely thought of as only being three or four years old, but it dates further back to those heady days of hope in the late 1980s, when all things seemed possible and the prospect of "mutually assured destruction" through nuclear confrontation between the US and the Soviet Union was ended. Purists will argue that there have been previous examples of globalization, notably around the beginning of the twentieth century, an experiment that as we all know ended badly, but for our purposes we focus only on this more recent exercise.

The breaking down of those barriers — firstly those made of brick and subsequently those economic barriers to free markets — triggered an explosion in trade and capital flows, which in turn triggered a parallel explosion in the size of the currency market as the BIS surveys from 1989 to 2001 confirm. At a daily turnover of around USD1.2 trillion a day, the currency market now dwarfs the US stock or bond markets. As the pulling down of trade and capital barriers has led to investors and corporations seeking to expand and diversify in other countries, so the global currency market has been the facilitator of that, and in the process increased in size exponentially.

When the experiment began in late 1971, most economists viewed favourably this new-found exchange rate flexibility. Subsequently, to some, the experiment that started 30 years ago appears to have created a monster. The last decade in particular has seen much talk of a need to bring exchange rates back under control, either through a tax on currency trading (the so-called "Tobin Tax" idea) or a move to re-peg exchange rates, perhaps even using gold as the monetary anchor. From my perspective, while exchange rate volatility is frequently unwanted, empirical studies have noted that over the long term it is lower than equity market volatility and few are trying to shackle similarly the equity markets. Equally, the explosion the world has seen in trade, finance and most of all growth simply would not have taken place were it not for the currency market, acting as the facilitator of that growth.

Whatever one's view on the matter, there is no debate as to the global effect the currency market now has, nor that currency risk is now a crucial consideration. At the level of the ordinary man or woman on the street, the most obvious expression of this is through travel. When travelling abroad, most people consciously or subconsciously translate "foreign" prices back into their home currency terms to give them a frame of reference. Thus, the price of foreign goods can seem "cheap" or "expensive" relative to the price of the same good in the home country. Economic models can be more effectively explained sometimes through example and analogy rather than through complex mathematical formulae. For instance, Americans generally regard the UK as "expensive". If a New Yorker, who is used to paying a dollar fifty for his morning cappuccino comes to London and has to pay three pounds sterling (USD4.5 at a sterling–dollar exchange rate of 1.5) the UK price is clearly expensive. In our example, the price differential reflects the sterling–dollar exchange rate, the relative supply/demand dynamics of cappuccino in New York and London and the different cost prices. The "law of one price" otherwise known as Purchasing Power Parity suggests that over time the exchange rate between two countries must alter so as to correct any imbalance between the price of the same basket of goods in those two countries. In our cappuccino example, if we use a cup of coffee as reflective of the general price differential for a representative basket of goods between the US and the UK, a combination of a sterling depreciation over time against the dollar and a fall in the domestic London price of cappuccino relative to that in New York should occur in order to narrow the price differential. In theory, this works fine over the long term. Readers will note that in 1992, the sterling–dollar exchange rate was briefly above 2.00. At the start of

2002, it was around 1.45. Over the short term, however, the record of PPP is decidedly more patchy, which is of course no consolation to London coffee lovers nor to our New Yorker guest! Relative pricing can be further distorted by other factors such as barriers to trade and different cultural tastes. For instance, some people may not like coffee while to others it may be against their religion. That said, it holds true that the exchange rate is a key determining factor for how one defines "expensive" or "cheap" in the first place.

The same premise is also evident at the corporate level. When the US dollar was appreciating to multi-year highs against European currencies during the period of 1999–2001, this together with the fact of strong US consumer demand made it very attractive for European manufacturers to export their production to the US at increasingly competitive prices. The strength of the US currency deflated the dollar price of these products, thus making them more competitive and encouraging US consumers to buy more European goods. For US exporters, however, the picture was the opposite, as their exports to Europe became less competitive as the dollar strengthened, reducing their market share or pricing them out of some markets entirely. Thus, the US trade deficit ballooned, not just with Europe but with the world as a whole, reaching a level of some USD400 billion in 2001. Yet, just as the US trade deficit was expanding, so more competitive exports to the US together with a slowdown in US demand in 2001 forced US manufacturers in turn to cut their prices, reducing inflationary pressures. However, as corporate executives are painfully aware, just as domestic currency weakness can lead to more competitive exports and thus higher profits, causing a benign circle, so a vicious circle can result from domestic currency strength, hurting one's export competitiveness. From the perspective of a European exporter, a weak dollar is not a good thing, as it causes the exporter's prices to rise in dollar terms. At some stage, those higher prices will cause US consumers to buy American instead of European. This will cause the US trade deficit with Europe to shrink, but it will also bite hard into the profits of European exporters.

Exporters are of necessity keenly aware of the importance of exchange rate movements. However, companies that have no exports but simply produce and sell in a single country are also affected. A company that has no direct export exposure and thus thinks itself blissfully exempt from currency risk is in for a nasty shock. As we have seen in the above example, changes in the exchange rate — the external price — cause changes in turn in the *domestic* price of goods and services. Thus, if your currency strengthens against that of your competition, you face a competitive threat — and assuming all else is equal, the choice of either cutting your prices, thus reducing your margin, or losing market share.

Currency movements can also have a profound effect on investing. Fixed income and equity portfolio managers, in investing in another country's assets, automatically take on currency exposure to that country. Frequently, fund managers view the initial decision to invest in a country as being one and the same with investing in that country's currency. This is not necessarily the case for the simple reason that the dynamics which operate within the currency market are frequently not the same as those that govern asset markets. It is entirely possible for a country's fixed income and equity markets to perform strongly over time, while simultaneously its currency depreciates. My favourite example of this phenomenon is that of South Africa. From the autumn of 1998, when the 5-year South African government bond yield briefly exceeded 21%, this was one of the world's most outstanding investments until November 2001. By then, this yield had made a low of around 9.25%, a direct and inverse reflection of the degree to which its price soared over the previous three years. In that time however, the value of the South African rand has fallen substantially from around 6 to the US dollar to almost 14. Here is a clear example where the currency and the bond market of the same country have been going in opposite directions over a period of three years! An investor in the 5-year South African government bond in the autumn of 1998 would have seen their excellent gains in the underlying fixed income position over that time wiped out by the losses on the rand exposure. The lesson from this is that currency risk should be an important consideration for asset managers and moreover one that is managed *separately and independently from the underlying*. Empirical studies have shown that currency volatility reflects between 70 and 90% of a fixed income portfolio's total return. Thus, for the more conservative fund managers, who cannot take such swings in returns but do not take the prudent step of hedging currency risk, it can be the main reason why they stay out of otherwise profitable markets. Conversely, currency risk can also enhance the total return of a portfolio. When the US dollar was falling from 1993 to 1995, this made offshore investments more attractive for US fund managers when translating back into dollars. It was no coincidence that this period also saw a substantial increase in portfolio diversification abroad by this investment community.

There is little doubt that currency exposure can be unpredictable, frustrating and infuriating, but it is not something one has the luxury of ignoring. In John Maynard Keynes' reference to the "animal spirits", that elemental force that drives financial markets in herd-like fashion, he was referring to the stock market. More than most, he should have defined such a term as he was one himself, having been an extremely active stock market speculator as well as one of the last century's most pre-eminent economists. However, he might as well have been referring to the currency market, for the term sums up no other more perfectly. A market that is volatile and unpredictable, a market that epitomizes such a concept as the "animal spirits" surely requires a very specific discipline by which to study it. That is precisely what this book is aimed at doing; providing an analytical framework for currency analysis and forecasting, combining long-term economic valuation models with market-based valuation techniques to produce a more accurate and user-friendly analytical tool for the currency market practitioners themselves. In terms of a breakdown, the book is deliberately split into three specific sections with regard to the currency market and exchange rates:

- Part I (Chapters 1–4) — Theory and Practice
- Part II (Chapters 5 and 6) — Regimes and Crises
- Part III (Chapters 7–10) — The Real World of the Currency Market Practitioner

We begin this process with **Chapter 1 (Fundamental Analysis: The Strengths and Weaknesses of Traditional Exchange Rate Models)** which as the title suggests examines the contribution of macroeconomics to the field of currency analysis. As we have already seen briefly in this Introduction, economics has created a number of equilibrium-based valuation models. Generally speaking, such models try to determine an equilibrium exchange rate based on the relative pricing of goods, money and trade. In turn, this concept of relative pricing can be broken down into four main types of long-term valuation model, which focus on international competitiveness, key monetary themes, interest rate differentials and the balance of payments. I would suggest that while such equilibrium exchange rate models are an indispensable tool for analysing long-term exchange rate trends, their predictive track record for short-term moves is mixed at best. Moreover, as we noted above, they are based on the concept of an equilibrium, which rarely exists in reality and if it does exist is in any case a moving target. This is in no way to attempt to downplay the immense contribution that economics has made to currency analysis, rather it is to emphasize the different focus of the two disciplines. Whereas economics seeks to determine the "big picture", currency analysis seeks specific exchange rate forecasts over specific time frames. Neither is "better" or "worse". They are merely different analytical disciplines responding to a different set of requirements. In the very act of attempting practical modifications to the classical economic approach towards exchange rates, one pays homage to the original work.

Precisely because currency markets are affected by so many different factors, it has proved an extremely difficult (if not impossible) task for economists to design fundamental equilibrium models with predictive capacity for exchange rates for anything other than the long term. Thus, **Chapter 2 (Currency Economics: A More Focused Framework)** seeks to go beyond these theoretical models outlined in Chapter 1 to capture those elements of economics relevant to the currency market and tie them into a loose analytical framework capable of giving a more relevant and accurate picture of short- and medium-term currency market dynamics. Whereas the classical economic approach has been to start with general economic rules and impose them on exchange rates, the emphasis here is to start with the specific currency market dynamics and use whichever aspects of economics are most appropriate to these, as characterized by the label "currency economics". The attempt here is not to create or define a new economic discipline, but instead to use the existing qualities of economic and other analytical disciplines to create a framework of exchange rate analysis that is more relevant and useful for currency market practitioners.

For this purpose, we cannot rely on economics alone. As we analyse the specific dynamics of the currency market we see that other analytical disciplines may also be relevant. In **Chapter 3 (Flow: Tracking the Animal Spirits)** we look at the first of these, namely that of "flow" analysis. It is interesting to note that where once this discipline was not even recognized as having worth, it is now at the forefront of financial analysis. As barriers to trade and capital have fallen over the last three decades, so the size and the *importance* of investment capital has grown exponentially. While the classical approach has traditionally taken the view of the efficient market hypothesis, namely that information is perfect and that past pricing holds no relevance in a market place where all participants are rational and profit-seeking, there have been a number of recent academic works looking at how "order flow" can in fact be a crucial determinant of future prices. Thus Chapter 3 seeks to take this view a stage further and look at using order flow — that is the sum of client flows going through a bank — as a tool for forecasting and trading exchange rates.

The tracking of capital flows of necessity involves looking for apparent patterns in flow movement. Linked in with this idea is the discipline of tracking patterns in price. This discipline is that of technical analysis. While the economic community appears to have finally taken the discipline of flow analysis to its heart, there remains considerable resistance to any similar acceptance of technical analysis. **Chapter 4 (Technical Analysis: The Art of Charting)** looks at this discipline, how it evolved and how it professes to work. Whatever the scepticism and criticism of this discipline, the reality is that flow and technical analysis have succeeded to a far greater degree where equilibrium exchange rate models have failed in seeking to predict short-term exchange rate moves. Technical analysis has come a very long way, even to the point where some market practitioners base their investment decisions solely on the basis of technical signals. Several public institutions have sought to investigate the phenomenon of technical analysis and why it works, including no less than the Federal Reserve Bank of New York. The reasons vary from market herding patterns, as noted by the field of behavioural finance, to economic and financial cycles matching each other. Whatever the case, the results of technical analysis are impressive, enough to persuade investment banks and hedge funds to trade off them.

Having looked at flow and pricing patterns in Chapters 3 and 4, it is also important to examine the structural dynamics that determine those patterns, which is the focus of Chapters 5 and 6. Currency markets are widely viewed as volatile, yet there is also the perception that a clear differentiation can be made between "normal" and "crisis" trading conditions. The structural dynamics of the currency market can determine when and how this differentiation occurs. A key structural dynamic concerns the type of exchange rate regime, which can significantly distort both fundamental and technical signals. Thus, in **Chapter 5 (Exchange Rate Regimes: Fixed or Floating?)** we look at how the type of exchange rate regime can have potentially major impact on the business decisions of currency market practitioners. To most modern-day readers, at least those within the developed markets, the exchange rate norm is and has always been freely floating. While this is now true for the most part within the developed markets it is not so much the case in the emerging markets where the series of currency crises in the 1990s would appear to confirm that the type of exchange rate regime remains a pertinent issue for investors and corporations alike. This chapter takes a brief but illuminating look at the history of exchange rate regimes, noting a clear trend within the dynamic tension between governments and the market place towards either completely freely floating exchange rate regimes or hard currency pegs since the break-up of the Bretton Woods system in 1971–1973. There remains a rich debate within academia as to the optimal currency regime, with free market ideologues calling for freely floating exchange rate regimes as the only solution in a world of free and open trade and capital markets, while at the other end of the spectrum some still call for a return to fixed exchange rates. Where there appears at least some degree of agreement is the idea that within these two extremes semi- or "soft" currency peg regimes are no longer appropriate in a world without barriers to the movement of capital. We touch on this academic debate only for the purpose of seeing how the issues are relevant for currency market practitioners. Indeed, to round off the chapter, we look at the issues of "exchange rate sustainability" and the "real world relevance of the exchange rate system", noting points that currency market practitioners should be on the lookout for with regards to the relationship between the exchange rate regime they are operating under and the specific currency risk they are exposed to.

The implicit assumption in Chapter 5 is that "normal" trading conditions apply. Yet, within currency markets, there are periods of turbulence and distress so extreme that the dynamics of "normal" trading conditions may no longer apply. Logically enough, we term this hurricane or typhoon equivalent in the currency markets a "currency crisis". As with our meteorological counterparts, currency analysts have tried to examine currency crises in order to be able to predict them. As with hurricanes, this is no easy task. **Chapter 6 (Model Analysis: Can Currency Crises be Predicted?)** takes a look at the effort by the economic community to model and predict currency crises. For the reason that I have worked on this subject for some years, I enclose my own effort entitled the Classic Emerging Market Currency Crisis (CEMC) model, which looks at the typical emerging market *pegged* exchange rate regime. In addition, I enclose a model focusing on the "speculative cycle", which takes place in *freely floating* exchange rate regimes. Here, I make no claim to a definitive breakthrough. However, I do feel these two models capture the essential dynamics of the currency crisis on the one hand and the currency cycle on the other. The emphasis in this chapter is on the emerging markets for the most part, largely because ever since the 1992–1993 ERM crises the developed markets have no longer presented such easy targets. All major developed market exchange rates have been freely floating, and the 15% ERM bands in the run up to the creation of the Euro on January 1, 1999 were sufficiently wide to eliminate the risk of a repeat attack on the mechanism. Under freely floating exchange rates, currency crises take on a different form and are more reflective of a loss of market confidence rather than an actual crisis involving a pegged exchange rate which ultimately involves desperate and futile defence followed by de-pegging and devaluation.

One could well argue that one of the prerequisites for developed country status is a freely floating currency, though to be sure the creation of the Euro somewhat clouds the issue. In any case, the emerging markets have provided a rich if unwanted source of currency crises to study, including those of Mexico (1994–1995), Asia (1997–1998), Russia (1998), Brazil (1999) and most recently Turkey (2001). Needless to say, following these violent and destructive events the attempt at generating models able to predict currency crises has been greatly accelerated, albeit with mixed success to date.

In Chapters 5 and 6, we have looked at exchange rate regimes, how they might affect currency risk and in turn how they might drive the ultimate expression of currency market tension, the currency crisis. In Chapters 7–10, we again seek to take the study of currency markets to the next level and try to apply many of the lessons that we have learned to the real world of the currency market practitioner. The first chapter in this section, **Chapter 7 (Managing Currency Risk I — The Corporation)** looks at how the multinational corporation should manage currency risk. Before looking at currency hedging strategies and structures, we first have to establish what kinds of currency risks exist. For the multinational corporation, there are three types of currency risk or exposure: transaction, translation and economic, each of which requires a different approach. As with some investors, there are corporations ideologically fixated with the idea of not hedging. Others focus on the "natural" approach to hedging through the matching of currency assets and liabilities. There is an understandable desire on the part of some corporate executives to leave the issue of currency risk to the likes of currency dealers and speculators and to "just get on with the company's underlying business". Unfortunately, few things in life are as simple as one would like them. Whether it likes it or not, a corporation that has currency exposure is by definition a currency market practitioner. It may not seek to manage currency risk but even by doing so it is taking an active decision. *There is no opt-out with regards to currency risk or exposure.* Fortunately, most major corporations have realized this and have gone to great effort to establish sophisticated Treasury operations. There are still some who hold out, and in any case even for these "progressives" there remains work to be done in developing and maintaining skill levels to match those of their currency market counterparties. Finally, after establishing what currency risk should be managed and why, we shall look at the "how" by examining such concepts as optimization, balance sheet hedging, benchmarks for currency risk management, strategies for setting budget rates, the corporation and predicting exchange rates and a menu of advanced hedging strategies.

The worlds of the corporation and the investor may seem very different on the face of it, but in fact they are very similar in a number of ways. Both view currency risk as an annoyance and indeed there remain some on both sides who refuse to acknowledge it exists. Still to this day, I come up against investors who have an almost ideological aversion to the idea of managing currency risk. For the most part, this is on the view that investing in a country is equivalent to investing in that country's currency. If **Chapter 8 (Managing Currency Risk II — The Investor)** succeeds in nothing else than to disabuse readers of such a view, then it will have succeeded utterly and entirely. The case of South Africa already mentioned in this Introduction may be seen as an extreme example, but it is far from unique. The structural dynamics of asset market risk and currency risk are fundamentally different, and thus they should be managed separately and independently. This is not to say that they have of necessity to be managed by different people. However, the crucial point to be made is that these risks should be managed differently and separately from one another, reflecting those different dynamics. When pressed, both the investor and the corporation for the most part seek defensive strategies which can manage currency risk by reducing that exposure, limiting the vulnerability of either the income statement or the portfolio. Indeed, readers will note that some strategies mentioned in Chapters 7 and 8 are interchangeable between the corporation and the investor. Thus, in this chapter, we will take a look into the world of the sophisticated institutional investor and how they manage currency risk. As with the corporation, investors can choose both passive and active currency risk management approaches for this purpose. Investors can also use optimization as an important risk management tool, and the setting and use of currency benchmarks is a further similarity. For both, the bottom line is that the currency exposure should be managed in such a way as to limit any reduction and potentially enhance the total return.

The third set of currency market practitioners that we will examine is on the one hand the largest grouping within the currency market and on the other the most misunderstood — the currency "speculator". For many, the very term triggers an instinctive reaction, frequently one that is far from positive. For our purpose here, I define currency speculation as the *trading of currencies with no underlying attached asset within the transaction*. Clearly, such a definition is inexact, but it provides nonetheless a useful framework with which to analyse the subject. **Chapter 9 (Managing Currency Risk III — The Speculator)** takes a look at the fascinating but much misunderstood world of the currency speculator, how it works and how to be a better speculator! Speculators have periodically been demonized by governments of the developed and emerging countries alike, frequently in the wake of violent currency crises. Such crises are however rarely caused by speculators, who are I would contend a symptom rather than the disease itself. Indeed, in some cases speculation can actually be the cure, as when sterling was ejected from the recessionary shackles of the ERM in September 1992, only for the UK economy to recover strongly thereafter. Speculation can be both a positive and a destructive force, but its intention is neither, rather to make a profit. In this, it is neither moral nor immoral, but rather amoral.

Currency speculation does not take place within a vacuum, but instead is a market and indeed a human response to changes in ordinary fundamental and technical dynamics. For the most part, currency speculators follow the same economic and technical analytical signposts as corporations and investors. On occasion, both investors and corporations can act as currency speculators. The term is certainly not limited to dealers or hedge funds. Moreover, currency speculators generally provide exchange rate liquidity for the more productive elements of the economy. It is my hope that readers of whatever hue will find this chapter both interesting and informative, concerning a subject which deserves at the least a chapter of its own if not an entire and separate book. Undoubtedly, the issue of currency speculation is likely to remain controversial for the foreseeable future. The aim here has been to take out some of the emotional aspects of the issue and try to look at it coolly and dispassionately.

Speculators can accelerate change but they cannot cause it in the first place. Moreover, speculation provides a valuable need for the rest of the market in the form of liquidity. Yet, speculation also remains only one part of the overall picture of the currency markets. As the title might suggest, **Chapter 10 (Applying the Framework)** seeks as the final chapter to bind together all the strands of thought that we have looked at up to now into a coherent framework for analysing the currency markets. One can have a reasonably informed idea about the prevailing currency economics, the technical picture and the flows, but it is only by combining those that one sees the whole picture and therefore can come to an informed decision about how to manage currency risk. For this purpose, I use a very simple "signal grid", which combines the individual signals of currency economics, technical analysis, flow analysis and long-term equilibrium model valuation, into a combined currency view. The signal grid should provide an informed view as to exchange rates but at its most basic it will only say "buy" or "sell". What it cannot do is to suggest the type of currency instruments or structures needed. For that, we need to apply the combined result of the signal grid to the currency market practitioner's own risk profile. For both the corporation and the investor, their risk profile is a function of their tolerance of the volatility of their net profit or total return.

No book should claim it can by itself make the reader an expert in its subject. Rather, this is a book aimed at those who are already experts in their own respective fields, whether that it is in fixed income or equity investment, managing multi-billion dollar corporations, or trading currency pairs such as Euro–dollar or dollar–rand. The purpose therefore of this book is to help these experts become more proficient in currency risk management to the extent where it makes a real and measurable difference to their bottom line. In sum, this book aims a lot higher than most written to date on exchange rates. I leave it to the reader to decide whether or not it has succeeded in this regard.

Callum Henderson
London
May 2002

Part One
Theory and Practice

1
Fundamental Analysis:
The Strengths and Weaknesses of
Traditional Exchange Rate Models

The starting point of "fundamental" currency analysis is the exchange rate model, or the attempt by economists to provide a logical framework with which to forecast exchange rates. In response to the break-up of the Bretton Woods exchange rate system, the economics profession has spent the last three decades trying to improve its exchange rate forecasting ability, mainly by refining the traditional exchange rate models and occasionally coming up with new ones. To date, the results of this worthy effort have been mixed at best. We will go into why this is the case later. In the meantime, it is worth spending some time looking at the various models, their practical uses and individual track records, for to say their results have been mixed is not to suggest they are without use. On the contrary, traditional exchange rate models provide a valuable framework for analysing exchange rates, without which strategists would have few long-term guides as to where exchange rates should be priced.

Most traditional exchange rate models derive from some form of equilibrium, which is based on the relative pricing of a given commodity. Since an exchange rate is made up of two currencies, it should logically reflect the relative pricing of a commodity between the two countries concerned. Traditional exchange rate models are identified by the approach they take towards determining or forecasting exchange rates, and therefore by the commodity whose relative pricing they use for this purpose:

- The exchange rate as the relative price of goods — Purchasing Power Parity
- The exchange rate as the relative price of money — The Monetary Approach
- The exchange rate as the relative price of interest — The Interest Rate Approach
- The exchange rate as the relative price of current and capital flows — The Balance of Payments Approach
- The exchange rate as the relative price of assets — The Portfolio Balance Approach

Many readers will be familiar with some or all of these models. The attempt here is not merely to describe them, thus perhaps going over old ground, but to discover their individual strengths and weaknesses by relating them to the real world of currency trading.

1.1 PURCHASING POWER PARITY

Purchasing Power Parity (PPP) or the "law of one price" is probably the best known exchange rate model within currency analysis. The basic idea behind PPP is that in a world without barriers to free trade the price of the same good must be the same everywhere over time. As a result, the exchange rate must move towards a long-term equilibrium value that ensures this is true. PPP or the law of price should hold if:

- There are no barriers to trade or arbitrage in the good
- There are no transaction costs
- The good being traded is perfectly homogeneous

This is best shown by an example. Say, for argument's sake, the price of exactly the same sports car in the Czech Republic and Germany is CZK1 million and EUR100,000. If we use this sports car as broadly representative of the price differential between these two countries, then we derive from this that the PPP equilibrium value of the Euro–Czech koruna exchange rate should in turn be 10 (i.e. 1,000,000/100,000). Obviously, the prices in this example are not meant to be representative of the actual price of a sports car. Rather, we have used these numbers to illustrate the basic concept more easily.

If the PPP equilibrium value of the Euro–Czech koruna exchange rate is 10, we can derive from this firstly that the actual exchange rate should revert towards this over time and secondly that the actual exchange rate reflects a quantifiable degree of over- or undervaluation relative to that PPP value. At the time of writing, the actual Euro–Czech koruna exchange rate was around 31.50. If we used our example to reflect the Euro–Czech koruna's PPP value, this would suggest the Czech koruna was significantly undervalued relative to PPP and should appreciate over time to eliminate that undervaluation. In a world where there are no barriers to trade or knowledge, a German car buyer will be fully aware that the same car is cheaper in the Czech Republic. Hence, if there are no laws against such practice, he or she will travel there, buy the car and drive back. Whether or not this is realistic misses the point. Rather, it is meant to illustrate the principle at work within the PPP concept. The transmission mechanism that is at work in this example and more generally that would cause an eventual elimination of that Czech koruna undervaluation is as follows:

> Cheap currency → Attracts buyers → Increased demand to buy goods →
>
> Currency appreciates

In this book, every effort will be made to spare the reader from complex mathematical formulae, which though impressive do little to advance the argument in the face of incomprehension. There are however a few basic mathematical constructs which have to be defined, and PPP is one of those. Thus, the basic mathematical expression of PPP is:

$$E = \frac{P}{P*}$$

Or, another way to express this is:

$$P = E \times P^*$$

where

E = The PPP long-term equilibrium exchange rate value
P = Domestic price level of goods
P^* = Foreign price level of goods

This reflects the fundamental view of PPP, which is that the long-term equilibrium value of an exchange rate is a direct function of the ratio between the "internal" prices of the same tradable goods between two countries. Currency market practitioners, however, think of exchange rates with regard to the base and the term currencies, naturally using the base currency first, as the point of reference. Thus, the exchange rate between the US and Japan is not seen as yen per dollar, but expressed instead as dollar–yen. This is how foreign exchange traders quote and this is how clients ask for those quotes. Thus, in our PPP formula, we could express this slightly differently as:

$$E = \frac{P_t}{P_b}$$

where:

E = The PPP long-term equilibrium exchange rate value
P_t = Price level in the term currency
P_b = Price level in the base currency

Returning briefly to our sports car example, this is indeed how we derived the supposed PPP value of the Euro–Czech koruna exchange rate using the price levels given.

1.1.1 Reasons for "Misalignments"

Exchange rates which do not reflect the PPP value are said to be "misaligned" and it is assumed therefore that they have to revert towards PPP. Such misalignments are seen as being caused by temporary distortions, either to the price of the good or the exchange rate, which should quickly be eliminated by a rational, profit-seeking market. In reality, such "misalignments" can last for months or even years. In other words, traders, investors or corporations who base short-term financial decisions on the PPP model of exchange rate value do so at their own risk. The track record of the PPP model *over the short term* leaves a lot to be desired, to the extent it is known in the market as the "Pretty Poor Predictor". How can such misalignments occur in a free market economy where the price adjustment mechanism should be immediate? If there is free trade between nations, a price differential in a good (or basket of goods) should create an arbitrage opportunity — you buy the good in the cheaper country. Such buying should push up the currency in the cheaper country relative to the more expensive one. Yet still, this is not necessarily what happens over the short term. Why?

- **We do not have perfectly free trade** — Such a concept would imply zero import tariffs, zero export subsidies and perfect competition across all business sectors. Needless to say, this is not the case. Whatever progress we have made, we are not there yet. As a result, there remain significant trade-related price (and therefore exchange rate) distortions.
- **The adjustment mechanism is not necessarily immediate** — During periods of market volatility, corporations may delay setting prices and budget exchange rates until they have a better idea of where the appropriate levels should be to retain competitiveness and margin.
- **The price of goods may not be the most important exchange rate determinant** — A basic PPP assumption is that the relative pricing of goods is the main driver of exchange rates. However, since the liberalization of capital markets, this may no longer be the case.
- **The good or basket of goods may not be exactly the same in different countries** — The consistency of the good should not be taken for granted as the same good may vary between countries in terms of quality, cost and speed to market.
- **Base-year effects** — There is also the question of when to start the PPP analysis. Logic might suggest starting from the end of the Bretton Woods exchange rate system in the 1971–1973 period, yet this took place at a time of very high inflation, thus significantly distorting the results.

1.1.2   Tradable and Non-Tradable Goods

There is a further point, which is that clear differentiation has to be made between tradable and non-tradable goods. PPP may not hold for non tradable goods such as services. The dry world of economics is frequently best explained through example and anecdote. Thus, a haircut might be cheaper in New York than London (most things are and this is not one of the exceptions), but few people would be prepared to fly to New York from London just to get that cheaper haircut. This is not just because to do so you would have to pay for a London–New York return flight, which would negate any haircut-related gains you would make. Even supposing the air ticket was free would you really fly 8 hours for a cheaper haircut? The PPP concept assumes there are no barriers to the arbitraging of price differentials, yet with non-tradable goods this may not be the case. Granted, there may always be some wayward individuals who would actually take that flight!

PPP or the law of one price holds better of necessity for homogeneous commodities that are traded internationally, with arbitrage opportunities being quickly eliminated. However, even here, care is needed. While PPP may hold generally, prices even of homogeneous commodities may vary widely between countries depending on local supply/demand dynamics. Indeed, the very fact that the price of a McDonalds Big Mac, which is a homogeneous commodity, can vary between countries for even a short period of time proves this point.

1.1.3   PPP and Corporate Pricing Strategy

The law of one price assumes the exchange rate will move over time so that the price of the same good is the same everywhere. However, corporations do not necessarily follow this as they may vary national prices of the same good to reflect a variety of factors in those countries such as local supply/demand dynamics, delivery costs, cultural tastes, customer price tolerance, target margin, competitor prices, market share considerations and so forth. To an economist, such price variations represent temporary distortions, which should over time be eliminated by market efficiency. To a corporate executive, faced with the frequently competing real-world priorities of profit maximization and raising market share, there may be nothing temporary about such "distortions". As a result, PPP may in some cases not hold over the "short term" for homogeneous goods since such pricing strategies may not allow it to hold.

Example 1

In the mid-1990s, US–Japanese trade relations went through one of their periodic bouts of bitter dispute, with the US side accusing Japan of a host of uncompetitive practices including "price dumping". Having followed this situation closely when I was a foreign exchange analyst living in New York, I think it is a good practical example of the theoretical principle of PPP faced with the real world of corporate pricing strategy. It was certainly a heated time, with news headlines from trade representatives of both sides causing wild gyrations in the dollar–yen exchange rate.

From a purely objective viewpoint, it should be instructive to look at the various transmission mechanisms that were at work. PPP, of course, states that the price of the same good should be the same everywhere over time and that the exchange rate should adjust to ensure this. How then does an economist deal with a clear disparity in pricing? PPP suggests that this disparity is unsustainable and that the market will move to eliminate it over time. Corporate pricing strategy may however be an obstacle to this. In the case of the US–Japan trade deficit, a key issue — undoubtedly only one of many — was the US view that Japanese auto manufacturers were selling their export production to the US at cheaper prices than those charged domestically in Japan for the same production. Whatever the merits of this view, this makes perfect economic sense. A Japanese manufacturer's cost base is likely to be considerably higher than elsewhere. Thus in order to maintain margin domestically it has little choice but to charge higher prices domestically relative to those that would be tolerated elsewhere, such as in the US. A trade negotiator, fixated with the idea that trade is some kind of national war-game, would cry foul. However, a higher domestic cost base means of necessity that a manufacturer of whatever nationality either deliberately undercuts the domestic price structure, thus making a loss, or keeps export prices lower than domestic ones.

The higher cost base and consumer price tolerance work hand in hand. In the US, because US consumers are used to a system which exemplifies a very high level of competition, this drives down retail prices, reducing consumer "price tolerance". PPP theory states that the exchange rate should adjust for price differentials in the same good. Thus, the currency where the good is priced cheaper should appreciate relative to that where it is priced more expensively. In this case, the US dollar should appreciate relative to the yen. Assuming that trade in autos can affect exchange rates over a sustained period of time, this is what should take place in the exchange rate as a result of the relationship between PPP and a potential price disparity between Japanese autos sold in the US and Japan.

In reality, this is of course not what happened, confirmation if such were needed that PPP can be distorted by "temporary" factors. Between 1993 and 1995, the dollar–yen exchange rate fell sharply from around 120 to a record low of 79.85, a decline of some 33%. A rise in the yen against the US dollar should push Japanese export prices higher in US dollar terms. As Japanese domestic prices are substantially higher than those tolerated in the US, such an appreciation in the yen's value would merely compound an existing problem. Our Japanese manufacturer would face the dilemma of either maintaining the Japanese domestic price in the US and thus losing market share — and pleasing the US trade negotiator — or cutting the US dollar price sharply, sacrificing its margin on the alters of sales and market share.

In the first case, one would assume US consumers would not tolerate Japanese domestic prices, that Japanese exports would fall as a result and that if PPP holds the yen would fall to the extent that Japanese export production becomes competitive once more. In the second case, the Japanese manufacturer could either cut its US price to the extent it attracted US consumers or else to the extent it believed the *perception* of superior quality would offset a price differential relative to its competitors. The natural inclination would be the latter, in which case PPP would again be distorted because price would be "distorted" by the influence of consumer taste. Hence, from an exchange rate perspective, one would not expect the dollar–yen exchange rate to move to offset the price differential. Indeed, if anything it might actually move in favour of the yen if there were a US preference for Japanese autos that offset price considerations, until yen appreciation put the manufacturer's US dollar prices under such upward pressure that it was forced to raise them.

For such a dramatic move in the dollar–yen exchange rate, there is of course a third alternative for our Japanese auto manufacturer, which is in the face of inexorable yen appreciation, to move production out of Japan to the US. This is indeed what happened in specific cases and to an extent how the two sides found some degree of compromise. From the perspective of PPP, this did not end the issue because the newly US-made auto would still be cheaper than its counterpart made back in Japan. However, it would no longer be exactly the same auto, taking into account differences in quality, cost and so forth, thus one could argue that the law of homogeneity no longer applies. This is splitting hairs. The important thing is to demonstrate how PPP plays a part in the real world of merchandise trade and corporate pricing strategy.

Thus, care needs to be taken with PPP as it can be distorted by a wide variety of factors, particularly over the short term. Over the long run, however, PPP serves as an extremely useful benchmark. Indeed, another example should hopefully put the PPP model in a better light.

Example 2

The Economist newspaper uses a well-known method of monitoring PPP levels, the "Big Mac Index". This model of "burger-nomics" examines the domestic price of a McDonalds Big Mac in a range of countries, translates that into US dollars and seeks to measure the disparity between the price of a Big Mac in the US and that in other countries as a reflection of medium-term under- or overvaluation.

To some, this may seem a jovial if spurious exercise, but it is PPP in its simplest and purest form, not least because a Big Mac is a homogeneous product — it is the same wherever you go. This is exactly what you need for PPP analysis in order to avoid distortions. Moreover, the Big Mac Index actually has an impressive record of forecasting exchange rate trends over long periods of time and as a result has been the subject of several academic research papers. For instance, when the Euro came into being in January 1999, most currency forecasters predicted the Euro–dollar exchange rate would appreciate over time — that is, the Euro would appreciate against the dollar — based on anticipation of capital flows and the view that the new single currency was undervalued. The fact that most currency forecasters in turn got this prediction entirely wrong shows the danger and the limitation of valuation considerations. You can be looking at the wrong measure of valuation, and even if you are looking at the right one you can get the wrong time horizon. To be fair to my fellow currency forecasters in the industry, the Euro–dollar exchange rate did rise initially, reaching a high of 1.1885. From then, however, it fell like a stone, grinding lower remorselessly, greatly disappointing not only the expectations of the market, but also those of European Union officials. One must give credit where it's due, however. In early 1999, not everyone was a raging bull on the Euro. On January 7 of that year, *The Economist* published the latest readings of its Big Mac Index, suggesting the Euro was not undervalued, but actually *overvalued* by some 13%! In order to calculate the Big Mac PPP for the Euro–dollar exchange rate, you simply translate the Euro price of a Big Mac into US dollars at the prevailing exchange rate and divide that by the US dollar price of a Big Mac in the US. Clearly, if you had followed that forecast and run your position over the next two years, you could have made a lot of money. The usefulness of PPP applies not just with industrial country currencies but also with those of the emerging markets.

In order to give a slightly more up-to-date edition of this entertaining — and informative — variation on the theory of PPP equilibrium theory, I include Table 1.1 from *The Economist* as of April 19, 2001. At the time, these results would have suggested a number of interesting possibilities for currency valuation, some of which have proved largely accurate, others that have yet to show such accuracy. Within the industrialized world, these results suggested at the time that the Euro was still undervalued by around 11% as of mid-April 2001, estimating the PPP level for the Euro–dollar exchange rate at 0.99. In addition, it suggested that the Japanese yen was around 6% undervalued against the dollar, implying a PPP rate for dollar–yen of around 116. Subsequently, it should indeed be remembered that since then the

Table 1.1   McParity

| | Big Mac prices | | Implied PPP of the USD | Actual USD exchange rate (17/04/01) | Undervaluation (−)/ overvaluation (+) against the USD (%) |
	Local currency price	USD price			
United States	USD2.54	2.54	—	—	—
Argentina	ARS2.50	2.50	0.98	1.00	−2
Australia	AUD3.00	1.52	1.18	1.98	−40
Brazil	BRL3.60	1.64	1.42	2.19	−35
Britain	£1.99	2.85	1.28	1.43	+12
Canada	CAD3.33	2.14	1.31	1.56	−16
Chile	CLP1260	2.10	496	601	−17
China	CNY9.90	1.20	3.90	8.28	−53
Czech Republic	CZK56.00	1.43	22.0	39.0	−44
Denmark	DKK24.75	2.93	9.74	8.46	+15
Euro area	EUR2.57	2.27	0.99	0.88	−11
Hong Kong	HKD10.70	1.37	4.21	7.80	−46
Hungary	HUF399	1.32	157	303	−48
Indonesia	IDR14,700	1.35	5787	10,855	−47
Japan	JPY294	2.38	116	124	−6
Malaysia	MYR4.52	1.19	1.78	3.80	−53
Mexico	MXN21.9	2.36	8.62	9.29	−7
New Zealand	NZD3.60	1.46	1.42	2.47	−43
Philippines	PHP59.00	1.17	23.2	50.3	−54
Poland	PLN5.90	1.46	2.32	4.03	−42
Russia	RUB35.00	1.21	13.8	28.9	−52
Singapore	SGD3.30	1.82	1.30	1.81	−28
South Africa	ZAR9.70	1.19	3.82	8.13	−53
South Korea	KRW3000	2.27	1181	1325	−11
Sweden	SEK24.0	2.33	9.45	10.28	−8
Switzerland	CHF6.30	3.65	2.48	1.73	+44
Taiwan	TWD70.0	2.13	27.6	32.9	−16
Thailand	THB55.0	1.21	21.7	45.5	−52

Source: The Economist (April 19, 2001). © The Economist Newspaper Limited, London.

Euro–dollar exchange rate has indeed appreciated from 0.88 through 1.00. Meanwhile, the dollar–yen exchange rate fell from 124 to 116. Readers will no doubt claim that a plethora of factors could have been at work, irrespective of goods' price differentials and undoubtedly that was the case. That said, there is no getting away from the fact that the Big Mac Index in this case showed the way in terms of the forthcoming trend for these exchange rates.

As with every model, there are also cases where it has not worked so well and there are indeed cases of that in Table 1.1 (e.g. the South African rand was undervalued by 53%). In response, I would say that broadly speaking any type of PPP model should only be viewed from a long-term perspective. In addition, it has to be acknowledged that PPP can be distorted for substantial periods of time. Thus it may have differing levels of importance and relevance depending on the type of currency market practitioner. For instance, a corporation that is looking to hedge out a year's worth of receivables may find PPP a very useful valuation consideration come January. That said, an investor would most likely not be able to wait that long. For a trader, medium-term valuation considerations such as PPP cannot be afforded in a world of split-second timing.

In the Big Mac example, "McParity" can be significantly distorted by cultural and religious considerations, notably in India and Israel. That said, while some in the market like to ridicule PPP measures such as but not exclusive to this, the beauty of it is in its simplicity and trans parency. Furthermore, its results have been impressive, certainly to the extent that it should be taken seriously.

1.1.4   PPP and the Real Exchange Rate

The real exchange rate is a function of the price or inflation differential and the nominal exchange rate. The relationship between the concept of PPP and the "real exchange rate" — or the nominal exchange rate adjusted for price differentials — is of necessity a close and important one. In line with this relationship is the core idea that if PPP is seen to hold over the long term, then the real exchange rate should remain constant. This is the case because if PPP holds relative price differentials between two countries will over the long term be offset by an appropriate nominal exchange rate adjustment. Granted, the real exchange rate may fluctuate significantly over the short term, with the result that such fluctuations can have potentially important economic impact, however, it should revert to mean over time assuming PPP holds.

When the real exchange rate is constant, the international price competitiveness of a country's tradable goods is maintained. Another way of expressing this is to say that when a country experiences high inflation, its tradable goods become proportionally uncompetitive. In order to restore price competitiveness, there has to be a depreciation of the nominal exchange rate. In order to gain competitiveness, a country needs a real depreciation, not simply depreciation in the nominal value of the exchange rate.

The behaviour of the real exchange rate and its components can be broken down into that existing under fixed and floating exchange rate regimes. Under a **fixed exchange rate regime**, the nominal exchange rate's ability to move is of necessity limited, hence changes in the real exchange rate must be a direct function of the change in the inflation differential, and this is indeed what we find empirically. By contrast, under a **floating exchange rate regime**, both the nominal exchange rate and the inflation differential can change or "adjust" in economists' jargon. Thus, the relationship between the real and the nominal exchange rates is considerably closer. Indeed, because inflation differentials adjust relatively slowly in floating exchange rate regimes, most of the adjustment to the real exchange rate comes from an adjustment in the nominal exchange rate. Hence, the same cautions of applying PPP to nominal exchange rate valuation should also apply to real exchange rate techniques.

To summarize this concept of PPP or the law of one price, it is a poor predictor of short-term exchange rate moves. However, it is considerably more accurate on a multi-month or multi-year basis. Note that in the case of the Euro–dollar forecasts, the 13% overvaluation noted in January 1999 and the 11% undervaluation noted in April 2001 was a multi-month guide to the future nominal exchange rate. Thus, a corporate Treasury department or a long-term strategic investor can find a PPP model highly useful in terms of providing a directional framework for medium- to long-term currency forecasting. A "macro" hedge fund or leveraged investor might also find this highly useful for spotting disparities between fundamental valuation and market perception. On the other hand, this is clearly less so for short-term traders whose perspective is measured in days or weeks.

Some final points to note with regard to PPP:

- PPP provides a useful medium- to long-term perspective of currency valuation
- If PPP holds, the real exchange rate remains stable over the long term

- There can however be substantial short-term divergences from PPP
- PPP may thus be particularly useful in currency forecasting for corporations, long-term investors and also leveraged investors, but much less so for short-term traders

1.2   THE MONETARY APPROACH

Linked in with the concept of Purchasing Power Parity is the second type of long-term equilibrium model we will look at, the Monetary Approach to determining or forecasting exchange rates. In this, there are two transmission mechanisms, the first through the price, the second through interest rates.

According to classical theory, a country's price level is a function of the quantity of money. However, according to PPP, exchange rates adjust to equalize domestic tradable goods prices between countries. Thus, if monetary factors determine prices, they also play a part in determining exchange rates. The transmission mechanism for this would be as follows:

(i) Change in money supply → Change in price → Change in exchange rate

(ii) Change in money supply → Change in interest rate → Change in exchange rate

---

For instance, if money supply was rising, one would presume this was due to relatively loose monetary policy from the central bank. That rising money supply would in time lead to rising prices *as too much money chases too few goods*. PPP suggests that under the law of one price, the price of freely tradable goods must be the same everywhere over time and that the exchange rate must adjust to achieve that. Hence, as prices rise in a country relative to prices for the same goods elsewhere, so the currency must depreciate to restore equilibrium.

Similarly, a rise in money supply should lead to a reduction in interest rates. Money supply is presumed to be known and a function of central bank activity. Money demand is somewhat more complex and is determined by interest rates, real income and prices. A decrease in interest rates should logically cause an investor to increase their portfolio weighting in money/cash and decrease it in interest-bearing securities.

The basic premise behind this is that a change in money supply will eventually be offset by a similar change in money demand to restore balance. Within this, the point at which real money supply is equal to real money demand should logically equate to an "equilibrium" interest rate. Given that the Monetary Approach is focused on determining exchange rates, this point should simultaneously reflect the equilibrium exchange rate. However, it should come as no surprise that this point where money supply and demand equate is rarely if ever achieved. Indeed, like any "equilibrium" level, it is a moving target, which is why central banks can get monetary policy "wrong", and the fact that it can change is clearly a factor in interest rate and currency market volatility.

Looking at it logically, it is all about incentive. As interest rates rise above this supposed equilibrium level at which real money supply and demand equate, money demand should fall as the incentive to hold interest rate-bearing securities should rise relative to the incentive to hold non-interest-bearing money. Here, "money" refers to cash, which is assumed to have no interest-bearing component. Thus, reduced money demand should eventually reduce money supply. Equally, as interest rates fall below the equilibrium level, so the incentive to hold interest-bearing securities falls and the incentive to hold money rises. Rising money demand therefore should eventually cause rising money supply.

Within this premise however, and indeed within the Monetary Approach as a whole, is the idea that the transmission mechanism from monetary impulse through prices to the exchange rate is perfect and immediate. In the real world, this is simply not the case. There can be significant lags between the monetary impulse and the change in the exchange rate, not least because the prices of tradable goods do not necessarily respond immediately to changes in the dynamics that affect them. This is the idea of prices being "sticky", which is the economists' response to the apparent disparity between what should happen according to the standard monetary flexible price model and what actually does happen. Thus, instead of the theoretical transmission mechanism, we get something more akin to:

Change in money supply → Delayed price change → Delayed exchange rate change

Eventually, the same transmission mechanism takes place, but the model by itself does not tell us when the exchange rate changes in response to a change in money supply or to what extent. In an attempt to deal with these practical issues, there have been a significant number of variations on the original Monetary Approach to exchange rates, most of them involving a blizzard of formulae. Given this book's practical emphasis, we do not go through these here. This effort to determine exchange rates using the Monetary Approach owes much to the brilliant work of Rudiger Dornbusch, Jeffrey Frankel and Paul Krugman.[1] However, despite this effort, the Monetary Approach is far from a complete predictor of exchange rates. This failure to be able to predict accurately short-term exchange rate moves can logically be ascribed to one of two things, either that the transmission mechanism is significantly delayed and allowing for such delays improves the results, or rather the Monetary Approach does not predict exchange rates because exchange rates do not respond to monetary impulses in the way economists believe — in other words that the theory does not work.

While the results of the Monetary Approach to trying to predict exchange rates have been far from satisfactory, we cannot reject it out of hand, not least because we know that most of the building blocks of the theory are correct. Rising supply will eventually meet rising demand of any commodity. The key lies in the transmission mechanism. We know that there are delays, but why is that so? The usual component of the model which is blamed is PPP, which makes sense given that we know that PPP itself involves delays. However, this is not the whole story. After all, if none other than the Federal Reserve accepts that recent changes within the financial system, notably the much greater public involvement in the equity market, mean that money supply data can no longer be relied on as an inflationary indicator, then why should we suppose that changes in money supply can be used to predict exchange rates? In 2001, money supply growth exploded, with no adverse impact on the US dollar, which in fact had another stellar year in the face of the worst recession in the US for at least 30 years. At present, the best answer we can come up with is that the transmission mechanism will work, but it takes time. Whatever such changes, rising money supply (of a currency) should eventually lead to a depreciation of that currency until such time as that rising money supply creates rising money demand, at which point the currency should stabilize and recover lost ground.

---

[1] Readers who are interested in delving deeper into their work on exchange rates may care to read some or all of Rudiger Dornbusch, *Exchange Rates and Inflation*, MIT, 1992; Jeffrey Frankel, *On Exchange Rates*, MIT, 1993; Paul Krugman, *Currencies and Crises*, MIT, 1992.

As with any market, an exchange rate is a function of supply and demand. In a freely floating exchange rate regime, the market sets both the prevailing and the equilibrium exchange rate levels. In a fixed exchange rate regime, however, a central bank determines the prevailing level of the exchange rate. In committing to a fixed exchange rate regime, the central bank most likely would seek to commit to an exchange rate value which mirrors the equilibrium level at which exchange rate supply and demand meet. However, we know that equilibrium levels themselves can and do fluctuate. Therefore, it should be safe to assume that at some point the prevailing exchange rate level and the equilibrium level will not match. Indeed, this is likely to be the case the majority of the time. As a result, one should also assume an excess of demand or supply for the local currency to be the norm. The central bank has to offset that excess supply or demand by buying or selling its own currency. If there is excess demand for the currency within a fixed exchange rate regime, this forces market interest rates higher than they otherwise would be, obliging the central bank to "sterilize" the effect of excess money demand by injecting money supply into the system. Equally, if there is excess supply of the local currency, the authorities must drain that excess. The ability of a central bank to achieve either of these goals is limited. In the first case, if there is excess local currency demand, its ability to sell local currency is limited by its willingness to print that local currency. To do so could be inflationary, which might necessitate higher interest rates, yet higher interest rates might result in even higher levels of local currency demand. Thus, maybe it should cut interest rates in order to reduce the attractiveness of its currency? Yet, if it does that, it might spark inflation. The ability to cope with massive capital inflows — excess demand for the local currency — is an issue which is very familiar to many emerging market countries.

Equally, if there is an excess supply of local currency within a fixed exchange rate regime, this forces market interest rates lower than they otherwise should be, obliging the central bank to drain that excess local currency supply and force interest rates back up — in other words to conduct unsterilized intervention. This time, its ability to achieve this is limited by the extent of its foreign exchange reserves and its willingness to tolerate sharply higher interest rates. When a central bank runs out of reserves in its attempt to offset excess local currency supply, de-pegging and flotation (devaluation) become inevitable. The general rule for this is that the longer the central bank tries to defend a fixed exchange rate regime that is experiencing an excess supply of local currency, the greater the degree of local currency devaluation and "overshooting" relative to that equilibrium once it is de-pegged and floated. This is one of the reasons why emerging market currencies such as the Indonesian rupiah, Thai baht, Korean won, Russian rouble and Brazilian real substantially overshot any approximation of their equilibrium level using a monetary approach before finally recovering some ground. Thus, while the Monetary Approach may not be able to make accurate short-term exchange rate forecasts, it should be able to provide insight into future exchange rate "events", such as the de-pegging and devaluation of a fixed exchange rate regime.

1.2.1 Mundell–Fleming

Thanks to the work of Robert Mundell and J. Marcus Fleming we know that certain combinations of monetary and fiscal policy create specific exchange rate conditions. The Mundell–Fleming model illustrates how specific combinations of monetary and fiscal policy changes can cause temporary changes in the balance of payments relative to an equilibrium level. The exchange rate therefore becomes the transmission mechanism by which equilibrium is restored to the balance of payments. It must be noted within this that the degree of capital mobility is crucially important.

In an economy with high capital mobility, suppose that a central bank decides to loosen monetary policy by cutting interest rates. One must assume that it does this because of weak growth conditions and benign inflation. As we saw before when looking at money demand, lowering interest rates reduces the incentive to hold interest-bearing securities, thus on a relative basis increasing the incentive to hold money or cash. This increase in money demand can be put to work buying goods and should reflect a future rise in national income and growth. The standard monetary model thinks of this in terms of rising demand causing price increases, which in turn causes the exchange rate to depreciate via the concept of PPP. Looking at it another way, rising domestic demand will cause rising import demand, which should mean deterioration in the trade balance. This in turn should eventually lead to depreciation in the exchange rate to allow the trade balance to revert back towards an equilibrium level. Another way of expressing the same thing is that lower interest rates cause capital outflows, which in turn cause depreciation in the exchange rate. Conversely, the basic assumption is that tighter monetary policy through higher interest rates should lead either to weaker domestic demand and a positive swing in the trade balance, or capital inflows, both of which should cause exchange rate appreciation.

On the fiscal side, much depends on whether trade or capital flows dominate. On the one hand, looser fiscal policy, either through tax cuts or spending increases, should cause rising domestic demand, which in turn should cause deterioration in the trade balance. On the other hand, looser fiscal policy causes higher domestic interest rates, which in turn attract capital inflows. If trade flows dominate, then the exchange rate should depreciate. However, if capital flows dominate, then the exchange rate should appreciate.

Conversely, tighter fiscal policy should, according to Mundell–Fleming, lead to weaker domestic demand. On the trade flow side, this should result in reduced import demand, causing a positive swing in the trade balance. On the capital flow side, tighter fiscal policy should lead to lower interest rates, which in turn lead to capital outflows. Here, if trade flows dominate, the exchange rate should appreciate, whereas if capital flows dominate, the exchange rate should depreciate. In a world of perfect or at least high capital mobility, it is assumed that capital flows dominate over trade flows. Therefore, we can express the likely impact on exchange rates via specific combinations of monetary and fiscal policies through Table 1.2.

This model can be used for developed economies and the leading emerging market economies which have deregulated and liberalized barriers to trade and more importantly capital. The classic example of this used in text books is that of the US dollar in 1980–1985, when it appreciated dramatically as the Reagan administration's military spending programme dramatically boosted the budget deficit, while the Volcker-led Federal Reserve waged war against inflation (caused at least in part by those budget deficits). The Plaza Accord of 1985, which helped to

Table 1.2 The policy mix impact on exchange rates in an economy with high capital mobility

	Loose monetary policy	Tight monetary policy
Loose fiscal policy	Offsetting impact	**Exchange rate appreciation**
Tight fiscal policy	**Exchange rate depreciation**	Offsetting impact

Table 1.3   The policy mix impact on exchange rates in an economy with low capital mobility

	Loose monetary policy	Tight monetary policy
Loose fiscal policy	**Exchange rate depreciation**	Offsetting impact
Tight fiscal policy	Offsetting impact	**Exchange rate appreciation**

bring down the value of the US dollar, worked only because it was accompanied by significant policy changes. In the 1993–1995 period, the US had a somewhat different problem to 1980–1985. While the new US government was moving towards the idea of balancing the budget, and thus tightening fiscal policy, the Federal Reserve was in 1993 keeping a relatively loose monetary policy. Indeed, one could argue that the Fed maintained an inappropriately loose monetary policy for much of 1994 up until its tightening of November 1994, before policy was seen as appropriately tight. Perhaps not coincidentally, in 1994 the US Treasury market had its worst year on record. In line with this, the US dollar weakened up until November of that year.

The above model and examples assume either perfect or high capital mobility. However, not all economies are like this. While the move towards liberalization of trade and capital has broadly increased capital mobility, there remain specific countries in the emerging markets where capital mobility remains low (e.g. China). In this case, therefore, one must assume that trade flows dominate over capital flows. Thus, the results are altered as in Table 1.3.

The Mundell–Fleming model has done much to explain how combinations of monetary and fiscal policy should affect exchange rates. Indeed, their model is the standard for this kind of work.

1.2.2   Theory vs. Practice

However, as ever with exchange rate models, in an open economy with high capital mobility there remains the issue of delay in the transmission mechanism. Monetary models suggest that an increase in interest rates should lead to an increase in the investor's weighting of interest-bearing securities and a corresponding reduction in the weighting of money/cash. This in turn should lead to a reduction in the demand for and therefore the price of goods, which according to PPP should result in an offsetting appreciation of the nominal exchange rate in order to restore equilibrium.

In practice, it may not take place exactly like this, at least in the short term. Say you are an investor in US Treasuries and the Federal Reserve tightens monetary policy by increasing interest rates. Depending on what were market expectations for Fed policy prior to that and also depending on where you were positioned on the US yield curve, you may be facing losses on your position due to the simple inverse relationship between bond yields and bond prices. Eventually, the incentive to hold interest-bearing securities will rise as interest rates rise, but only at the point where the investor believes interest rates have stopped rising. Until that time, the investor may in practice do the opposite of what the model suggests, by reducing their position in interest-bearing securities and reverting to money/cash in order to preserve capital. Theoretically, the investor will have more money/cash to spend on goods and this should push up prices, which in turn should lead to depreciation — rather than appreciation — of the exchange rate according to PPP to restore equilibrium.

Equally, the natural reaction of our US Treasury investor to a fall in interest rates is not necessarily to reduce the position, given that falling yields equal rising prices. Eventually, the reduction in income will not be offset by the capital gain, at which point the investor will indeed reduce the position in favour of other assets such as money/cash. Before that, they may well maintain or even increase the position in interest-bearing securities in order to reap the capital gains impact. Thus, a reduction of interest rates may at least initially lead to an actual reduction in money/cash within portfolios, in turn causing money demand and prices to fall and the currency to appreciate according to PPP to restore equilibrium.

I suspect that the very suggestion that a reduction in interest rates may lead to a reduction rather than an increase in money/cash may cause one or two economists reading this to foam at the mouth. The point is a serious one however, and it is this — the assumption that a change in monetary policy leads directly and automatically to a parallel change in the exchange rate is flawed for the following reasons:

- There may be a delay in the transmission mechanism
- The initial exchange rate reaction may be the exact opposite of what standard models assume

This is not in any way to reduce the importance of the original work. Rather, it is to bring it into the context of modern-day trading and investing conditions. Over the medium to long term, the Mundell–Fleming model of policy combinations is an invaluable guide to future exchange rate direction. In the short term, however, as I have tried to show, there may be delays and distortions, which at least put off the anticipated results.

1.2.3   A Multi-Polar rather than a Bi-Polar Investment World

The results we have looked at so far with regard to this model assume a bi-polar world of money/cash or interest-bearing securities. Suppose however that our investment world is much more complex than that, involving equities, fixed income securities, money market funds and money/cash. As a central bank cuts interest rates, the effect of this should be spread across these asset classes, which in turn react in different ways. If a central bank cuts interest rates, this should cause the investor to cut their portfolio weighting in money market funds and increase it in equities. In the short term, it should also cause an increase in the weighting for fixed income securities as the capital gain should offset the lost income. Eventually, however, we should assume that it causes a reduction in the weighting for fixed income securities. Finally, a rate cut should also lead to an increase in the weighting of money/cash. The reduction in money market funds and fixed income securities should logically equal the sum of the increase in weighting in equities and money/cash. Since money/cash has to share its gains with equities, one should assume that the effect on money demand and therefore prices is reduced. Prices should rise less than they would otherwise do without the influence of equities. Consequently, as prices rise by less, the exchange rate should also depreciate by less than one would otherwise expect. In the same way, an interest rate increase should in this multi-polar investment world lead to less of an exchange rate appreciation than would be expected in a bi-polar investment world.

1.2.4   Two Legs but not Three

The final word on the Monetary Approach and the exchange rate impact from policy combinations concerns the idea from the Mundell–Fleming model that a central bank can in a world of high capital mobility target the exchange rate or the interest rate but not both. Another way of expressing this is that you can have two of the following but not all three:

- A fixed exchange rate regime
- Monetary policy independence
- High capital mobility

The first assumes the targeting of the exchange rate, while the second assumes the targeting of inflation and interest rates. The discovery of this rule was the stuff of brilliance, the monetary equivalent of the discovery of penicillin, yet history is littered with examples of policymakers who ignored it to their cost. While the example of Asia and the subsequent Asian currency crisis may spring to mind, there are also examples within the developed world, notably that of the ERM crises of 1992–1993. Here, there was indeed a commitment to a type of fixed exchange rate regime under conditions of high capital mobility. At the same time however, ERM members were allowed monetary independence. In practice, some, notably the Benelux countries, appeared to all but abandon monetary independence in favour of adopting the harsh benchmark of Bundesbank monetary policy. Others, such as the UK, Italy and Spain, sought a greater degree of monetary independence. Is it any coincidence that these were either forced out of the ERM altogether or forced to devalue within it? While the argument is frequently made that the UK pound sterling went into the ERM at an overvalued level to the Deutschmark, a contrary argument could be made that sterling would have been forced out of the ERM no matter what its entry level because the UK authorities refused to relinquish monetary independence to the Bundesbank.

1.2.5   Implications for EU Accession Candidates

This simple rule of being able to maintain two policy focuses but not three has potentially important implications for the EU accession candidate countries such as Poland, Hungary, the Czech Republic and Slovakia, particularly during their transition phase between membership of the EU and entry into the Euro. During that period, it is assumed that these countries will be part of an "ERM II" grid, featuring a narrow exchange rate band, whose limits are defended by the commitment of the central bank to intervene.

For example, if in January 2005 Poland becomes a member of the EU and as a result the Polish zloty enters the ERM II grid, Poland must renounce its monetary independence at the same time. If Poland does not, it must either put limits on capital, which would be against both the spirit and the letter of the treaties of Maastricht and Nice, or eventually be forced to relinquish its fixed exchange rate peg. The only way to avoid this is for ERM II to have a very wide band, otherwise at the very least EU accession candidate currencies are (once again) in for an extremely wild — and potentially unpleasant — ride.

1.3   THE INTEREST RATE APPROACH

A further approach to trying to determine or predict exchange rates is that involving the analysis of interest rate differentials (the Interest Rate Approach). This involves a number of different principles and we shall go through them briefly and in turn. The first principle involves the basic *interest rate parity theory*, which is that:

An exchange rate's forward % premium/discount = its interest rate differential

Thus, for instance, the traditional forward discount on the dollar–yen exchange rate should equal the interest rate differential between the two currencies. This is seen as the equilibrium reflecting the relationship between the exchange rate and interest rates. Because forwards are a traded instrument and thus subject to supply and demand, the forward premium or discount can vary briefly from this equilibrium, but should always revert to norm. After all, if for argument's sake the forward premium/discount for some reason did not equal the interest rate differential between the two currencies an arbitrageur could in theory make risk-free profits by borrowing in one currency, investing in the securities of the other currency and simultaneously opening a forward contract in the exchange rate for the same period as the initial loan. This is called *covered interest rate arbitrage*.

The theory of interest rate parity is a guiding principle for several economic and financial models. Under this theory, it is assumed that the expected (interest rate) returns of a currency should be equalized through speculation in another country once converted back to the first currency. This may sound like gibberish, but basically this is an interest rate version of PPP — and like PPP its results are decidedly mixed. Indeed, there can be significant violations of the interest rate parity theory for substantial periods of time without the immediate reversal that covered interest rate arbitrage might suggest. Not too surprisingly, this is a dismal predictor of exchange rates.

Indeed, before we go further into the theory, it is important to point out a practical flaw in the theory involving incentive, which is undoubtedly a key contributing factor to its poor predictive track record — the theory supposes an automatically causal relationship between interest rates and the exchange rate, yet in practice most currency market practitioners trade currencies with directional rather than interest rate considerations in mind. Even this statement is a generalization. On a simple numerical basis, the majority of currency market practitioners are made up of interbank dealers, thus it is important and necessary to look at their motivation for trading. Spot traders for the most part care not one whit about a currency's interest rate, in part because they hold positions for too short a time for it to matter, in part because they are seeking to predict direction — and thus make capital gains on their position, not primarily to make interest income. Forward traders are a different breed entirely and more akin to money market or interest rate traders. Indeed, the way they hedge out their forward exposure frequently involves an array of interest rate-related instruments. Eventually, interest rate parity violations will be reversed, but there is little incentive to do so in the immediate term if you don't care about the interest rate in the first place.

Returning to the theory for now, interest rate parity theory states that the difference between a spot and forward exchange rate expressed as a percentage should equal the interest rate differential between the two currencies. Yet, we know from the PPP principle that exchange rates and inflation rates are linked. Can we not link these also with interest rates? Indeed we can, thanks to the seminal work of the economist Irving Fisher. Thus, according to what has become known as the "Fisher effect:"

The difference in interest rates = the difference in expected inflation rates

Thus, we have gone from the difference between the spot and the forward exchange rate equating to the interest rate differential through the interest rate parity theory, which in turn equates to the difference in expected inflation rates through the Fisher effect. Yet, PPP tells us that absolute or relative price growth levels can be used to forecast future exchange rates.

Thus, through PPP we can extrapolate this one stage further to suggest that:

The difference in expected inflation rates = the expected exchange rate change

Bringing all these together, we get:

(1) The difference in spot and forward rates = the difference in interest rates
(Interest rate parity theory)

(2) The difference in interest rates = the difference in expected inflation rates
(Fisher effect)

(3) The difference in expected inflation rates = the expected change in spot exchange rate
(Purchasing Power Parity)

Logically from this, one may conclude that the difference between the spot and forward rates expressed as a percentage should equal the expected change in the spot exchange rate. This is known as the expectations theory of exchange rates.

Finally, there is the theory that:

(4) The difference in interest rates = the expected change in the spot exchange rate
(International Fisher effect)

On the face of it, the ideas presented above seem logical and follow a clear and persuasive train of thought. There is only one small problem — this clear train of thought rarely works in practice. More specifically, the difference in interest rates or expected inflation rates may be equal to the theoretical construct of the "expected change in the spot exchange rate", but in practice it is of the future exchange rate. In line with this, the forward rate is also a very poor predictor of the future exchange rate, a fact that economists have labelled "forward rate bias" or the "forward premium puzzle". As Bansal and Dahlquist (2000)[2] confirmed in their exhaustive study, in contrast to the theory, empirical evidence suggests that in fact current interest rate differentials and future spot exchange rates are frequently *negatively correlated*. This is particularly the case within the developed economies, though the picture is somewhat more mixed within emerging market economies.

Over the long term, the interest rate parity theory is seen to work as enough market partici-pants can be found to "discover" the opportunities available for covered interest rate arbitrage between currencies and interest rates, thus in the process eliminating such disparities. However, there are much longer lags than the theory might suggest is possible. Here again, the issue of incentive must be a focus. As noted earlier, it should behove the theorists to know that the majority of currency market practitioners are currency interbank dealers and moreover that the main incentive for these to trade is directional gain rather than interest income. Currency markets do focus on interest rate differentials for extended periods of time, but equally they focus on other factors, in many cases completely disregarding interest rates.

1.3.1   Real Interest Rate Differentials and Exchange Rates

Currency strategists do however use models comparing the real interest rate differential with either the nominal or the real exchange rate between two countries. The logic behind this relates

[2]Ravi Bansal and Magnus Dahlquist, The forward premium puzzle: different tales from developed and emerging economies, *Journal of International Economics* 51 (2000) 115–144.

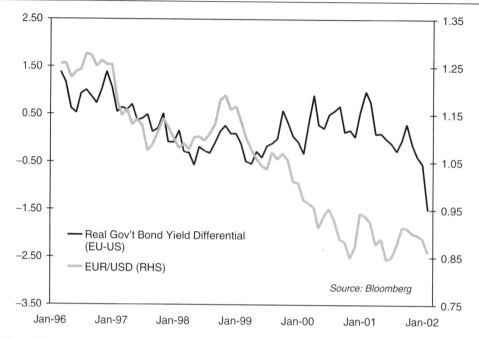

Figure 1.1   Euro–dollar exchange rate vs. 10-year bond yield differential

to both the international Fisher effect and to PPP, where on the one hand the difference in interest rates should, if not be exactly equal to an expected change in the spot exchange rate, at least be an important driver of it, and on the other hand where nominal interest rate differentials are adjusted for inflation (i.e. domestic price growth) and thus relate to the exchange rate through the law of one price.

The link or correlation between real interest rate differentials and the exchange rate appears to have grown exactly in line with the gradual move since the end of the Bretton Woods exchange rate system to liberalize capital flows globally. As barriers to capital movement have fallen, so the overall importance of capital flow has grown exponentially relative to that of trade flow. Exchange rate models that focused solely on the current account no longer seemed appropriate in such a world, those that focused on capital flows seemed increasingly so. As capital flows have gained in importance, so their importance within overall currency market flows has grown and thus the correlation between the two increased. Thus, currency strategists across the market continue to track this relationship between real interest rate differentials and nominal exchange rates as one of many useful and important indicators of currency over- or undervaluation. Figure 1.1 compares the Euro–dollar exchange rate against the 10–year bond yield differential from 1996 through to the end of January 2002.

1.4   THE BALANCE OF PAYMENTS APPROACH

The core idea behind the Balance of Payments Approach is that changes in national income affect both the current and the capital account and through this cause a predictable reaction in the exchange rate in order to restore balance of payments equilibrium. The best way of looking at this is to examine the transmission mechanism from the change in national income through to the exchange rate reaction. When considering the Balance of Payments Approach to exchange rates, it is good to keep in mind the classic accounting identity for economic adjustment:

$$S - I = Y - E = X - M$$

where:

S = Savings
I = Investment
Y = Income
E = Expenditure
X = Exports
M = Imports

Within economics, this is an unequivocal law which governs how economies adjust to changes in economic dynamics.

1.4.1 A Fixed Exchange Rate Regime

Under a fixed exchange rate regime where capital mobility is extremely limited, the focus is on the current account rather than the capital account. Assume for the purpose of this exercise that national income is rising. As national income rises, so stronger demand sucks in an increasing amount of imports, which in turn causes current account balance deterioration. The exchange rate cannot be the transmission mechanism for restoring balance of payments equilibrium since the exchange rate is fixed. Hence, the monetary authority has the choice of either selling its foreign exchange reserves in the market to alleviate pressure on the exchange rate or more practically tightening monetary policy in order to dampen domestic demand, thus reducing import demand and restoring the balance of payments equilibrium.

Equally, within that same fixed exchange rate regime, say national income was falling. This would imply that weaker domestic demand would cause a decline in import demand, which would paradoxically cause an improvement in the current account balance. Because the capital account would not be a consideration given our premise that capital mobility is highly restricted and the exchange rate is fixed, equilibrium in the balance of payments can only be restored through a reversal of that current account balance improvement. Such an improvement would pressure the fixed exchange rate to appreciate. The monetary authority could either absorb this pressure by increasing its foreign exchange reserves and selling the domestic currency in the market to do so, or by loosening monetary policy. Either way, this would cause market interest rates to fall, spurring domestic demand and thus import demand, which in turn would cause the current account balance to move back to a position such that the balance of payments equilibrium would be restored.

The dynamic whereby a change in national income is transmitted within a fixed exchange rate regime through the current account balance is expressed in the following diagram:

> Change in national income → Change in current account balance → Monetary reaction →
>
> Reversal of current account balance change → Balance of payments equilibrium restored

In theory, a fixed exchange rate regime should automatically be in balance as left to its own devices it should be self-correcting through changes in capital flows and interest rates. An imbalance of one kind or the other should automatically be corrected, albeit after a lag. Yet, in reality, fixed or pegged exchange rate regimes have faced an increasingly turbulent time during the 1990s to the extent that many of them have collapsed in the face of seemingly irresistible speculative pressure. Why has this been the case? Many of the reasons for this are case-specific. However, the underlying theme is that frequently countries simply have not been prepared to maintain the degree of economic discipline that is required to maintain the fixed exchange rate regime. In addition, many appeared to forget the core rule established by the Mundell–Fleming example that you can have only two but not all three outcomes with a fixed exchange rate regime, high capital mobility and an independent monetary policy. Under the misguided influence of the official community in Washington, many emerging market countries, which had fixed or pegged exchange rate regimes, opened up their economies to high capital mobility at the same time they sought to maintain some degree of monetary independence. Looked at from this perspective, the result was inevitable.

Maintaining a fixed or pegged exchange rate regime within a world of high capital mobility requires a considerable degree of economic discipline given that the transmission mechanism for restoring imbalances to the equilibrium of the balance of payments cannot be the exchange rate but instead must be the real economy. Furthermore, global financial markets must be convinced that the monetary authority of this fixed exchange rate regime will hold the line come what may. In the case of Asia, countries like Thailand, Indonesia and Korea were ultimately either unwilling or unable to maintain that discipline. Interestingly, China, Hong Kong and Taiwan were all able to weather the storm, not least because they upheld the principles of the Mundell–Fleming rule. In the case of China and Taiwan, both had monetary independence and a fixed or pegged exchange rate regime (Taiwan's cannot be called a freely floating exchange rate regime by any stretch of the imagination), but maintained significant restrictions on capital mobility. In the case of Hong Kong, on the other hand, it had very high capital mobility and a fixed exchange rate regime in the form of a self-balancing currency board, but its monetary authority, at least in theory, abandoned monetary independence in favour of following the monetary policy of its peg currency, namely that of the Federal Reserve. Granted, Hong Kong, China and Taiwan perhaps had both greater resolve and ability to resist speculative pressures, but the structure of their exchange rate regimes was crucially more secure. As the example of Argentina shows in 2002, following this two-but-not-three model is not a guarantee of success. However, one could well say that not following it is more or less a guarantee of failure.

1.4.2 A Floating Exchange Rate Regime

Under a floating exchange rate regime, we have to consider the capital account as well as the current account. Here, as national income rises, so import demand rises, in turn causing the current account balance to deteriorate. So far, this is just like the fixed exchange rate regime. However, in the case of the floating exchange rate regime, the exchange rate is able to be the transmission mechanism for restoring the balance of payments to equilibrium. On the capital account side, a rise in national income, causing the current account balance to deteriorate, must be accompanied by a rise in real interest rates. The higher real interest rate will dampen import demand, which will in turn cause the current account balance deterioration to reverse. As that happens, national income will fall back, causing real interest rates also to fall back. If we start off with national income falling, we achieve the same transmission mechanism, only in reverse, with real interest rates falling, causing capital account outflows and current account balance improvement to the extent that these developments cause on the one hand a revival in domestic demand and on the other a loss in export competitiveness. Thus, the current account improvement reverses and real interest rates rebound. We can express this transmission mechanism from a change in national income through the balance of payments within a floating exchange rate regime with the following diagram:

Change in national income → Change in current account balance → Change in real interest rates → Change in capital flows → National income change reversed → Current account reversed → Capital flows reversed → Real interest rates reversed → Balance of payments equilibrium restored

1.4.3   The External Balance and the Real Exchange Rate

Similar to the Balance of Payments Approach to exchange rates is that which focuses on the relationship between a long-term equilibrium value for the real exchange rate and the external balance. Under this, the long-term equilibrium exchange rate is that which generates both internal and external balance, where internal balance is defined as full employment and external balance as the current account. Since the creation of this model, the emphasis has shifted away from focusing on full employment to concentrating on achieving a sustainable current account balance — not necessarily zero — which will achieve a perceived economic and exchange rate equilibrium.

As with the Balance of Payments Approach, the current account is seen as the transmission mechanism for the exchange rate, albeit this time under both fixed and floating exchange rate regimes. If the current account balance is showing an unsustainably high deficit relative to historic deficit levels, this will require a real exchange rate depreciation to restore equilibrium. Conversely, if it is showing a very high current account surplus, this will require a real exchange rate appreciation to restore equilibrium.

The example that is often used with regard to this is Japan, which has had a structurally high current account surplus. Using the external balance approach, if that current account surplus is seen as unsustainably high relative to historical norms, it requires a rise in the yen's real exchange rate to restore equilibrium. Barring periodic reversals, this is what we saw from 1971 to 1995. Since then, the yen has reversed course, not least because the strengthening of the nominal yen exchange rate to a record dollar–yen low of 79.85 caused such a real shock to the current account balance that it in turn required a significant real exchange rate depreciation to restore equilibrium once more.

Within the emerging markets, another good example is that of Russia. Before the Russian rouble crisis of August 1998, Russia continued to record significant current account deficits. The external balance approach suggested that at some point a real exchange depreciation would be required to restore equilibrium. However, the Russian rouble was pegged to the US dollar and in order to maintain that peg real interest rates were kept high. Eventually, the costs of defending the Russian rouble peg — yet another case of trying to have all three of monetary independence, reasonably high capital mobility and a fixed exchange rate regime — proved too much and the rouble was de-pegged and devalued, and for good value Russia defaulted on its domestic debt.

1.4.4   REER and FEER

In line with the external balance approach, the Real Effective Exchange Rate (REER) is the trade-weighted exchange rate (NEER) adjusted for inflation. As with PPP, the purpose of using REER is to try to gauge an exchange rate's over- or undervaluation relative to a given norm. As with PPP, using REER is far from an exact science and in fact PPP and REER run into similar problems. For instance, a major problem with PPP is which base year to choose. REER has the same problem and for similar reasons. Using a particular base year with which to begin one's analysis can significantly distort the results. On the face of it, it would seem logical to start both PPP and REER analyses in the 1971–1973 period when the Bretton Woods exchange rate system broke up, yet this was a highly inflationary and therefore distorting period as far as such analyses are concerned.

The transmission mechanism is again the current account balance. Significant REER over-valuation relative to a given norm of 100 tends to produce a widening current account deficit or "external imbalance" in the jargon of economists. In order to restore balance or equilibrium, there has logically to be a REER depreciation. This can be achieved either by a depreciation of the trade-weighted exchange rate — that is to say by a depreciation of the nominal exchange rate — or by a sharp decline in inflation.

So far, this seems relatively logical and deceptively predictable. However, significant REER overvaluations can last for substantial periods of time. In some cases it can take several years before an adjustment process takes place to eliminate such overvaluation. A good example again is that of the Russian rouble, whose REER value was overvalued by around 60% for three years — depending on the base year used — before it finally succumbed to gravity. The REER values of both the Mexican peso and the Venezuelan bolivar have indicated significant overvaluation for several years now, and in the case of the Mexican peso to a greater degree than before the 1994–1995 "Tequila" crisis. The lesson of REER is that it can be a useful tool for diagnosing over- or undervaluation and a consequent need for an adjustment to restore equilibrium — but what it cannot do is tell you when that will happen.

Another way to estimate a real exchange rate's equilibrium is FEER, or Fundamental Equilibrium Exchange Rate, pioneered by the writer and economic scholar John Williamson in 1985. Recognizing the imperfections of the PPP concept, FEER reflects the exchange rate value that is the result of a current account surplus or deficit that is in turn appropriate to the long-term structural capital inflow or outflow in the economy, assuming that the country does not have barriers to free trade and is also trying to pursue internal balance. Assessing the appropriate level of long-term structural capital inflow or outflow requires a considerable degree of value judgement. Even if it did not, it assumes that such capital inflows or outflows should persist simply because they have occurred in the past. Given this construction, it is not surprising that estimates of an exchange rate's FEER value vary widely. This is not to say that it is not a useful model. Indeed, models based on the FEER concept have been widely used within the private sector for some time. However, it is to say that using such a type of exchange rate model puts a considerable degree of emphasis on the value judgement of the analyst concerned, thereby undermining the point of using a model in the first place.

Looking at exchange rate models in general that use some variation of the external balance approach, we see that considerable "misalignments" in the external balance — and therefore presumably in the exchange rate — can persist over significant periods of time. The fact that this can happen suggests equally that for substantial periods of time the importance of the external balance to the exchange rate can be more than offset by capital flows. Eventually, it appears that the misalignment in the external balance reaches a level which produces a loss of market confidence and capital outflows. As capital outflows occur, this by necessity must reduce the current account deficit. The problem of course is that this level, this trigger point which causes a loss of market confidence, is not static but changes. Thus, as with all exchange rate models, those which focus on the external balance should be used for long-term exchange rate considerations rather than for the short term.

1.4.5   Terms of Trade

Another important aspect of the external balance approach to exchange rate determination is the so-called "terms of trade", which is the relationship between a country's export and import prices. A country's terms of trade can be an important determinant of its long-term equilibrium real exchange rate. We find this particularly the case for countries that are major commodity exporters and therefore whose economies are particularly sensitive to swings in commodity prices. An improvement in a country's terms of trade, that is a rise in its export prices relative to import prices, should lead to a rise in the real exchange rate equilibrium value. Rising export prices should be reflective of rising global demand for that country's exports, both on an absolute basis and relative to domestic demand levels. Consequently, one should assume that an improvement in the terms of trade should lead to an improvement in the current account balance, which in turn requires a real exchange rate appreciation to restore equilibrium. Equally, a deterioration in the terms of trade leads to a current account deterioration, which requires a real exchange rate depreciation to restore equilibrium. For the sake of clarity, we can express this transmission mechanism using the following simple diagram:

Change in terms of trade → Change in current account balance →

Real exchange rate change to restore equilibrium

Taking oil as an example, the terms of trade concept is an important determinant of the long-term real exchange rate equilibrium value for the countries of the Gulf, Mexico, Venezuela, Colombia, Nigeria, Indonesia, Russia, the UK and Norway. Note that these are just the exporters. The terms of trade concept also works for the importers as well, which is why when the international price of oil experiences a significant uptrend, this causes a terms of trade deterioration for the major oil importers, leading to current account balance deterioration. All else being equal, this should require a real exchange rate depreciation to restore equilibrium.

1.4.6   Productivity

Last but not least, we look at how productivity growth can affect the equilibrium real exchange rate. What is productivity? We have a vague concept of this in our work place, but it has a precise definition — output per man hour. Rising productivity growth causes increased supply of a good. Supply/demand dynamics require that increased supply relative to demand leads to a fall in price. The principle of Purchasing Power Parity requires however that falling prices in one country relative to another lead to an offsetting exchange rate appreciation under the law of one price. Thus higher productivity growth in tradable goods should lead to exchange rate appreciation to restore equilibrium to the current account.

The issue of productivity growth was much in debate in 2001 as economists sought to explain the US dollar's inexorable rise against the Euro. Indeed, both the Federal Reserve Bank of New York and the Bank of England produced reports on the issue of whether higher US productivity growth explained the US dollar's strength and indeed whether or not the US did in fact produce higher productivity growth. Despite the presence of such eminent scholarship, the jury is still out. There does however seem to be greater clarity at least as regards the broader issue of whether or not productivity growth should produce exchange rate appreciation. Just as PPP is not a good short-term predictor of exchange rates, so productivity growth should not be used as a short-term trading model. However, both are profoundly useful in predicting medium- to long-term exchange rate trends. Here, the fact that the US has had consistently higher productivity growth in the wake of the "re-engineering" drive within the US economy in 1994–1995, and the fact that the US dollar has been on a long-term uptrend ever since, should not be seen as coincidence. Similarly, Japan during the 1970s and 1980s had consistently higher productivity levels than either the US or Europe, and this should be seen as at least one of the major reasons why we saw trend appreciation of the Japanese yen during that period.

Yet, at some point productivity growth becomes unsustainable. After all, it deals with the issue of increased supply, presuming that there is always demand for that increased supply. At some point, the levels of supply will exceed demand. When that happens a hitherto unforeseen "inventory overhang", as per the economists' jargon, appears. The natural dynamics of supply and demand suggest that the excess supply should instantly be eliminated to restore "equilibrium" supply levels relative to demand. Yet, we know from painful experience that this is not what happens. If we view productivity as supply and wages as demand, the standard economic model suggests that higher productivity growth automatically results in higher wages. Yet, during periods of major technological change, which tend to produce the strongest levels of productivity growth, the fact that competition is greatly increased produces such downward pressure to prices to the extent that the only way some can compete is to cut wage growth. At the very least, wage growth does not keep up with productivity growth. In other words, demand does not keep up with supply — which brings us back to the idea that this excess supply will rather quickly have to correct automatically to match the level of demand.

However, this is not what happens in reality because this simple model of productivity (supply) growth and wage (demand) growth does not take account of the very modern concept of debt. Inadequate demand growth in the form of wages can be artificially propped up to meet ever increasing supply growth in the form of productivity through debt or borrowing. Eventually, of course, the gap between supply and demand becomes too wide even for debt to bridge. When that happens, supply crashes. At the microeconomic level, faced with a massive inventory overhang, companies cut costs and the easiest way of doing that is to cut jobs. Demand falls as well. This is how financial crashes happen, whether we are talking about Japan in 1990 or the US in 2000. Does this automatically lead to an exchange rate reaction? Not necessarily so. After all, the yen continued to rise for another five years after the "bubble economy" burst. Similarly, the US dollar has continued to rise despite the bursting of the "internet bubble economy" in 2000. Some explanation for this can be given by the fact that productivity rates have remained extremely high in the US — as they did in Japan — despite the financial and economic distress that has been seen in the last two years. What we learn from this however is that productivity growth appears to be in part cyclical in nature, in so far as it does not go on for ever but instead reaches unsustainably high levels which lead ultimately to a violent correction. The bursting of a productivity bubble should eventually lead to lower

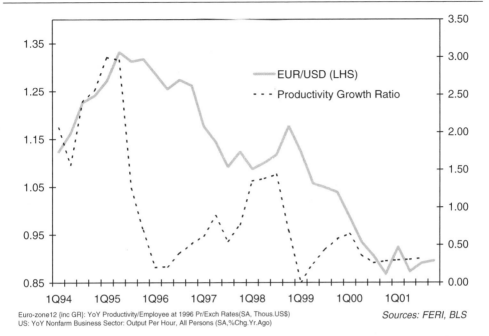

Euro-zone12 (inc GR): YoY Productivity/Employee at 1996 Pr/Exch Rates(SA, Thous.US$)
US: YoY Nonfarm Business Sector: Output Per Hour, All Persons (SA,%Chg.Yr.Ago)

Sources: FERI, BLS

Figure 1.2 Euro–dollar exchange rate vs. relative productivity growth levels

trend productivity growth for a period of time and higher prices, thus requiring according to PPP an exchange rate depreciation to offset this price disparity under the law of one price.

This is of course not what we have seen in Japan to date. Instead, debt/GDP has continued to rise inexorably as the real interest rate has consistently exceeded the real GDP growth rate. The rising debt burden, along with the rising real interest rate, has acted not only to keep a lid on price growth but also to cause actual price deflation. Under PPP, if anything this should lead to yen appreciation, which is of course the last thing Japan needs. Turning to the US, corporate and consumer debt levels are extremely high. For now however, productivity growth remains extremely high as well, certainly higher than the EU. Both of these factors support the idea that the US dollar should remain a strong currency near term.

In Figure 1.2, we again use the Euro–dollar exchange rate, this time compared with relative productivity growth levels. As the figure shows, there is an important relationship between the two, though admittedly the degree of correlation has declined sharply for periods of time. In this regard, relative productivity growth levels are an important indicator of exchange rate direction, but apparently not capable of providing a more sophisticated analysis in terms of either the timing or degree of the chosen direction.

1.5   THE PORTFOLIO BALANCE APPROACH

Having dealt so far with the relative price of goods, money, interest and current/capital flows, the last model we will look at in this chapter deals with the relative price of assets. This is the Portfolio Balance Approach and it deals specifically with the relationship between the relative price of domestic and foreign bonds and the exchange rate. Within this model, it is presumed that a change in monetary and/or fiscal conditions will in turn lead to changes in the supply and demand for domestic currency bonds and the demand for foreign currency bonds, which will in turn trigger a reaction in the exchange rate between the two currencies.

On the monetary side, assume that a cut in interest rates by the central bank causes outflows from domestic interest rate-bearing securities into money/cash, as per the Monetary Approach we looked at earlier. If one assumes for the sake of this simple model that domestic bond supply is unchanged, demand for those bonds should be reduced because of the lower interest rate. This effect should cause increased demand for the foreign currency bonds, which in turn should cause the domestic currency to depreciate against the foreign one. Equally, if one starts from the premise that the central bank raises interest rates, this should, according to this simple model, cause a domestic currency appreciation.

Looking at this question from the fiscal side, assume that a government expands fiscal policy in the face of an economic downturn. In terms of the domestic bond market, this should lead to an increase in domestic bond supply. Holders of existing domestic bonds will only support such an increase if it leads to a higher interest rate to compensate for the increased supply. Thus, increased domestic bond supply should eventually result in increased domestic bond demand, reduced foreign currency bond demand and an appreciation in the domestic currency against the foreign currency. Similarly, according to this model, decreased bond supply should eventually lead to depreciation in the domestic currency due to outflows by investors in favour of foreign bonds.

This Portfolio Balance Approach appears overly simplistic and it is. Indeed, it has been a very poor predictor of exchange rates, not least because it does not deal with the real-world realities of a fixed income fund manager who has to make asset allocation decisions.

Example

Assume for argument's sake that our fixed income fund manager invests only in US Treasuries and Japanese government bonds ("JGBs"). The Portfolio Balance Approach assumes money/cash is not interest-bearing, but this is not in fact true. Thus, the fund manager can also have a cash allocation, which he/she can put on a modest deposit rate. The fund manager starts the year with a 60% allocation in US Treasuries, 35% in JGBs and 5% in cash. If the Federal Reserve cuts interest rates, our fund manager does not immediately reduce his/her allocation in Treasuries in favour of JGBs as the model assumes. Much depends on the relative policy mixes in the US and Japan and also the prevailing nominal and real interest rate differentials between the two countries. There are far too many uncertainties within this situation for us to be able to assume that JGBs would automatically be favoured over US Treasuries due to a US interest rate cut. If Japanese interest rates are already substantially below those of the US, one US interest rate cut might make no difference whatsoever to the asset allocation. Therefore, one cannot assume that the US dollar would fall against the Japanese yen.

Looking at this from a fiscal policy perspective, again let's suppose that the government expands fiscal policy in order to boost a flagging economy. This implies increased bond supply. If we assume that this economy is that of the US, then our fund manager has a dilemma. Increased bond market supply will of necessity push interest rates higher — and bond prices lower. Depending on where the fund manager is positioned along the US Treasury curve, this may result in painful losses. Thus, if anything the fund manager may in fact initially reduce his/her allocation in US Treasuries. In our example the fund manager can only invest in US Treasuries, JGBs and cash. As this example assumes a change in US fiscal policy but not US monetary policy, the fund manager may reduce his/her allocation initially in US Treasuries in favour of JGBs. Thus, assuming for the purpose of this example that our fictional fund manager represents the entire universe of institutional investors, the exchange rate reaction may at least initially be the complete opposite of what the Portfolio Balance Approach suggests.

Clearly, where theory and practice meet is not in the short-term reaction but in the long-term trend. A trend of rising domestic interest rates relative to foreign interest rates will attract rising foreign demand for domestic bonds and therefore in turn cause a domestic currency appreciation relative to the foreign currency. Equally, rising bond market supply should on a trend basis have the same exchange rate reaction by causing bond yields to rise, thus attracting increased foreign investor interest. Both of these exchange rate reactions may occur over the long term. Thus, we can use this approach, as with the Mundell–Fleming model, to explain the inexorable strength of the US dollar in the 1980–1985 period.

Over the short term however, what we may see is in fact the complete opposite exchange rate reaction. Indeed, the very concept of short term is subjective as such "disparities" relative to the model can go on for years. For instance, between 1996 and 2000 the US dollar rose dramatically against its major currency counterparts, despite tight fiscal policy and varying degrees of loose monetary policy. This should, according to both the Portfolio Balance Approach and the Mundell–Fleming model, have produced exchange rate depreciation, yet it did not. Indeed, it produced the complete opposite. Clearly, the model does not take account of such issues as existing investor positioning and the degree of policy credibility (which may cause investors to be more eager to buy a bond than simple yields would otherwise imply).

Thus, to summarize the Portfolio Balance Approach, use it sparingly in trying to determine or predict exchange rates and only for long-term trends. Furthermore, use it from the perspective of asset allocation. As fiscal policy expands, investors will gradually, after a suitable interval to allow for the rise in bond yields, increase their asset allocation in the bonds of that country, assuming that those bonds are already within their benchmark index. Thus, as Japanese fiscal policy has been expanded in the 1990s, so investors have increased their asset allocation of JGBs. This may be considered a further reason for the yen's appreciation from 1990 to mid-1995, but not thereafter as it fell back. Note however that such asset allocation shifts are also cyclical in nature as they will be increased within a particular bond market to the extent that monetary and fiscal policies are perceived as credible. When they are no longer seen as credible, not surprisingly the asset allocation shift goes into reverse. For instance, in 2001 and early 2002 investors started to perceive Japanese fiscal policy as out of control, causing most to reduce their JGB weightings and some to remove JGBs entirely from their portfolio.

1.6 SUMMARY

To conclude, the traditional exchange rate models, which are based on some form of equilibrium value, do offer an important and useful long-term guide towards exchange rate prediction. Indeed, without these long-term signposts, currency strategists might be quite lost in seeking to predict exchange rates past one year out. As a result, in terms of their usefulness to specific types of currency market practitioner, corporations, strategic "real money" investors or "macro" hedge funds with a multi-month or even multi-year perspective would probably find them most valuable as an analytical tool. On the other hand, these traditional exchange rate models are unlikely to be of more than passing interest or use to short-term speculators or interbank dealers whose time frame is far shorter. Lastly, it is a major theme of this book that currency analysis and strategy should be part of an integrated approach, involving the simultaneous use of several analytical disciplines. The apparent weaknesses of traditional exchange rate models, I would suggest, adds to this case that such an integrated currency strategy framework be adopted.

It has to be said that to date, when faced with the unsatisfying results that the traditional exchange rate models have produced as far as predicting exchange rates is concerned, the economic community has for the most part either ignored these inconvenient results or declared that it is impossible to forecast short-term exchange rate moves as they are determined by the so-called "random walk" theory. Occasionally, there has been a paper, illuminating in both its honesty as well as its intellectual acumen, which has "fessed up" to both the failure of these models as predictive tools and a lack of understanding as to why that may be the case. The majority of the time, however, the reaction to the obvious question has been denial or the random walk excuse. According to the latter, since traditional exchange rate models do not appear able to predict short-term exchange rate moves, it must follow logically that such short-term exchange rate moves cannot in fact be predicted at all and must therefore follow a "random walk" path, suggesting an equal probability of appreciating or depreciating over time. Fortunately, however, recent developments in technical and capital flow analysis have achieved significantly better results in predicting exchange rates than the random walk would imply. Thus, the correct approach to analysing and predicting exchange rates would seem to be to use market-based approaches such as technical and flow analysis for short-term exchange rate moves and the traditional exchange rate models for medium- to long-term predictions.

This is certainly not the whole story in trying to create an integrated framework for analysing currencies, but it forms a good start in our understanding of how we should approach exchange rates.

Building on this, going forward, it seems logical to assume that traditional exchange rate models should be modified to suit the modern structure of currency market flows. More specifically, trade flows, which form the premise behind the PPP, Balance of Payments and External Balance Approaches, were once seen as the main driver of currency market overall flow. However, nowadays, they make up only around 1–2% of the USD1.2 trillion in daily volume going through the currency market. Hence, as the overall importance of trade to total market flow has declined, so to a degree has the relevance of those exchange rate models that rely solely on shifts in trade flow patterns. Meanwhile, just as the pre-eminence of trade flows has declined, so the importance of portfolio flows has grown exponentially as barriers to capital have been lifted over the past two decades. The Portfolio Balance Approach is clearly an attempt to focus on asset markets and specifically the bond market as a driver of exchange rates, yet this model remains unsatisfactory as a predictor of exchange rates for the reasons given.

In order to try to get to a better answer of exchange rate movement over the short term, we have to define the main flow drivers of exchange rates:

- "Speculative" flow (without an underlying attached asset)
- Equity flow
- Fixed income flow
- Direct investment flow
- Trade flow

By far, speculative flow is the main driver of exchange rates over the short term. It is not sufficient to suggest that speculative flows follow a "random walk" for the simple reason that both technical and flow analysis have discovered consistent patterns in short-term exchange rates which should not exist under random walk theory. Within asset market flow, equity and fixed income flows continue to do battle for pre-eminence. For instance, from 1998 to mid-2000, net inflows to the US equity markets were a key driver of dollar strength. Equally, as the US equity market began to falter, the resulting equity outflows from the US market weighed on the US dollar. Eventually, however, these flows were more than made up for by fixed income inflows to the US fixed income markets as the Federal Reserve continued to cut interest rates to support the economy. Direct investment is also an increasingly important driver of exchange rates, both in the developed economies and in the emerging markets, as barriers to inward investment have also fallen away. In 2001, the top five performing currencies in the world against the USD were the Mexican peso, Polish zloty, Czech koruna, Hungarian forint and Peruvian sol, all of which benefited from substantial direct investment inflows which had a significant impact on their exchange rates.

The importance of all of these flow types continues to fluctuate in line with market trends. What is clear however, is that until there is a specific exchange rate model which focuses on the main flow dynamic of the currency market, namely speculative flow, it is unlikely that exchange rate models in general will be able to improve upon their current accuracy to any significant degree. In the next chapter, this is in fact what we will try and do — to build a simple exchange rate model which focuses on speculative flow. In addition, we also examine how to use "currency economics", or the bits of economic theory that are relevant to the currency market, in a practical manner for currency forecasting, trading and investing.

2
Currency Economics:
A More Focused Framework

In the previous chapter, we had a pretty detailed look at traditional exchange rate models. Significant research went into these models and indeed they are valuable in trying to predict long-term exchange trends. Where they fall down is their ability to predict short-term moves.

The reaction of economists to this realization in truth has been mixed. Of late, however, there seems to have been a gradual recognition that a greater focus is needed in applying the general rules of economics to the specific dynamics of the currency market. For want of a better term, I have called this greater focus "*currency economics*". I should say at the outset this is not an attempt to create an entirely new field of currency analysis. Rather, it is to create a more focused framework, using those existing economic principles that are relevant to the currency market and when necessary adding on other analytical disciplines to provide an integrated approach to currency analysis. After all, analysis is the means to an end. *It should not be viewed as the end in itself*. A certain degree of flexibility is needed to modify the theory to fit better the practice. As John Maynard Keynes himself is reputed to have said, "when things change, we change". To a trader, this is only common sense. However, to the modern economic community, such flexibility appears frequently elusive. Further, while the more flexible economists have pondered how to make the traditional exchange rate models more accurate in predicting exchange rate moves, other disciplines appear to have got there before them. To a considerable degree, technical and flow analysis have succeeded where classical economics has yet to. We will look at these in detail in Chapters 3 and 4, but for now the point has to be acknowledged that these disciplines have had success precisely because they have focused on solving the problem of predicting short-term exchange rate moves. Yet, if exchange rates are only subject to random walk theory over short-term periods, how can this be so? The answer is obvious and it is this — they are not subject to random walk theory, but instead can over short time periods demonstrate clear and identifiable patterns, patterns that can be used to predict their movements. This is not to say they will be predicted every time, but it is to say trying to forecast short-term exchange rate moves need not be the equivalent of a blind monkey throwing a dart at a dartboard, as random walk theory might suggest.

Suggesting that other types of analysis have succeeded to a degree in predicting short-term exchange rate moves does not mean we abandon the attempt to improve economic analysis to make it better able to do the same thing. To do this however, we have to get past the stage of relying solely on the traditional exchange rate models and focus more on the specific dynamics of the currency market. Only when we understand these can we hope to get measurably better results in applying economic analysis to the prediction of short-term exchange rates. Before that, we need to have a much better idea of the specific dynamics that are at work in the currency market itself.

2.1 CURRENCIES ARE DIFFERENT

The first thing to say about the currency market is that it possesses and obeys a different set of dynamics to other financial markets. Unlike in the case of equity or fixed income markets, the vast majority of currency market practitioners are *speculators* of one sort or another. Global merchandise trade going through the currency market makes up around 1–2% of total volume. Let's say we more than double that to allow for foreign direct investment, making a volume contribution of around 5%. Asset market volumes have risen sharply over the past 20 years as barriers to capital have fallen. Having made up only a small proportion of currency market volume before the end of the Bretton Woods exchange rate system, they probably now make up as much as 35% of total currency market volume on a daily basis. That still leaves 60% of daily currency market volume, which has to ascribe to "speculation". Granted, these are very rough, back-of-the-envelope figures, but they give a good idea of the proportions that are involved. Given this, is it any wonder that many of the traditional exchange rate models that are based on the current account and therefore on trade flows are poor predictors of exchange rates over the short term?! Equally, this gives some clue as to why the portfolio balance approach to exchange rates also achieves unsatisfactory results.

2.1.1 (In)Efficient Markets

As we know from Chapter 1, economic theory approaches the issue of exchange rates by trying to find a theoretical equilibrium level, against which one can measure over- or undervaluation relative to the actual exchange rate. Such theory relies on a number of important premises with regard to the information that might affect exchange rates:

- Exchange rates reflect all available knowledge at any one time
- There is perfect knowledge dispersal (such that no-one has an advantage)

While it is debatable whether or not these exist in other financial markets, we do know that these are not the reality in the currency market. Many people think of the currency or FX market as the "perfect market", being that in which knowledge dispersal is optimum and which responds with perfect efficiency to stimulus. This simply isn't the case. Information is not perfect and some market participants can indeed gain a knowledge advantage over their counterparts. Why is this so?

- The sheer weight of information affecting exchange rates at any one time is so huge that all currency market practitioners cannot possibly absorb all of it all of the time.
- Knowledge dispersal is not perfect and some do have an advantage over others. Such advantages may include knowledge about specific flows that may occur, a bank's own "order book" and finally the ability to do larger currency market transactions than other market participants.

If knowledge is power, then such power in the currency market is not distributed equally. This is no accident. Indeed, it is the very intention of normal and healthy competition to try to gain advantage over other market participants. While news information has never been as freely available as now, at some point that very availability swamps the ability of the users of such information to absorb it all. To some, we appear closer to a state of perfect knowledge than we have ever been, yet I would liken this to the speed of transportation. In 1900, the average speed of the leading mode of transportation in the city of London (the horse) was 11 miles an hour.

In 2000, the average speed of the now leading mode of transportation (the turbo fuel-injected car) was . . . 11 miles an hour. Progress begets more progress until you progress so far that you go nowhere. The more information that is available to us, the less we actually have the time (or the willingness) to read. If the good news is that we are closer to perfect knowledge than we have ever been, then the bad news is that we are never likely to get there!

Information costs money to deliver and therefore there is not "perfect" information delivery because not everyone gets it, either at all or at the same time. Even if it were free, "information overload" still means that not everyone reads and uses it at the same time. If you don't believe me, just think of your e-mail inbox! In sum, there is neither perfect information nor perfect information dispersal — and there never will be. In response, an economist might argue that we have "good" information, if not perfect information. It would be tough to argue with this, but then "good" is not "perfect" and "perfect" is a necessary aspect of the equilibrium concept.

Furthermore, this supposed equilibrium level is rarely ever reached. Real life is surely a constant state of flux and imbalance, so why should financial markets be any different? In turn, if one assumes that the economic fundamentals that can affect exchange rates are themselves in a constant state of flux, one must equally assume that the equilibrium itself is in a constant state of flux — which to an extent calls into question the idea of it being an "equilibrium" in the first place. In truth, it is a signpost on a road. It points you in the right direction, but it gives you no idea of when you will get there or where you might have to turn off along the way.

2.1.2   Speculation and Exchange Rates: Cause, Effect and the Cycle

As with the supposed efficiency of markets, which does not actually work in practice, so there is the idea that supply and demand are completely independent of one another. If this were so, price trends could not exist because markets would instantly work to eliminate any supply or demand imbalances. The fact that this does not happen and that price trends do occur suggests that there are lags, sometimes substantial lags, before such imbalances can be eliminated. In addition, supply and demand are not completely objective concepts. Rather, at least in part, they reflect the views expressed by those market participants that make up that supply and demand. In other words, supply and demand are both cause and effect.

So much for the theory, what does this mean in practice? Actually, to a market practitioner, these ideas are relatively obvious. Currency interbank dealers know full well that particular flows will have more effect than others and thus will materially affect the supply/demand dynamics. Say a large multinational corporation transacts an end-of-quarter hedge in the Euro–dollar exchange rate. Granted, this is the most liquid currency pair in the world, but if the flow is large enough it may affect both current market pricing and future market thinking. Of course the term "future" means different things to different people. To the multinational, it means months at least if not years. To the interbank dealer transacting the flow in the market place it means minutes or hours at most. Currency markets are essentially flow-driven over short time frames, and therefore it is vital to understand the relationship between supply and demand dynamics.

Just as supply and demand are not independent of one another and are both cause and effect, so the relationship between "speculation" and economic fundamentals is also not just one-way. Economic theory requires that markets eliminate "speculative excess", thus restoring equilibrium. However, we have already established that "equilibrium" is actually a moving target. If the "speculative excess" is the extent to which markets diverge from equilibrium, then that "speculative excess" is also a moving target. Finally, the presumption of economists is that economic fundamentals drive market pricing and thus to an extent speculative excess. Even if we accept this, it has also to be acknowledged that speculative excess can in turn affect economic fundamentals. This is best proven by example.

Example

Let's use an example from the emerging markets. From October 2000 through June 2001, the Polish zloty was one of the top three strongest currencies in the world, powering ahead on the back of the irresistible combination of portfolio and direct investment inflows. It is probably safe to assume that on the back of this trend — said trend proving that supply and demand are not independent — speculative flows also bought the Polish zloty to profit from anticipated capital and carry gains. Here, we define "speculative" flow as that which has no underlying commercial or financial market transaction behind it but instead is purely a currency market transaction for the purpose of a directional bet. For our example, we have used the Polish zloty's "basket" value, which is made up of 55% Euro and 45% US dollar against the zloty.

In Figure 2.1, the apparent "downtrend" in the Polish zloty against its basket actually represents currency appreciation rather than depreciation. It should be immediately obvious from this chart that the Polish zloty has been a highly volatile currency over the last few years. Equally clear should be the idea that as the Polish zloty has gradually "fallen" on a trend basis towards the right-hand side of the chart, so this reflects trend appreciation. As the price trend lasted for so long — October 2000 to June 2001 — then we should assume that this trend is fundamentally based. If this were not so, one must presume it would have ended a lot more quickly as an increasing number of market participants would have viewed it as unjustifiable. Yet, this trend of Polish zloty appreciation took place over a period of some nine months, apparently confirming that the sum of currency market participants viewed it as fundamentally justified.

To return to the theory, this states that exchange rates may diverge from their equilibrium levels, that speculative excess is responsible for this and that resulting extreme (under- or over-) valuation relative to the equilibrium will be corrected over time due to economic fundamentals. In our Polish zloty example, we see a rather different picture. In 2000, the Polish economy was still relatively strong, growing by 4.0%. In addition, Polish interest rates were still extremely high at around 20%. Investment flow seeks out the highest returns available and thus we must assume that strong growth and high interest rates were powerful incentives for both fundamental and speculative inflows into Poland at the time. For this purpose, we define "fundamental" flow as that related to underlying financial or commercial transactions — stocks, bonds, trade and direct investment.

Yet, those same high growth and interest rate levels which were attracting large capital inflows also reflected a significant tightening of monetary conditions by the National Bank of Poland to temper inflationary pressure. There are two aspects to overall monetary conditions. There is the cost of money — the interest rate — and the price of money — the exchange rate. As a currency appreciates, this also reflects a tightening of overall monetary conditions. Thus, in the last quarter of 2000, we had a situation whereby interest rates were extremely high and the Polish zloty also appreciated significantly. In effect, monetary conditions were tightened twice! The combination of interest rate- and exchange rate-related tightening of monetary conditions hurt Poland's economic growth, triggering a recession the following year in 2001.

However, to accept this fact is also to accept the suggestion that currency moves and this "speculative excess" can actually affect economic fundamentals, that they can both be cause

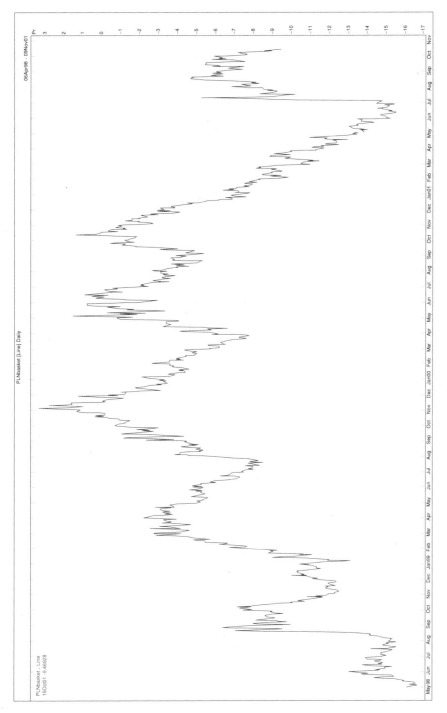

Figure 2.1 Polish zloty basket chart (up-moves reflect depreciation, down-moves appreciation)
Source: Reuters.

and effect, as is the case with supply and demand. Looking at this example, we can also see that the way "speculative excess" affects economic fundamentals follows a clear and discernible pattern. Indeed, if we compare how Poland's economy performed relative to the trend in currency appreciation of the Polish zloty, we see the following pattern or "cycle" at work:

- Fundamental market participants (e.g. corporations and asset managers) apparently deemed Polish zloty fixed income securities as good value around October 2000 and started buying them on a sustained basis, creating a trend in the Polish zloty itself.
- As the zloty continued to appreciate, this tightened overall monetary conditions even further, in addition to already high interest rates. Meanwhile, the longer the zloty trend continued the more self-perpetuating it became, with speculators joining their fundamental counterparts, anticipating more or less guaranteed returns.
- However, the longer the Polish zloty's trend appreciation continued, the more monetary conditions were tightened and the more this hurt Poland's economy. Exporters were hurt by the increasingly uncompetitive currency, while the domestic economy was hurt by high borrowing costs and cheap imports resulting from the currency's strength.
- As the currency trend extended and continued therefore, fundamental market participants became increasingly concerned about economic fundamental deterioration in the form of fading economic growth and widening current account deficits, and thus increasingly started to take profit on their positions.
- For a time, this fundamental selling was more than offset by speculative buying. Eventually, however, the combination of increasing selling pressure and clear and increasing evidence of major fundamental deterioration in the Polish economy proved too much and the speculative flow capitulated (as reflected by the sudden and dramatic spike higher in the Polish zloty basket chart in June–July 2001, reflecting a collapse in the zloty's value).

This cycle or pattern is not just reflective of one single example, but instead of a broader relationship between speculative flows and economic fundamentals within freely floating exchange rates. To some extent, this reflects the reaction of the current account to changes in national income, as shown in the external balance and balance of payments models, however, the advantage of this is that it specifically focuses on how speculative flows, which make up the majority of overall currency market flows, affect economic fundamentals. As a result, an appropriate title for this model would appear to be the **"speculative cycle of exchange rates"**, which we can break down into four key phases:

- Phase I — Fundamental market participants deem a currency good (poor) value and start buying (selling) it on a sustained basis, thus creating a currency trend.
- Phase II — The longer the trend continues, the more speculative it becomes in nature, as more and more speculative market participants (i.e. no underlying asset in the transaction) buy (sell) the currency trend.
- Phase III — However, as the trend of currency appreciation (depreciation) continues it creates increasing economic deterioration (improvement), encouraging an increasing number of fundamental market participants to sell (buy) their positions.
- Phase IV — For a time, speculative inflows (outflows) more than offset those fundamentals outflows (inflows), but eventually in the face of increasing economic deterioration (improvement) they capitulate and the currency collapses (rallies).

Economists may note that this model is not that dissimilar in essence from the belief that speculative excess will be corrected by fundamentals, back towards an equilibrium level. The crucial difference however is that the relationship between speculation and fundamentals is not one-way but two-way. What the two ideas have in common however is that they believe in a **cycle**. The cycle of foreign exchange activity may or may not be the same as the economic cycle, depending on a number of factors such as positional risk and investor asset allocation. In addition, there is no telling how long it will last. It could take weeks, months or even years. However, it is a discernible pattern, reflecting the key dynamics of the currency market and focusing specifically on speculative flows. In addition, it can be used as a framework for the analysis and prediction of exchange rates over the short to medium term.

2.1.3   Risk Appetite Indicators and Exchange Rates

Within such a cycle, there is obviously a substantial amount of intraday and intraweek volatility, reflecting swings in market sentiment. Traditionally, economists have either ignored such short-term periods or suggested they could not be predicted. While flow and technical analysis have done much to dispel such a view, recent work on the relationship between "risk appetite" and asset prices has made a real breakthrough in terms of being able to predict those short-term swings in sentiment and in turn how they affect currency and asset prices. Risk appetite or market sentiment are not easily definable concepts given that what these are focusing on is the investor's willingness or otherwise to invest — which is not always based on logic! Despite such difficulties, the private sector has over the past few years been hard at work creating "risk appetite indicators" to measure overall conditions for risk tolerance across currency and asset markets. Within the investment banks, JP Morgan created its "LCPI Index" Bank of America has its "Global Hazard Indicator" and Salomon Smith Barney its "**Instability Index**". For the purpose of an example, we will focus on the Instability Index. The index was originally created to track levels of risk appetite or conversely "instability" for fixed income investors. However, because it uses cross-market indicators for this purpose, we can also use it for managing and trading currency risk.

Risk appetite has become an increasingly important concept, not just because of the need to create more accurate models for forecasting short-term currency moves, but also because the last few years have shown a marked pick-up in cross-asset market volatility. Indeed, one can go as far as to suggest that as the globalization of capital flows has proceeded, so volatility has increased. Risk appetite is essentially a capital flow event and its relationship is directly proportional to the size of capital flows involved. For this very reason, just as capital flows across borders have grown exponentially, so the degree to which capital flows affect currency markets has grown proportionately. A crisis in one country is no longer isolated but is transmitted instantly around the global financial system. Investors who face losses in that one market may seek to take profit on other positions in order to offset those losses, thus creating a domino effect in hitherto unrelated markets.

Extreme bouts of cross-market volatility such as were seen in the wake of the ERM, Mexican and Russian currency crises prompted interest in creating risk appetite indicators which, if not predicting actual crises themselves, would at least be able to predict significant moves in terms of general investor risk tolerance. For this purpose, categories or levels of risk tolerance also had to be created. The three generally accepted categories within most such risk appetite models for this purpose are:

- Risk-seeking
- Risk-neutral
- Risk-aversion

As the focus of the *Instability Index* is on market volatility and "instability" for the purpose of alerting investors to such bouts of unwanted volatility, these categories can be modified slightly for the purpose of focusing on such instability:

- Stable
- Neutral
- Unstable

When market conditions are perceived as stable according to the market indicators used by the index, they are of necessity optimum for investors to be in risk-seeking mode. Equally, when market conditions are unstable, this is synonymous with investor risk-aversion or avoidance. The focus for such an analytical tool has been the investor community. However, currency speculators and corporations can also use a risk appetite or instability indicator with which to trade or manage their currency risk.

Using the context of the 1997–1998 crisis period, the *Instability Index* seeks to measure risk appetite using leverage, credit spreads and cross-market (equity, fixed income and foreign exchange) options' volatilities as its three benchmarks. The period of June 1997–September 1998 accelerated the focus in trying to measure risk appetite as first the Asian countries experienced currency crises one after another and then Russia devalued and defaulted in August 1998. Conceptually, everyone knew what it meant to be risk-averse, but measuring it was another matter, let alone trying to use that measurement to predict future phases of risk appetite. While investment banks needed analytical tools to track the overall risk appetite of clients across markets, particularly in times of stress, academics and policymakers also needed such a tool for the purpose of measuring just how orderly or disorderly market conditions were in order to help guide future policy responses. The *Instability Index*, which was formalized in 1999, is just such a guide and includes three main components:

- **De-leveraging** — There are two parts to this. The first looks at the relationship in the currency market between the US dollar (as an equity-linked, higher yielding asset) and the likes of the Swiss franc (as a traditional safe-haven currency) and Japanese yen (as a low interest rate, funding currency). During times of market stress, the US dollar tends to lose ground against these as "leverage" or risk is cut. The second component looks at US and European bank equities as a measure of market "leverage".
- **Credit spreads** — In the US dollar credit markets, this tracks the spreads between BBB-rated industrial credits, emerging market Brady bonds and swaps to Treasuries, while it also tracks Euro swap spreads to Bunds. The overall reading gives a very good indicator of investor risk-tolerance.
- **Implied volatilities** — Across the three asset classes of equities, debt and currencies, tracking three-month implied volatilities gives a good idea as to demand levels for option-related protection structures from investors. Option implied volatility tends to rise more sharply during asset market slumps than when asset prices are rising.

The advantage with the readings within this index is that they are relatively easily available and updated daily. Thus, using these three components to represent the degree of "stability" or "instability" in the market, we can have a daily indicator of risk appetite, which can in turn be used as a forecasting tool for currency markets.

The parameters of these readings were set in large part by the global market crisis that happened in the autumn of 1998. During that time, the *Instability Index* hit an all-time high of

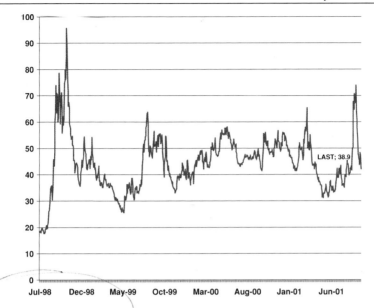

Figure 2.2   SSB Instability Index
Source: Citigroup.

95.6 on October 8, 1998. This crisis also lifted the index onto a higher plateau. Before the crisis, the index averaged 16.1 from January 1997 through July 1998. Since January 1999 through mid-2001, the index averaged around 45, spending much of the time between levels of 30 to 60. Since January 1997, the index has only spent 2.5% of the time above levels of 60–65. At such levels, we would expect to see extreme volatility and price action and that is indeed what happened. If we analyse the history of the index from July 1998–October 2001 (see Figure 2.2), we can clearly discern a corridor when market conditions have been in risk-neutral mode, that is when they were neither stable nor unstable. Indeed, a majority of the observations appear to have occurred in a corridor of between 40 and 50 according to this chart.

By creating a corridor for a risk-neutral stance, we can in turn create specific index parameters for both "risk-seeking/stable" and "risk-aversion/unstable" market conditions. Thus:

- Risk-seeking/stable: <40
- Neutral: 40–50
- Risk-aversion/unstable: >50

In turn, if we compare this index with a number of exchange rates, we find an important and specific correlation. During "risk-seeking/stable" market conditions, investors tend to buy credit product as opposed to Treasuries, equities as opposed to money market funds and in the currency world high carry emerging market currencies as opposed to low carry "safe havens" such as the Swiss franc or Japanese yen. When risk appetite conditions shift from risk-seeking/stable (below 40) in the index to neutral (40–50), many of these high carry currencies such as the Polish zloty, Hungarian forint, Slovak koruna, Mexican peso and Brazilian real tend to lose ground as investors become slightly more cautious, paring back their exposure. Frequently, the yen or the Swiss franc are used as funding currencies with which to buy these high yielders, hence as risk appetite is reduced so they tend to recover some ground as

Table 2.1   Currency decision template using a risk appetite/instability indicator

	Risk-seeking/stable (<40)	Neutral (40–50)	Risk-aversion/unstable (>50)
Asset managers	• Raise currency exposure to high carry currencies	• Reduce currency exposure to high carry currencies	• Eliminate currency exposure to high carry currencies
Currency speculators	• Buy high carry currencies • Short low carry safe haven currencies	• Close positions	• Short high carry currencies • Buy low carry safe haven currencies
Corporations	• Hedge high carry currency strategically	• Only hedge high carry currency exposure tactically	• Only hedge high carry currency exposure tactically

long high carry/short funding currency positions are reduced. Finally, when market conditions deteriorate to the extent the index moves into "risk-aversion/unstable" territory (above 50), high carry currencies are cut across the board, to the increasing benefit of safe havens such as the Swiss franc and the Japanese yen.

The relationship between risk appetite and specific currency performance has been proven statistically within academic research using correlation analysis. From this, we can come up with a rough template for currency trading, hedging and investing decisions using the index (Table 2.1). Note that this is not meant to be an exact list of recommendations. As with any model, there will be exceptions. Rather, it is meant as a template against which specific currency exposures should be measured on a case-by-case basis.

There is actual fundamental grounding for using a risk appetite indicator for currency hedging, trading or investing. Since the end of the Cold War, there has been much greater emphasis on tightening fiscal and monetary policies in order to bring inflation down. As a result, real interest rates have been rising. In the developed markets, capital flows over the medium to long term to those currencies with high real rates. The discipline associated with membership of the EU and the Euro has exacerbated this process, and the same should happen in Central and Eastern Europe ahead of accession to the EU. As a result of such global macroeconomic forces, the trend has been to hold high carry currencies in all conditions — risk-seeking/stable and neutral — apart from risk-aversion/unstable.

The link between risk appetite or instability and currencies comes through capital flows and therefore through the balance of payments. Countries with high current account deficits are dependent on capital flows and therefore dependent on high levels of risk appetite. Conversely, countries with current account surpluses are not dependent on capital flows or risk appetite. Therefore, during periods of risk-seeking, it should be no surprise that currencies whose countries have current account deficits tend to outperform. Equally, during periods of risk-aversion or avoidance, currencies whose countries have current account surpluses tend to outperform by default as capital flows are reduced or even reversed.

In the developed economies, currencies such as the US dollar, UK pound sterling, Australian dollar and New Zealand dollar are seen as risk-dependent currencies because of their current account deficits. Conversely, currencies such as the Swiss franc and the Japanese yen are not dependent on risk appetite because they have current account surpluses and therefore are seen as "safe havens" in times of risk-aversion. This is not an exact science, because there are exceptions such as the Canadian dollar, which tends to prosper during periods of risk-seeking despite the fact that Canada has historically run current account surpluses. Generally, however, within the developed economies the relationship between risk appetite and the current account tends to hold.

The principles that we have described here work for the developed market currencies. They also work very well within emerging market currencies, albeit with some caveats. Emerging market economies and currencies have some specific characteristics which need to be considered when using a risk appetite or instability indicator:

- **Most emerging market economies have current account deficits** — Because of high capital inflows, most emerging market economies run trade and current account deficits. As a result, most are risk-dependent, though one would assume this anyway.
- **Emerging market economies tend to have structurally high levels of inflation** — Due to economic inefficiencies and higher growth levels, emerging market economies have tended to be characterized by higher inflation levels.
- **Emerging market interest rates are more volatile** — Capital inflows to the emerging markets are frequently substantially larger than the ability to absorb them without consequent major financial and economic imbalances. Such inflows artificially depress market interest rates until such time as economic imbalances become unsustainable, at which point the currency collapses and interest rates rise sharply. Thus, such inflows can cause substantial interest rate volatility.
- **Political, liquidity and convertibility risk add to emerging market volatility** — Politics is no longer seen as a *primary* risk consideration within the developed markets, but it still is within the emerging markets however, given higher levels of political instability. Emerging markets are also considerably less liquid and some are not convertible on the capital account, both of which affect market pricing.

These caveats notwithstanding, asset managers, leveraged investors or corporations can use a risk appetite instability indicator as a benchmark for managing or trading emerging market as well as developed market currency risk. High carry currencies such as the Polish zloty, Hungarian forint, Brazilian real and Mexican peso tend to outperform when market risk appetite conditions are in risk-seeking/stable mode, while equally underperforming when market conditions are in risk-aversion/unstable mode. Similarly, low carry emerging market currencies such as the Singapore dollar and the Czech koruna tend to underperform during periods of risk-seeking/stable market conditions and outperform during periods of risk-aversion/unstable market conditions.

Neither the speculative cycle of exchange rates nor the risk appetite indicator is meant to represent exact science in terms of predicting exchange rates. They do however have the advantage of focusing on capital account rather than trade flows, in line with the elimination of barriers to free movement of capital. In addition, they are specifically useful for focusing on short-term exchange rate moves, an area where the traditional exchange rate models fall down. Finally, the results can be used specifically rather than just generally and tailored to the individual currency risk needs of asset managers, leveraged investors and corporations.

2.2 CURRENCY ECONOMICS

So far in this chapter, the focus has been on trying to create new exchange rate models based on capital flows to try to improve forecasting accuracy. As necessary as this is, it does not mean we abandon the traditional exchange rate models. Classical economic theory has provided the foundations for exchange rate analysis. The purpose of establishing a framework known as *currency economics* is to be able to combine the new with the exchange rate models and use both in a more targeted and focused way. Any major differences between this framework of currency economics and classical economics are more methodological than ideological. The traditional exchange rate models, focusing as they do on such factors as trade, productivity, prices, money supply and the current account balance, help provide the long-term exchange rate view. Capital flow-based models are considerably more helpful and accurate in terms of predicting short-term exchange rate moves.

However, these two types of exchange rate model should not necessarily be viewed as polar opposites. *The very purpose of establishing a specific framework known as currency economics is to create an integrated approach to exchange rate analysis, which is capable of answering the riddles of short-, medium- and long-term exchange rate moves.* The two sides do have some common ground, and it should be no surprise that this common ground is to be found in the balance of payments model — given that it focuses both on trade and capital flows. Within this, there are three specific analytical tools which should be of use to currency market practitioners in bridging the gap between short- and long-term exchange rate analysis:

- The standard accounting identity for economic adjustment
- The J-curve
- The REER

2.2.1   The Standard Accounting Identity for Economic Adjustment

We looked at this briefly in Chapter 1, but to recap it is expressed as:

$$S - I = Y - E = X - M$$

where:

S = Savings
I = Investment
Y = Income
E = Expenditure
X = Exports
M = Imports

This can actually be expanded by breaking down "savings" into public and private savings such that:

$$(S_p + S_g) - I = X - M$$

where:

S_p = Private savings
S_g = Government savings

Here, government "dis-saving" reflects having a budget deficit. Thus, from this, we can see immediately that there is a possible link between a budget deficit and a trade deficit. If a country's budget deficit continues to rise, this is reflected on the left-hand side of the equation by an increasingly negative value for S_g. Unless this is offset by a rise in private savings or a fall in investment, this will eventually mean that the left-hand side of the equation turns negative. Of necessity in this circumstance, the right-hand side of the equation must also be negative, which in turn means that the country has a trade deficit. Thus, a budget deficit can lead to a trade or a current account deficit. The link is not necessarily automatic. However, it should be assumed that widening budget deficits, if sustained over time, lead to widening trade and current account deficits. If we extend this, we see that at some stage widening current account deficits will become unsustainable, requiring a real exchange rate depreciation. Thus, widening budget deficits may *eventually* require real (and thus nominal) exchange rate depreciation.

Economists are not generally thought of as prone to high emotion. Yet, one has to say that the accounting identity is like a work of great art, hiding great intricacy and complexity behind the veneer of apparent simplicity. From this accounting identity, we can see how economies adjust to changes in fundamental conditions and therefore how exchange rates should adjust to those conditions. Again, this is probably best shown through an example.

Example 1

For the purpose of this exercise of showing how the accounting identity can work in practice, imagine *a purely theoretical example* whereby you are the corporate Treasurer of a South African mining company. For argument's sake, the company mines and exports precious metals to Europe, the US and Asia. Of course, those precious metals are for the most part priced in US dollars. However, the company is based in South Africa, thus its export revenues are in US dollars and its cost base is in South African rand. This may be an oversimplification but let's assume for the sake of this example that it is the case. In terms of currency risk, the Treasurer's main decision is whether to hedge forward receivables or alternatively allow them to be translated at designated intervals depending on exchange rate developments. In this specific example, it has to be pointed out that South African exporters have a regulated limit of a period of 180 days with which to repatriate export receivables.

If we look back at the first half of 2001, South Africa was recording tremendous trade surpluses, which is to say that the balance of exports to imports was robustly positive to the tune of over 20 billion rand in that period. Using our accounting identity, this can be expressed by:

$$(S_p + S_g) - I = +\text{ZAR20.5 billion}$$

Just as the right-hand side of the equation is strongly positive, so the same must be the case for the left-hand side. Thus, the inescapable conclusion from this is that the sum of $(S_p + S_g)$ must of necessity be considerably higher than I. At the same time, South Africa was actually running a budget deficit of around 2% of GDP. This represents government dis-saving, meaning that S_g is actually negative. Thus, we can in turn extrapolate from this that either South Africa's private savings (S_p) had become extraordinarily high or investment (I) was either low or negative. Those familiar with the South African economy know that low private savings has been a perennial structural weakness of that economy. Thus, the first suggestion is extremely unlikely. If we accept this, then in turn we must conclude from the accounting identity that low or negative domestic investment (I) in South Africa was the reason why the left-hand side of the equation was also strongly positive.

While precious metal exports have declined as a percentage of total South African exports in recent years, they still make up a considerable proportion at around 15%. Thus, the rising overall trade surplus may also reflect rising precious metal exports. Our corporate Treasurer, seeing mounting export receipts in US dollars, may presume that the sheer weight of the rising trade surplus may cause the rand to appreciate. If he or she does so, they may in turn decide to sell US dollars forward for rand to lock in at favourable levels and avoid having to hedge forward later at slightly less favourable levels. However, this may not in fact be the right decision to take. If we look again at the accounting identity in this specific example, we see a picture of low or negative domestic investment in the economy. Domestic investment in an economy is not the same concept as inward portfolio or capital investment. However, we may assume that if domestic investment is low or negative, inward investment is also likely to be low or negative. A currency market practitioner thinks not just in terms of trade or capital flows, but rather in terms of total flows going through the market; the common ground between the new capital flow-based and the traditional trade flow-based exchange rate models. Thus, in this example capital flows may be low or negative, potentially offsetting the positive impact on the rand of trade flows. As a result, the corporate Treasurer should think twice before hedging by selling US dollars for rand until such time as they have to since any trade-related benefit to the rand may be offset by investment-related losses.

In practice, the dollar–rand exchange rate traded in a relatively tight range through the first half of 2001, apparently confirming that net positive trade flows were offset by net negative investment outflows. Subsequently, of course, South Africa's trade balance swung from a substantial surplus to an even more substantial deficit due to the combination of strong domestic demand, boosted by loose monetary policy, and weak external demand. With domestic investment rising but inward investment still weak, those net negative trade flows became the dominating factor in subsequent rand weakness. From August 2001 through to the end of the year, the rand fell from around 8 to the US dollar to a low of 13.85. Ill-informed people have said it was due to speculation. The truth is somewhat less sinister, which is that it was due to fundamental factors at work that were evident within the standard accounting identity for economic adjustment.

This is an example of how a corporation can use the accounting identity to analyse their currency exposures. For good measure, we should try the same exercise for an investor.

Example 2

An institutional investor may also be concerned with currency risk, albeit from a slightly different perspective. Instead of mining precious metals out of the ground, our investor may be buying a portfolio of international equity and fixed income securities. Whether our investor likes it or not, the very act of international investment automatically assumes not only currency risk but also a specific currency view. What do I mean by this? If an investor in the UK decides to buy a 10-year US Treasury note, in order to do that they have to buy US dollars. In market parlance, they are whether they like it or not "long dollars, short sterling". If during the time in which they hold the investment, sterling falls against the dollar, this is a very favourable development which should help enhance the total return of the investment. Why? Because when the US dollar proceeds are translated back into sterling, a fall in sterling against the dollar means that the dollar is worth more sterling. The ensuing currency profit should thus boost the total return.

Say, however, that sterling actually appreciates significantly against the US dollar. In this case, any profit earned on the original investment in the US Treasury note may be reduced or even eliminated when the proceeds are translated back into sterling. The rise in sterling would mean that the US dollar proceeds would now be worth less sterling when translated. Seasoned international investors are of course well aware of such considerations, but however basic the example it is worth restating. Currency risk is not always a consideration of international investors, but it should be if they are concerned with the total return of their portfolio.

Returning to our accounting identity, let's consider an example, in this case the US in the second half of 2001. In social and human terms, the tragic events of September 11, 2001 caused tremendous grief and sorrow. They also had substantial economic impact, though that of course was not the immediate consideration. Using the accounting identity for economic adjustment, let's try and get a better idea of what was happening in the US at that time. Recapping the identity:

$$S - I = X - M$$

A UK investor looking at the US economy during the first half of 2001 saw that the US continued to run significant trade deficits. In other words, the right-hand side of the equation was substantially negative (to the tune of around USD160 billion). Equally, our investor would be able to assume that the left-hand side of the equation was also negative. At the time, the US was still running budget surpluses, so the combination of $(S_p + S_g)$ was positive, meaning that the culprit for the trade deficit was booming investment. This also reflected booming inward investment, more than offsetting the massive trade deficit. As a result, the US dollar rose substantially during the first half of 2001.

From July 2001 however things changed. Market participants began to question the ability of the Federal Reserve under Chairman Alan Greenspan to engineer the economic recovery miracle that everyone had been hoping for. Declining domestic demand in the US meant declining import demand. In terms of the accounting identity, this meant that M was declining relative to X, in turn reducing the trade deficit. This is indeed what we saw during the second half of the year, even before September 11. The US trade deficit shrunk from over USD30 billion a month to around 25 billion, a decline of over 16%. On the left-hand side of the accounting identity, as M fell relative to X on the right-hand side, so I declined relative to S. Lower domestic investment would surely be reflective of lower inward investment. Again, this is exactly what happened in practice. Domestic corporate investment was already falling sharply. In line with that, inward investment fell sharply. The improvement in the trade deficit was not a sign of economic improvement, but rather a reflection of a fall in import demand. As one might expect, the other side of the equation shows a fall in investment growth.

Such information could potentially be very useful for our investor. The immediate assumption is that a reduced trade deficit should be good for a currency, but this is not necessarily so. Indeed, in this case the fall in the trade deficit was due to a fall in import and domestic demand. It was a sign of economic weakness. Moreover, lower domestic investment also meant lower inward investment. In practice, this meant that inward investment fell below the level of the trade deficit. As a result, the dollar fell across the board. Sterling rose against the US dollar. If our investor had analysed the situation using the accounting identity, they may have been able to hedge that exposure to a rise in sterling against the US dollar, thus avoiding a currency loss to the portfolio's total return.

The purpose of both of these examples has been to show how currency market practitioners can use a key tool of currency economics, the standard accounting identity of economic adjustment, to manage their currency risk.

2.2.2 The J-Curve

This is a particularly useful concept because it deals with that frustrating delay between the change in the exchange rate and the adjustment to the economy. Equally, it deals with both trade and capital flows. Suppose international investors have been buying the equity and fixed income securities of an emerging market economy such as Korea. For some reason, those investors "lose confidence" in the Korean economic story and as a result the Korean won. What does that mean? In practice it means that international investors all try to sell at the same time. However, if investors all try and sell at the same time, chances are their orders will not be filled. The Korean won will fall like a stone, but on very little actual volume.

Classic economic theory suggests that a fall in the nominal exchange rate should lead to a reduction in the current account deficit by making imports more expensive and exports cheaper. However, this assumes that the transmission mechanism from the exchange rate to export and import prices is immediate. We know however that this is not the case. Corporations tend to take a wait-and-see attitude in times of market distress, delaying major price changes until financial and economic conditions become clearer. In economist jargon, as we saw in the monetary approach to exchange rates, prices are "sticky". Thus, in our example the Korean won may fall without any immediate benefit to the trade and current account balances. This is not completely a hypothetical example because this is exactly what we saw during the Asian currency crisis of 1997–98. Then, a crisis in Thailand focused investor concerns on much of the rest of Asia, triggering a general loss of confidence in Asian assets and currencies. Asian currencies collapsed but on far smaller volumes than the extent of their declines might have suggested. The Korean won collapsed along with the Thai baht, Indonesian rupiah, Philippine peso and at least initially the Malaysian ringgit. Despite this, there was no immediate reduction of Asian trade and current account deficits. Analysts of the Asian crisis will no doubt suggest that other factors were also at work, notably the high importer content within Asian exports. While this was undoubtedly the case, it does not detract from the fact that there was a clear and marked delay between the exchange rate move and the adjustment to the trade balance. For whatever reasons, Korean corporations delayed their price increases.

We can also see this at work from the angle of the exchange rate rather than the trade balance. As an exchange rate appreciates, it causes exports to become more expensive in the currency to which these exports are going and imports from that country to become cheaper. The initial reaction in the trade balance is not negative however. As the exchange rate appreciates, it causes export prices to rise and import prices to fall. This in turn causes the value of exports to rise vs. imports, thus the initial reaction in the J-curve is that the trade balance actually improves. While this is happening, however, the impact of higher export prices reduces demand for those exports, causing falling export volumes. In turn, falling export volumes eventually lead to a fall in the value of exports and thus to a deterioration in the trade balance. The delay between the fall in export volumes and export values and the subsequent impact on the exchange rate is reflected by the concept of the J-curve. That delay factor varies between exchange rates depending on specific export price sensitivity to changes in the exchange rate.

Example

The J-curve delay in the dollar–yen exchange rate has traditionally been two to three years. In other words, it has usually taken two to three years between a major move in this exchange rate and a subsequent reaction in Japan's trade and current account balances. The delay can vary even within the same exchange rate depending on the predictability of the exchange rate move.

For instance, during 1993–1995, the dollar–yen exchange rate fell consistently amid market concerns that the US administration was trying to devalue the US dollar deliberately as a trade ploy to bring Japan to the negotiating table on opening up their economy to US exports. Yen exchange rate appreciation caused a real economic shock to Japan's economy. Japanese export values rose initially as the value of the yen rose. While the higher value of the Japanese yen pushed Japanese export prices higher, theoretically Japanese manufacturers would be reluctant to pass that price rise on for fear that US consumers would not tolerate it and that as a result they would lose significant sales and market share. Indeed, they tried to keep price increases limited as much as possible, sacrificing margin for sales and market share. Eventually, however, they had to pass on some of the price rise to offset declining export volumes. The result was of course that trend appreciation of the Japanese yen led to a significant decline in Japan's current account surplus, but only from 1995 to 1996, some two to three years after the yen appreciation had begun. Similarly, the yen trended lower from the end of 1995 to mid-1998 in response to the deterioration in the current account balance, eventually to the point whereby it caused renewed recovery in that current account balance, providing at least part of the reason for the yen's dramatic recovery against the US dollar in August and September of 1998.

2.2.3 The Real Effective Exchange Rate

As noted in Chapter 1, the REER is the trade-weighted exchange rate (NEER) adjusted for inflation. It is viewed as a good indicator of medium- to long-term currency valuation. If we look at the Russian and Turkish crises, we see beforehand that the Russian rouble and Turkish lira were around 50–60% overvalued on a REER basis. This provides extremely useful information in that it actually suggests that the rouble and the lira will have to experience significant real exchange rate depreciations to restore equilibrium. That's the good news. The bad news is that it does not tell you when that significant real — and therefore nominal — depreciation will take place. In both cases, the rouble and the lira were overvalued for two to three years before the inevitable happened.

However, there are important clues as to when that REER appreciation may be about to end. Such REER appreciation usually causes significant trade and current account balance deterioration. The fact that this does not have an immediate reaction in the exchange rate confirms not only the existence of the J-curve but also the presence of significant capital inflows. Such inflows can offset a widening trade deficit for a period of time, but eventually are not able to. When they reverse, or rather when they just stop, the exchange rate comes under ever increasing pressure until such time as it collapses to restore equilibrium. This process can also work equally well with real depreciations. From the end of 1995 to mid-1998 the Japanese yen experienced an increasing REER depreciation. Capital outflows offset an increasingly improving current account balance until such time as they could no longer do so, whereupon the Japanese yen rallied significantly, resulting in one of the most dramatic collapses in the dollar–yen exchange rate — or any exchange rate — in history. REER valuation and the external balance are both cause and effect. It takes a REER depreciation of a currency to narrow significantly a large external imbalance. That said, an excessive REER appreciation can cause that imbalance in the first place.

2.3 SUMMARY

In sum, the aim of establishing an analytical discipline called currency economics is to adopt an integrated approach to exchange rate analysis, pooling those existing strengths of classical economics together with newer ideas based on capital flows into a combined framework which seeks to analyse exchange rates right across the spectrum of short-, medium- and long-term exchange rate views. The field of currency economics also seeks to differentiate between short-term cyclical factors such as monetary and fiscal policy and long-term structural factors such as persistent trends in the current account balance, REER valuation and PPP, in affecting the exchange rate. Currency economics seeks to make the economic analysis of exchange rates more relevant to short-term exchange rate moves, particularly in its attempt to focus on the capital account and capital flows. In doing so, it provides better exchange rate forecasting results than is the case with the traditional exchange rate models. However, the delay to the adjustment mechanism that bedevils the attempt by classical economic analysis to forecast exchange rates is also present within currency economics. For a truly real-time, market-based focus on forecasting exchange rates, we have to turn to analytical disciplines that are specifically targeted at short-term exchange rate moves, such as flow and technical analysis.

3
Flow:
Tracking the Animal Spirits

Within financial circles, it has become commonplace to talk about the importance of "flow" in forecasting exchange rates. International organizations and academic bodies now publish an increasing number of research papers on capital flow and how it affects economic policies. For instance, the IMF publishes its quarterly review of *Emerging Market Financing*, looking at trends over the quarter in equity, fixed income and foreign exchange flows, syndicated and official loans and direct investment. Looking at a slightly different time frame, several bank research departments now use intraday flow in the fixed income and foreign exchange markets to predict short-term exchange rate moves.

All of this marks a major departure from the previous orthodoxy. As we looked at in the first two chapters, the traditional exchange rate models are based on several important assumptions, including the view that markets are essentially rational, that information is perfect (i.e. available to everyone, all of the time) and that divergences from fundamental equilibrium levels will eventually be eliminated. Because of this, it was also assumed until quite recently that there was little point in studying financial market "flow". If a price is the result of all available information at one time, and if all information is equally available to all concerned within the financial markets, flow information cannot add any value or have any price effect as that information is already known. Moreover, economic fundamentals will dictate over time that capital flows so as to eliminate fundamental imbalances and price over- or undervaluation. In sum, the economists deemed themselves as being in full control of what they appeared to perceive as the rather unseemly elements of the financial markets, i.e. the actual participants. Economics was the "cause" and capital flow the "effect".

Some within the economic community diverged somewhat from this polar view, notably one John Maynard Keynes, who coined the term "the animal spirits", referring to the stock market and the way in which economic theory and financial market prices interacted. More recently, perhaps within the last decade, there has been a fundamental realization within the economic community, albeit perhaps a grudging one, that capital flow can be both cause and effect in its relationship with economics, that it is just as likely to change as to be changed by economic fundamentals.

In short, there has been a realization that the efficient market hypothesis, which has long dominated economic theory, is itself flawed. While we looked at this issue briefly in Chapters 1 and 2, it is important here to examine its specific flaws given the context of how capital flows can affect price. To recap, an efficient market is one where all relevant market information is known to market participants, who act rationally in accordance with economic fundamentals to quickly eliminate any divergences from fundamental equilibrium. This idea is ultimately flawed for the following reasons:

- Information is perfect — As we saw in Chapters 1 and 2, this is a nonsense. There are consistent inefficiencies in information availability and usage.

- Markets are efficient — If financial markets were fully efficient, there would be no such thing as a sustained divergence from fundamental equilibrium.
- Market participants are inherently rational — Rationality is itself inherently a subjective term, as is fundamental equilibrium.
- Market imbalances are eliminated and prices return to fundamental equilibrium — The reality is rather different. A host of academic papers have looked at the issue of exchange rate valuation and generally found that the traditional exchange rate models have had poor results, leading some to conclude exchange rates are not determined by economic fundamentals over the short term.[1]

Efficient market theory essentially suggests that it is impossible to make excess returns in exchange rate markets because efficient markets should eliminate profitable opportunities before investors are able to capture them. Empirical evidence suggests this is simply not the case. Investors have been able to make consistently good excess returns in the currency markets over time. Some would see this as being due to market inefficiency, while others see it as being due more practically to good trading technique, as in any financial market. Information is imperfect, market participants are not necessarily rational in the sense the theory demands and ultimately markets are frequently inefficient. For these very reasons, analysts and investors can indeed recognize and capture profitable opportunities. The fact that some achieve better results than others is explained simply by the fact that some are better analysts, traders or investors than others.

The subject of this chapter deals specifically with the concept of "flow", and therefore it is the inefficiency of market information that we are interested in here. If we accept that market information is imperfect, that not all information is available to all at the same time and therefore that the price does not reflect all information, then we must try and determine two things:

- What specific types of information are "in the price" at any one time?
- What types of information are important for price movement on a sustained basis?

It is probably best to look at these two issues as one. In the real world of a foreign exchange dealing room in London or New York, prices are indeed affected by the types of information that economic theory might expect, such as macroeconomic data, specific trends in microeconomic performance and so forth. However, to provide liquidity for customers and also to make a trading profit for themselves, currency dealers have to trade, irrespective of whether there have been changes in economic fundamentals. Hence, currency interbank dealers, who make up the majority of currency market participants — interbank dealing makes up around 65% of all spot transactions — seek out other types of information, perhaps more suited to their ultra short-term time horizon. Technical analysis is one of these, and we shall look at this fascinating discipline in Chapter 4. In addition, currency dealers look at a bank's "order book", at the book containing all the bank's customer orders in an attempt to gauge prevailing market "sentiment" towards specific exchange rates. *The sum of those orders* may give a very useful indication of how specific *client types* feel about specific currencies. *Note that this is not in any way trying to gauge specific client orders in order to trade ahead of those ("front-running").* Rather, it is achieving an understanding of how the client base *as a whole* views certain exchange rates.

---

[1]Readers who are interested in pursuing this further should look at Kenneth Froot and Kenneth Rogoff, *Perspectives on PPP and Long-Run Real Exchange Rates*, NBER Working Paper 4952, 1994; Rudiger Dornbusch, *Real Exchange Rates and Macroeconomics*, NBER Working Paper 2775, 1988; Jeffrey Frankel and Andrew Rose, *A Survey of Empirical Research on Nominal Exchange Rates*, NBER Working Paper 4865, 1994.

People talk about "the market" in a rather abstract sense in terms of market sentiment towards a specific asset or currency. However real this term may be to the user, it is still excessively vague. Far more useful for our purposes is to look at trends in actual transactions or the sum of orders that have been put in the market for the dealer to execute when the price hits the order level. The sum of orders or actual transactions of a major commercial or investment bank can be a far more accurate and representative gauge of "the market". There have been several important papers about this very subject, notably one by Evans and Lyons (1999),[2] which looked at the principle of "order flow", as being a key determinant of short-term exchange rate fluctuations. Another by the Federal Reserve Bank of New York (Osler, 2000)[3] looked at the same issue. Both focus on the idea that there is information surrounding actual currency transactions and orders to be transacted which can not only explain exchange rate movements, but also be helpful in forecasting future exchange rate moves — something which would be impossible if the efficient market hypothesis were correct.

The Evans and Lyons paper found that order flow accounted for about two-thirds of daily variation in the US dollar–Deutschmark exchange rate over the time studied. The main cause of the exchange rate variation was shifts in private capital flows. Interestingly, these shifts appeared to take place in the absence of major changes in economic information. Such private capital flow shifts can happen as a result of changes in investor risk tolerance, liquidity, portfolio balancing needs, hedging needs and so forth. In other words, they can happen for microeconomic as well as macroeconomic reasons, reasons that are due to the specifics of the investor's own risk tolerance profile and attitude to the market. The trade exchange rate models are not really designed to take account of such factors, and thus it would appear others are needed that are able to do so.

If exchange rates can be affected by the specifics of an individual investor's risk tolerance profile — something we know intuitively, but have now seen proven empirically — then such models need to track not fundamental equilibrium but the actions of the investors concerned. At a broader level, the idea that we need to track the sum of investor behaviour and intentions has sprung the school of thought known as **behavioural finance**. This field seeks to examine how and why investor "herding" takes place, how to anticipate it and finally how to anticipate reversion to fundamental mean. More narrowly, models have been developed to track the sum of client orders and transactions. These actions are compared to exchange rate prices on a real-time, live basis. If there is a good correlation between the sum of client orders and transactions and those exchange rate prices, then one effectively has a model which can not only track the relationship between the two, but also forecast future exchange rates based on those actions.

This intellectual shift in favour of behavioural finance has happened in part because of the need to find models that are more appropriate to market needs and also to try and explain how market "sentiment" or "psychology" can affect prices. In addition, major trends within finance itself have also provided support for the view that the "behaviour" of financial markets needs to be studied, that capital flows are not just "effect" but can also be the "cause" of market movement. These trends can broadly be divided into two main ones. Firstly, as barriers to capital have been pulled down over the last 30 years, the size of those flows and therefore their effect on the global economy has grown exponentially. Today, we more or less take for granted

---

[2]For more on this see Martin D.D. Evans and Richard K. Lyons, Order flow and exchange rate dynamics, *Journal of Political Economy*, August 1999; or Martin D.D. Evans and Richard K. Lyons, Why order flow explains exchange rates, *Journal of Political Economy*, November 2001.

[3]Carol L. Osler, *Currency Orders and Exchange Rate Dynamics: Explaining the Success of Technical Analysis*, Federal Reserve Bank of New York Staff Report No. 125, April 2001.

the fact that we can buy a mutual fund or unit trust that focuses on Thai or New Zealand stocks, safe in the knowledge that money transfer, clearing, settlement and broker account processes are all seamless. Where we travel, we presume now also that we can invest. All this, we take for granted. Yet, to our grandparents, this would be a wholly foreign idea. It was not that long ago that capital investment focused domestically rather than abroad. Over the last 30 years, just as trade has expanded so has the means by which to finance that trade, which is of course where capital flows come in. Indeed, since the war, it is only in the last 30 years that the proportion of trade within the overall US economy has grown significantly, from around 10% to 15%. As US companies have expanded abroad, so their need for financing abroad has also grown. So-called "natural" hedging involves the matching of assets and liabilities. Thus, a US company may invest in a factory in Poland and wish to finance that asset by raising Polish zloty debt, as an example. Previously, it was not possible to do this kind of funding operation given regulations against foreigners within emerging markets. In the developed world, also, regulations against capital raising and movement also inhibited commercial trade for much of this century. As barriers to trade have fallen away, so have the barriers to capital as a means to finance that trade. Further, as these barriers have fallen, capital flow growth has been a multiple of trade growth. This can only be sufficiently explained by an anecdote. *Every day*, the equivalent of a year's worth of global trade passes through the global currency market! Every week, the currency market trades the equivalent of the Gross Domestic Product of the United States! The development of capital flow began as a natural ally and accompaniment to commercial trade. In the past two or three decades, it has far outgrown it.

A second trend has been the realization of the growing importance of capital flow with respect to the various emerging market crises that have occurred in the 1990s. It had also been assumed that capital flows were a wholly beneficial thing, that they helped a country to grow, indeed that they were the fuel for economic growth, not just at a national but at a global level. For this reason, when capital outflows were seen as responsible for the financial and economic collapse of Mexico in 1994–1995, much of Asia in 1997–1998, Russia in 1998, Brazil in 1999 and Turkey in 2001 there was an understandable backlash. Having been seen as the saviour of emerging markets, helping them to emerge from the poverty of the early post-war years, capital flows were suddenly portrayed as a heartless villain, preying on the weak. The reality of course is that they were never an entirely beneficial force in the first place, just as they are not now the villain. To ascribe to capital flows human characteristics is to miss the point. Capital flows are neither trying to benefit nor are they trying to hurt a country. The only reason for them to be there is to make a return, to make money. If they can make a sufficient return, they will be attracted to a country and stay there. If they cannot make a return, they will leave. It is that simple. They are neither moral nor immoral. They are amoral — and that is exactly how it should be.

When national leaders have not been busy blaming money or "capitalism" — or the most efficient way of exchanging money — for all manner of ills, they have been blaming the money "changers". This is nothing new. National "leaders" have been doing this since before Christ. Historically, "traders" or "moneychangers" have been looked down upon by polite society from the time of the Romans. Thus, it was no surprise to see during the "big bangs" that took place in the 1970s and 1980s in the US and the UK that people from less privileged backgrounds grabbed the opportunity to participate in those financial revolutions with both hands. Skills that were learned in the back streets of Brooklyn or the East End were every bit if not more useful — if given the opportunity — than belonging to the right school or club. Only when these individuals made enough money at trading to be noticed did that polite society pay attention, but only grudgingly. Society was not alone in looking down on such people. Governments and national leaders did the same and always have done — and probably always will do. Thus, when the Prime Minister of Malaysia, Dr. Mahathir, railed against foreign exchange speculation, shouting that it should be "banned", at the IMF meetings in Hong Kong in 1997, this should not be seen as an isolated incident but part of a rich seam and history of conflict between governments and traders. Mahathir is far from alone in thinking or voicing such views. Some years earlier, after the 1993 ERM crisis, none other than the Chancellor of Germany at the time, Helmut Kohl, was reported as saying foreign exchange speculation was an Anglo-Saxon conspiracy against the goal of a united and single Europe, presumably forgetting in the process the origin of the word "Saxon".

When economic or financial calamity occurs, it is not surprising that governments react against this, not least because they do not want to seem to be blamed themselves and thus seek to blame others. In the context of capital flows, however, there seems to be a double standard. Governments are usually quite happy to receive large amounts of capital inflow. It is only when that capital starts to flow out again, putting pressure on exchange and interest rates, that governments protest against "speculation". From this, we arrive at a simple capital flow model:

A buyer = an investor

A seller = a speculator

This is of course nonsense and a gross simplification of what is actually a complex issue. Nonetheless, it is an attitude that is widely prevalent among national governments. Whatever the case, the perception that capital outflows have been behind the economic and financial collapse of a number of countries has produced outrage in these countries. Meanwhile, it has also had the somewhat more beneficial effect of causing supranational organizations such as the IMF and the World Bank, along with central banks, to spend a substantial amount of time and effort in studying capital flows and their effect.

3.1 SOME EXAMPLES OF FLOW MODELS

The field of currency analysis has in the past few years developed a number of models to track capital flows, the number of which has grown in line with increasing transparency of the available data. Most currency trading takes place in the "over-the-counter" market; that is to say over the phone between bank dealers. However, until relatively recently banks did not think to track their own transactions for the purpose of prediction. The market was thought to be a vast pool of transactions and sentiment, which it was virtually impossible to track. No one model could hope to track the entire currency market. In addition, it was doubtful that banks would be prepared to hand over their flow data to an outside party and risk it getting into the hands of their competitors. Thus, the first flow models came from the available data at the time, either from the "open outcry" exchanges such as the New York Stock Exchange, the Chicago Board of Trade or the Chicago Mercantile Exchange, or from official data sources such as the Federal Reserve Bank of New York, the US Treasury or the Bank of England. For instance, the Chicago Mercantile Exchange produces every week its IMM (International Money Market) Commitments of Traders report.

3.1.1   Short-Term Flow Models

The IMM Commitments of Traders Report

Unlike the OTC data that is currently available, there are two major advantages with data from open outcry exchanges — it is available relatively quickly after the trade is made and it is transparent. The rules of the exchange concerned require not only full documentation for each trade, but also the type of account making the trade. The weekly IMM Commitments of Traders report collates trades made in currency futures contracts through the IMM trading pit in Chicago by various types of accounts. For our purposes, the most useful type of account that we are interested in is what the IMM euphemistically calls "non-commercial accounts". In layman's terms, this means speculators or accounts that trade currencies on their own with no attached underlying asset.

Granted, the volumes that go through the IMM currency futures' contracts pale by comparison with the regular interbank market. However, here again, the advantage is that the IMM data is transparent. Moreover, given that the non-commercial account trades represent the activity of the speculative community on the IMM, this can be used as a reflection of overall speculative activity in those currencies. Indeed, one can go further and say that precisely because IMM volumes are small relative to the interbank market, a notable speculative position in a currency pair on the IMM may actually be reflective of a similar but much larger position in the interbank market. Before going on further, it is probably useful to take a look at an actual IMM Commitments of Traders report and seek to analyse it, just as a currency analyst would for their traders and clients. In Table 3.1 we present the IMM Commitments of Traders report as of November 20, 2001.

As the table shows, this report reflects the total long and short open positions that IMM speculators have in these currencies at any one time (in this case as of November 20, 2001). This is very useful information. If a speculative position becomes too large, we know from our work looking at the speculative cycle that it may eventually be reversed. Thus, using this information, traders, investors or corporations can position accordingly to anticipate such a reversal. In addition, it is a relatively simple matter to graph this against the spot exchange rate. If we accept that the speculative community's open position in IMM currency futures is a rough reflection of what it might be in the much larger interbank market, this might well give us a much more useful picture of what are the outstanding positions in the market, and thus the outstanding risk and vulnerability.

Table 3.1   IMM Commitments of Traders (non-commercial accounts) as of November 20, 2001

	EUR	JPY	CHF	GBP	CAD	AUD	MXN
Gross longs	17,899	13,491	8,473	3,162	3,288	3,729	16,393
Gross shorts	18,185	32,377	8,234	9,220	28,663	428	1,064
Net position	−286	−18,886	+239	−6,058	−25,375	+3,301	+15,329
Net position from prior week	+484	−4,231	+5,219	+1,755	−28,089	+12	+14,322
Five-year high (longs)	31,666 (28/08/01)	67,229 (08/31/99)	48,332 (10/19/99)	48,014 (10/19/99)	46,780 (11/12/96)	20,859 (05/11/99)	12,641 (03/20/01)
Five-year high (shorts)	34,328 (02/01/00)	69,715 (05/18/99)	54,553 (05/04/99)	43,767 (07/13/99)	41,327 (10/17/00)	11,484 (08/31/99)	4,159 (07/01/97)

From this table, we can extract a variety of specifically useful information. For a start, we can compare the net speculative position of the week being analysed to the previous one. In addition, we can compare this figure with multi-year highs and lows. Moreover, if we overlay this data with the actual spot rate, we can see how net changes in the IMM speculative position for each exchange rate correlate with the actual price action. To be sure, the IMM data is not a perfect representation of what goes on in the currency market as a whole, as its volumes are small on a relative basis and IMM-based speculators are not necessarily the same ones that operate in the larger currency market context. That said, the fact that one can use IMM data to generate excess returns suggests that the strong correlation, albeit with a lag, between the IMM data and the actual exchange rate price action does indeed reflect a predictive capacity of the data itself. A large number of banks now regularly use the IMM Commitments of Traders report, both as an analytical and a predictive tool for their own trading desks and for their clients.

For example, if we look at the available data we see that the speculative community has built up a substantial short yen position (against the US dollar). The base currency for the IMM data is always the dollar, thus if they were short yen futures, that means they were short yen against the dollar. IMM net positions can of course be easily graphed, either on their own or perhaps more usefully against the dollar–yen exchange rate. If we do that, we see that speculators had in fact been substantially long yen futures for October and much of November. This is also useful to know as it suggests that a potentially important trend reversal has just happened. If we consider this as a reflection in the overall currency market, we get a picture of speculators having been substantially short dollar–yen (i.e. long yen) and of that speculative short position having been gradually eliminated initially and then increasingly reversed. This actually occurred in line with a move higher in the dollar–yen exchange rate, as one might expect as a result of the buying required to close out those short positions. One thing that can be noticed from this example is confirmation that the IMM speculative position was indeed reflective of a much larger outstanding position in the overall currency market. After all, if that were not true, the closing out of the IMM position would have had no effect whatsoever on the price action. You might think this coincidence, but the correlation between changes in IMM speculative positions and short-term moves in the spot exchange rate is too high to be that.

While the reversal in the IMM speculative position in the yen may be a notable change and thus may last for some time, there is a further point to be made, namely that the larger the speculative position becomes, the more vulnerable it in turn becomes to reversal and retracement. Indeed, this is entirely in line with the conclusions of our speculative cycle model, which suggests that the longer a currency price trend lasts, the more speculative it becomes and the more vulnerable to a sharp and violent reversal. In line with this, the larger the outstanding speculative position, the more laboured the price action becomes in favour of the prevailing trend. This is not to say the prevailing trend cannot continue for some time. It is to say however that the momentum of that trend will continue to slow as the size of the outstanding position in favour of that trend increases. It is also to say the longer the trend lasts, the more explosive the eventual reversal.

Returning to our IMM example, looking at the dollar–yen exchange rate, the IMM data tells us that speculators were at the time becoming increasingly bullish on the dollar vs. the yen. Here, it helps to add some fundamental explanation to the available flow information. It is a key theme of this book that analytical disciplines, which focus on the currency market, are best used in combination rather than in isolation. That way they give a much more powerful — and therefore potentially profitable — signal. In this example, the Japanese authorities, in the form of both the Bank of Japan and the Ministry of Finance, had signalled that they were in favour of a weaker yen, in line with the weak Japanese economic picture. The ability of either monetary or fiscal policy to be eased further had been all but eliminated. The only lever left for further policy easing was the yen itself. This idea caught on within the speculative community, with the result that speculators closed out their short dollar–yen positions and created an increasingly large long dollar–yen position, as reflected by the IMM data. As an analyst or as a currency market practitioner such as a corporation or an investor, one can use this information in the following ways:

- Analyst — Review the flow and fundamental economic data to come up with an overall picture of the short-term flow and fundamental dynamics in the dollar–yen exchange rate and thus the ability or not of the prevailing trend to continue.
- Trader — As the prevailing trend continues and increases in the dollar–yen exchange rate, position to take advantage of the reversal when it comes.
- Investor — Use the combination of flow and fundamental data as a guide in determining yen exposure and hedging policy with regard to that exposure.
- Corporation — Use the combination of flow and fundamental data as a guide for short-term hedging policy.

To reinforce the point of the usefulness of this data, let's quickly look at another example. If we look at the position in Euro futures, we see that the net position as of November was net short −286 contracts. On the face of it this may suggest that there is no directional bias for the Euro–dollar exchange rate near term. However, it is important to note that the speculative community had a net long Euro position in the IMM futures contract for much of August through mid-November. Indeed, the Five-year high for Euro longs was hit on August 28 at 31,666 contracts. Since then, there was a gradual reduction in the speculative long position in Euro futures. In line with this, spot Euro–dollar came under increasing selling pressure. Thus, noting that there was such a large net long Euro position at the end of August, one could have positioned to anticipate a retracement in spot Euro–dollar in anticipation of those positions being closed out. Equally, the fact that this net long Euro position switched to a small net short conversely gave the Euro-dollar exchange rate some support as this overhang of long positions had thus been eliminated.

Proprietary Flow Models

Nowadays, a large number of commercial and investment banks have their own proprietary flow models, which track the foreign exchange activity of their global client base. Depending on the size of the bank and therefore of that client base, these can be very useful and informative models. The model that largely started this process off is the *CitiFX Flows* advisory service, which tracks the foreign exchange flow activity of the Citigroup global client base. Within this, there are three types of model, which are used concurrently to generate the results:

- Simple linear models — These are autocorrelation models, which are based on the short-term momentum of flow. Thus, this type of model suggests for instance that if there were buyers yesterday in a specific currency, there is consequently an increased chance of buyers appearing tomorrow and so forth.
- Complex non-linear models — These are error-correction models, which focus on flow that has been carried out in the past, but is not yet fully reflected in the price.

- Time-delay models — This focuses on the flow that has passed through in the recent past having important information about the future movement in the exchange rate.

CitiFX Flows analyses foreign exchange client flows globally in order to try to decipher two hidden trends:

- Client flow as an indicator of the underlying currency market momentum
- Client flow as an indication of outstanding positions in the currency market

Client flow has become an important component of the overall strategic view, in line with the increasing opinion to see flow as an important explanatory factor for price change. Liquidity has become a much-discussed topic and flow models are now a critical input of the overall currency strategy process.

Proprietary FX flow models generally produce:

- Trading signals based on one month's worth of flow data
- Overweight or underweight indicators based on six months' or one year's worth.

In line with this, such FX flow models are also frequently used as trading models, using the client flow data as trading signals.

In the example in Figure 3.1, *CitiFX Flows* shows global client flow going through the Euro–dollar exchange rate over the time period from August to October 2001, comparing that flow against the spot Euro–dollar exchange rate. Looking at the last month's worth of flow in this example, we see a consistent picture of the flow model's client base selling the Euro–dollar exchange rate. As an example, in the wake of this, the flow model issued a sell recommendation on Euro–dollar. Such sell recommendations last for one month. Since their inception, such bank proprietary flow models based on client flow have frequently generated consistent excess returns.

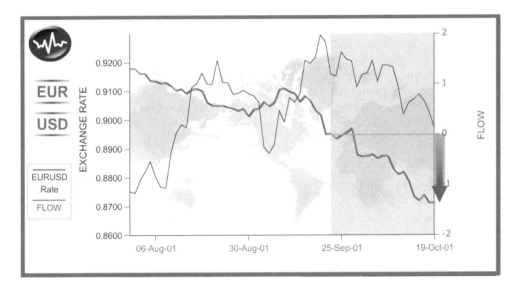

Figure 3.1 *CitiFX Flows*: example 1a

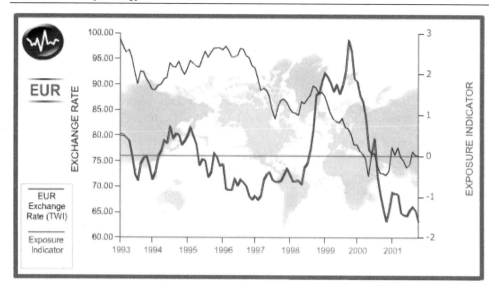

Figure 3.2 *CitiFX Flows*: example 1b

Such flow models also frequently publish more medium-term exposure indicators, the aim of which is to look for large over- or underexposures which may over time "revert to mean". This is again most easily explained using a chart. While Figure 3.1 provided a good flow picture over the short term, showing increasingly heavy selling of the Euro–dollar exchange rate by the flow model's global client base, Figure 3.2 takes a longer-term perspective of flow trends. More specifically, it compares the Euro trade-weighted exchange rate against the medium-term Euro exposure indicator. Obviously, before the January 1, 1999 start to the Euro as a tradable currency both measures are synthetic. Here we see that the model's client base exposure to the Euro has continued to move to a medium-term underweight from mid-2000 onwards, despite the fact that during this time the *trade-weighted* Euro remained relatively stable. We can derive from this that at some stage reversion to mean will require Euro buying to close that significant underweight exposure of 1.5 standard deviations. What such a chart does not tell us, unfortunately, is when that might happen. Combining the two charts, however, we get a picture both of the short-term flow momentum and of the medium-term positional considerations. Together they can help to provide a relatively exhaustive flow picture of an exchange rate. This in turn can provide both trading and hedging signals.

In order to reinforce the point, it is probably useful to conduct the same exercise using another currency. In the following example, we look at the Japanese yen. Figure 3.3 looks at the short-term flow picture against spot price action in the dollar–yen exchange rate. Figure 3.4 looks at the medium-term exposure indicator of the market as reflected by the model's client base as against the medium-term trend in the trade-weighted value of the yen.

Comparing the two charts, we get a very informed picture of the flow vs. the spot price action in the Japanese yen. In the case of Figure 3.3, the thing to note is that the flow was largely in line with the spot dollar–yen price action. More interesting is the fact that the flow continued to show heavy selling of dollars against the yen even in the face of adverse

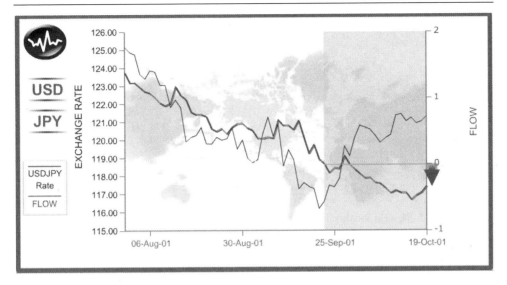

Figure 3.3   *CitiFX Flows*: example 2a

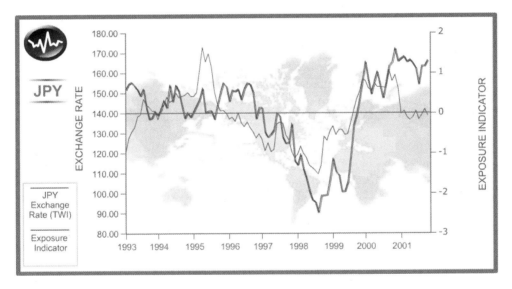

Figure 3.4   *CitiFX Flows*: example 2b

price action. From this, the *CitiFX Flows* team put out a recommendation to sell the dollar–yen exchange rate. Figure 3.4 shows the more medium- to long-term flow picture in the yen. Through mid-1998, the exposure indicator showed an increasing underweight position in the yen. From then on, the underweight was continually reduced until mid-1999 when it flipped to an overweight position. Medium-term exposure indicators are useful in that they imply a reversion to mean, and in this case that would mean the flow moving back to a more neutral reading, which would require significant selling of yen. Thus, combining the two, we get a picture of short-term flows favouring a lower dollar–yen exchange rate, but the medium-term flow picture favouring a potentially significant rebound in favour of the dollar.

Short-Term Emerging Market Flow Models

The academic community and financial market participants have finally come around to the idea that tracking capital or order flow in the developed world currencies was an important thing to do. Given the depth and liquidity of developed world markets, this fact may be surprising to some. However, as we have attempted to show above, this is nevertheless the case.

Where it is true in the developed world markets that watching flow is an important pursuit in determining the exchange rate path, this is even more the case in the so-called emerging markets. Here, the relationship between individual capital flows and overall market liquidity is much more in favour of individual flows. Liquidity in emerging markets is by definition substantially less than in the developed world. Thus, individual flows can cause substantial price disruption in emerging markets, whereas they might be more easily absorbed in the developed markets. For this very reason, it is important for currency market participants who are involved in or exposed to emerging market currencies to have a reasonably accurate idea of the prevailing type of flows going through the market. One such is the *EMFX Flow* model (Robert Lustberg and Callum Henderson, 2001) created to track client flows going through the global dealing rooms of Citigroup in emerging market currencies. The type of information that one can glean from this is the following:

- Total flow — The total flow indicator looks at cumulative transactions in the currency concerned against all the major base currencies (such as the Euro, dollar, yen, sterling and Swiss franc) combined. This gives an accurate indication of the client's base total exposure to that currency.
- Short- and medium-term flow indicators — The short-term flow indicator examines flow going through a specific exchange rate over the period of one month, while the medium-term flow indicator does this over six months.
- Client-type flow — It is also useful to look at what types of clients are doing what. For instance, one can see whether or not corporate hedgers are being particularly active in a currency or not, or whether or not there is substantial speculative flow.

The use of such a flow model is to realize flow trends, in some cases confirming through the model what one knows anecdotally, and then make formal trading recommendations on the back of that. Some of the major finds in 2001 from this work were the following:

- Brazilian real — Corporate hedging was the main flow dynamic of the dollar–real exchange rate for much of 2001. Examining the model's findings we saw that the consistency of hedging activity, which entailed buying of dollars, and the quality of the types of corporations hedging, strongly suggested the dollar–real exchange rate would continue to appreciate. Equally, during November–December, when these corporations were no longer rolling their hedges it was no coincidence that the dollar–real exchange rate stabilized and retraced lower in favour of the real.
- Mexican peso — Through the first eight months of 2001, client flows going through the dollar–peso exchange rate were largely in favour of the peso, confirming the anecdotal view

that foreign direct investment remained a major supportive factor for the peso, more than offsetting the current account deficit. From October on, however, local corporations as a group turned net buyers. This did not cause an immediate appreciation in the dollar–peso exchange rate, but did put a floor under it and caused it to appreciate over time.

- South African rand — There has been over the past few years much controversy regarding the flows going through the rand. Local market participants in South Africa have largely blamed the offshore market for rand weakness, while the economic community has been at a loss to explain rand weakness given the country's "strong economic fundamentals". From the *EMFX Flow* model, we discovered that the client flow of the bank had an asymmetric relationship with the price action of the dollar–rand exchange rate. That is to say, when clients were net sellers of dollar–rand — which was most of the time — the exchange rate remained largely range bound. On the other hand, during rare periods when clients became net buyers of dollars against rand, the exchange rate exploded higher. From this we can deduce a simple explanation for the rand's weakness according to flow — locals are responsible for rand weakness.

Such findings can help greatly, not just in terms of providing trading recommendations for the speculative community, but in helping investors or corporations to plan their hedging strategies. Proprietary FX flow models focus generally on the short-term flow picture. However, there are flow reports that focus on the medium-term structural flows that go through asset markets. These also reflect useful information. As examples of such medium-term flow analysis, we now focus on the US Treasury's "TIC" report and the Euro-zone capital flows report.

3.1.2   Medium-Term Flow Models

The US Treasury TIC (Treasury International Centre) Report

The second way we can approach this general issue of flow analysis is to look at the specific capital flows going into equity and fixed income markets. Here the availability and quality of the data vary widely. For instance, there are data reports focusing on what amounts of money are going into mutual funds. From this, we can of course break those mutual funds down into investment types — equity or fixed income, the destination of the investment and so forth.

Why these flows move over shorter periods of time depends as much on market psychology as economic fundamentals — but how does market psychology work? Moreover, why does a market that is impacted by some political and economic factors at one time then completely ignore them at another? To a large extent, the answer must lie in the very *structure* of the global currency market. While many people focus — rightly or wrongly — on hedge funds as being dominant currency market players, on any given day the vast majority of transactions are between banks, or "interbank" in market jargon. Hence, bank spot and forward dealers are by a long way the largest single player in the currency market. No one model has been able to forecast exchange rates accurately, because no one model has been able to predict accurately the sum of their intentions, behaviour or feelings towards the market. Yet, while that is the case there are some generalizations we can make about market behaviour given its participants. Firstly, traders have to trade in order to make a living. Hence, even in the absence of market-moving news or economic data, these traders still have to trade. This is of course linked in with the increasing use of technical analysis. As more people use this and more people watch certain levels, so those levels become more important. Needless to say, a break of those levels, one way or the other, thus leads to herding activity.

There is another aspect to market psychology and it is that markets, just as economies, also trade in cycles. This is not necessarily to say that the two cycles occur over the same time period. Obviously, this is a subject that will be covered more fully in this chapter, but to summarize briefly the longer a cycle continues, the more self-fulfilling it becomes. Speculative elements are increasingly attracted by what appears to be a one-way bet. Of necessity, the type of activity that this reflects is trend-following. The rule of trends is that they have not ended until they have ended. In other words, until there is clear evidence that the trend is over, the market continues to buy into that trend. However, such financial market trends have impact in the real economy. If the trend represents capital inflows, then it causes the current account balance to become an increasingly large deficit. Increasing fundamental deterioration is initially ignored, but after an extended period of time two things start to happen — the size of the current account deficit becomes alarming and investors start to get nervous as a result. Real money investors start to pare back their positions, but speculators continue to pile in. Towards the end of a trend, volatility starts to pick up markedly, until such time as an unforeseen catalyst causes the trend to end abruptly and violently. Indeed, the longer the trend has gone on, the more people are in the trend, and thus the more violent the trend reversal. Yet, just as trends are self-fulfilling, so are trend reversals, which in turn become new — if opposite trends; so works the market cycle, according to technical rather than economic factors.

Cross-border flows are also driven by fundamental considerations such as:

• Portfolio diversification
• Maximizing total returns
• Specific investor risk tolerance levels

When it comes to investment, these are important incentives and guidelines. Our purpose here is to track not incentives but actions. Thus in our first example we look at the US Treasury's "TIC" report, which examines portfolio flows by non-residents of the US going into the US equity and fixed income markets. As we have seen, as barriers to capital have fallen across the world, so capital flows have become increasingly important in determining exchange rates. The usefulness of this report is in explaining and confirming medium-term flow trends either in favour or against the US dollar in this case. Thus, as an example, Table 3.2 shows the TIC report from August 2001.[4]

From this we can tell a lot of useful information. For instance, we can note that total foreign investor inflows to the US asset markets rebounded in August to USD37.6 billion, after falling sharply in July to USD26.8 billion from USD39.5 billion in June. There are both negatives and positives from this. On the negative side, this USD37.6 billion was a rebound from a 14-month low in July and also well below the USD48 billion monthly average for the first half of the year. On the positive side, this month-on-month increase happened at a time of USD weakness. A major positive swing in favour of US Treasuries was largely behind it, from a total of –USD11.5 billion in July to +USD4.4 billion in August. Agencies, corporates and US stocks all saw modest declines in net inflows from non-US accounts.

Looking at the regional breakdown, the largest swing in favour of Treasuries was by European accounts, though the largest absolute buying was by Latin American/Caribbean accounts, which are usually dominated by offshore hedge funds. For the US dollar to trend lower requires that

---

[4]US Department of Treasury TIC Report, August 2001.

Table 3.2   US Treasury "TIC" (Treasury International Capital) Movement Data as of August 2001

Net foreign inflows into long-term US assets (USD billions)

	Monthly net flows			Quarterly average net flows		
Asset class	August	July	June	Q2-01	Q1-01	Q4-00
Treasuries	4.40	−11.49	−3.45	−4.69	0.97	−8.96
Agencies	11.91	12.48	16.91	13.11	14.09	15.49
Corporates	12.71	14.37	15.56	23.97	23.28	17.15
Total fixed income	**29.02**	**15.35**	**29.02**	**32.39**	**38.35**	**23.68**
Stocks	8.59	11.48	10.44	11.46	13.89	12.17
Total US assets	**37.61**	**26.82**	**39.46**	**43.85**	**52.24**	**35.85**

	Europe		Asia		Latin America/Caribbean	
Asset class	August	July	August	July	August	July
Treasuries	0.31	−8.22	0.58	−3.94	3.72	1.89
Agencies	1.92	4.60	4.83	6.80	5.55	1.02
Corporates	7.64	7.31	2.72	1.67	3.40	5.21
Total fixed income	**9.86**	**3.68**	**8.12**	**4.53**	**12.67**	**8.12**
Stocks	9.06	6.70	1.44	3.73	−3.06	0.07
Total US assets	**18.92**	**10.39**	**9.57**	**8.26**	**9.61**	**8.18**

inflows to US assets also *trend* lower, and as of this report those conditions had not been met. Thus, comparing the spot price action in dollar exchange rates to the table, we see a flow confirmation of what many in the market called the "surprising" resilience of the US dollar. Subsequent TIC reports from the US Treasury confirmed the US dollar strength through early December, despite the accelerated deterioration in US economic fundamentals. The flow picture thus explained the strength of the US dollar where just using the fundamental picture did not.

The Euro-Zone Portfolio Flow Report

The Euro-zone capital flows report for September 2001[5] shows that the Euro-zone, which had been recording monthly capital outflows (combined direct and portfolio investment) from 1999 through the first half of 2001 started to record capital inflows in the second half of 2001 and in September of that year saw the second highest monthly inflow since the establishment of the Euro in January 1999. This was also the fourth consecutive net inflow. Comparing the first nine months of 2001 to 2000, the total net outflow fell to EUR51.3 billion from EUR87.5 billion, an important reason for the Euro's more stable performance. See Figure 3.5.

Within this overall flow picture, as we see in Figure 3.6, net fixed income inflows rose substantially to EUR16.6 billion in September, a five-fold increase from the previous month's small inflow. Indeed, for the first time since the inception of the Euro in January 1999, the assets side of total portfolio investment (Euro-zone-based investors) switched to net inflows in September 2001.

Finally, equity flows recorded a net inflow for the fifth straight month in September rising to more than double August's level at EUR28.3 billion. All of this helps to support a picture

---

[5]Euro-zone Capital Flows Report and European Central Bank, September 2001.

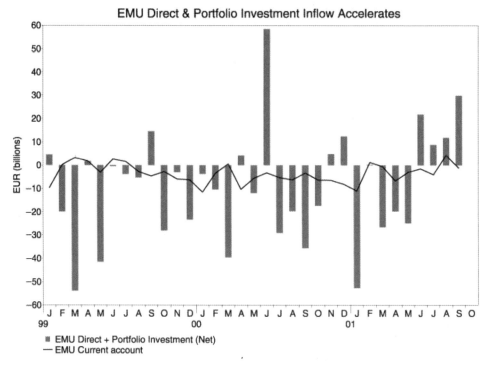

Figure 3.5   Euro-zone capital in flows

of an improving flow story for the Euro in the second half of 2001. This does not definitively suggest on its own that the Euro should appreciate against its major currency counterparts. It does appear to suggest however that the Euro should at the least be more stable — and this is more or less what happened, excluding the specific volatility caused by the tragic events of September 11.

The IMF Quarterly Report on Emerging Market Financing

Within the emerging markets, the International Monetary Fund produces a quarterly report on asset market-related flows, which is available on the IMF website. As an example of this, we can take a look at the Q3, 2001 report,[6] which appeared to confirm that the events of September 11 significantly increased investor uncertainty and reduced risk tolerance at a time when market concerns were already high about global slowing, emerging market fundamentals and the potential for credit events in particular emerging markets. There was an across-the-board sell off of emerging market assets and at least initially an ensuing drought in new bond issuance.

In terms of the flow trends at work, the major symptoms were a broad-based sell off in emerging market assets, thus increasing the correlation between individual market returns and a general "flight to quality" among investors within the credit spectrum. Treasuries outperformed credit product for this reason. Some credit or spread products outperformed others, suggesting

---

[6] IMF quarterly report on Emerging Market Financing, Q3, 2001.

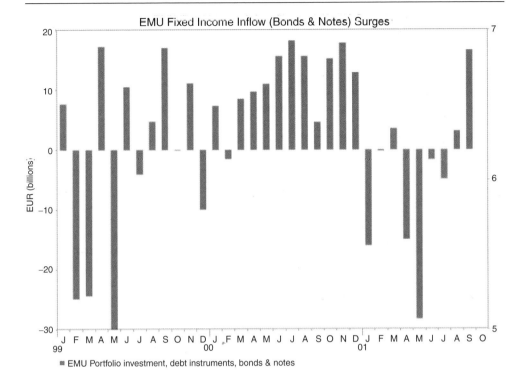

Figure 3.6   Euro-zone fixed income inflows

that the sell off was not entirely panic-driven and that some degree of differentiation was made. Not surprisingly, financing by the emerging markets on international capital markets fell sharply in Q3 to issuance levels not seen since the Russian crisis in the autumn of 1998. More specifically, bond issuance more than halved from levels seen in Q2.

The Emerging Market Financing report examined in depth two issues:

- The report examined in detail the investor selection and discrimination process within emerging fixed income markets. The sharp fall in investor risk tolerance was found to be a crucial determining factor in the parallel decline in bond issuance.
- The report suggested that, based on trends through the end of Q3, net capital flows to the emerging markets were set to turn negative for 2001 as a whole for the first time in more than 10 years, and then goes on to look at whether the rise in private sector capital inflows to the emerging markets in the 1990s was a cyclical phenomenon or due to temporary factors, the end of which may or may not have been signalled by the fact of negative inflows in 2001.

These are the kinds of issues that the IMF's quarterly review of Emerging Market Financing deals with. It is an excellent and exhaustive report, which shows the medium-term trends in equity, fixed income and lending flows for the emerging markets. It is useful not so much for short-term traders, but rather for corporations or institutional investors who require a detailed medium-term flow picture before making their investment decision, or alternatively require information that will help in deciding whether or not to hedge or reduce currency exposure.

Table 3.3   25 delta risk reversals

	EUR–USD	USD–JPY	GBP–USD	EUR–JPY	EUR–GBP	USD–CHF	AUD–USD	USD–CAD	EUR–SEK	EUR–CHF	GBP–JPY	USD–PLN
1M	0.15 EUR call	0.7 JPY put	0.4 GBP put	0.2 EUR call	0.2 around	0.15 CHF call	0.5 AUD put	0.5 USD call	0.3 EUR call	0.7 EUR put	0.35 GBP put	1.8 USD call
3M	0.25 EUR call	0.5 JPY put	0.2 GBP put	0.2 EUR call	0.25 EUR put	0.25 CHF call						
6M	0.25 EUR call	0.4 JPY put	0.35 GBP put	0.2 EUR call	0.15 EUR put	0.3 CHF call						
1Y	0.25 EUR call	0.35 JPY put	0.35 GBP put	0.2 EUR call	0.25 EUR put	0.2 CHF call						

3.1.3   Option Flow/Sentiment Models

Risk Reversals

In addition to flow indicators, there are also sentiment indicators. These do not reflect flows directly going through the currency market, but more indirectly by representing the market's bias towards exchange rates. A very useful indicator of market sentiment or "skew" is the option risk reversal. This is the premium or discount of the implied volatility of a same delta currency call over the put. For instance, a dollar–Polish zloty three-month risk reversal may be 3 vols, which means that the implied volatility on the 25 delta three-month US dollar call costs 3 vols more than the 25 delta dollar put against the Polish zloty.

Table 3.3 looks at the risk reversals for the major exchange rates and the US dollar–zloty exchange rate. Given that it provides risk reversals across tenors, this produces in effect a risk reversal "curve". How do we interpret this information? Clearly, the best way of doing so is by comparing current to historic levels. In this case, one should compare the current levels of option risk reversals as expressed by the table results to a historic measure of risk reversals for those same currency pairs.

Options are priced off forwards and through this option risk reversals are priced off interest rate differentials. How do we price interest rate differentials? A key determinant for both the level and trend of interest rates is the current account. A current account surplus results in greatly increased liquidity, which in turn pushes interest rates lower. Equally, a current account deficit is an important factor in pushing interest rates higher. From this, we can say that term currencies with current account surpluses usually have the risk reversal in their favour. Thus, the dollar–Swiss franc exchange rate risk reversal should usually be in favour of Swiss franc calls. In other words, Swiss franc calls should be more expensive than Swiss franc puts. Equally, the same should usually be the case for dollar–yen risk reversals. If at any one time they are not, then this *may* represent a profitable trading or hedging opportunity.

Looking at Table 3.3, we see that Euro–dollar risk reversals are bid for Euro calls, which should be the case given relative interest rate differentials and current accounts. However, comparing this situation with how Euro–dollar risk reversals traded in the prior weeks before this report, a picture emerges of the options' market gradually reducing its bias in favour of Euro calls. The risk reversal was substantially more in favour of Euro calls and has been reduced. Thus, it is important not just to look at current risk reversal levels, but also to compare them with where they have been in the past. Historically, the one-month dollar–yen risk reversal has usually been around 0.4 in favour of yen calls given the interest rate differential and Japan's structurally high current account surplus. In 2001, Japan saw its current account surplus decline from USD12.6 billion to USD9 billion, or from 2.5% of GDP to 1.8%. As a result, "fair value" for the dollar–yen one-month risk reversal probably fell to around 0.3 for yen calls. Note however that in the table the entire risk reversal curve is bid for yen puts. Hence, the options market seems temporarily out of line and may at some stage revert to mean — through yen appreciation and the risk reversal swinging back in favour of the yen. This is the kind of information that one can gain from the risk reversal table.

3.2 SPECULATIVE AND NON-SPECULATIVE FLOWS

While these flow and sentiment models vary, both in terms of the time span they focus on and the kind of information they look at, the basic premise behind them is the same — exchange rates are determined by the supply and demand for currencies, in other words by "order flow". Over time, economic fundamentals will dictate the order flow and therefore the exchange rate itself. However, currency market practitioners do not necessarily have that long to wait. Therefore, it is necessary to study order flow separately and independently from the fundamentals, and moreover it is necessary to study the drivers of that order flow. That is what we have attempted here in this chapter.

The key distinction between a speculative and a non-speculative capital flow, keeping to the definition that we are using for speculation — which is that speculation involves the buying and selling of currencies with no underlying attached asset — is the exchange rate itself. For a speculator, the exchange rate is the primary incentive for investing, using this definition. However, for an asset manager, the exchange rate is not the primary consideration, which is the total return available in the local markets. As the barriers to capital have broken down and as currencies have been de-pegged and allowed to float freely, so both speculative and non-speculative capital flows have grown exponentially. There remains a dynamic tension between the two, allowing one or other to be more important in terms of total flows at any one time.

Generalizing somewhat, one can say that speculative flows dominate short-term exchange rate moves, while non-speculative flows that are attracted by long-term fundamental shifts in the economy dominate long-term exchange rate moves. This is a nice, cosy definition of the dynamics affecting exchange rates, however there is a problem. Financial bubbles are seen as essentially speculative creations, yet they are generated not by short-term exchange rate or asset market moves but by long-term and increasingly self-perpetuating shifts. The essential lesson behind this is that it is in fact exceptionally difficult to differentiate the speculative from the non-speculative. It is easier to focus on the incentive rather than the result. The primary incentive behind speculative flow, using our definition of speculation, is that it is mainly driven by the exchange rate not the interest rate. If it were the latter, neither the Japanese yen nor the Swiss franc would ever have risen. Yet, since the 1971–1973 break-up of the Bretton Woods exchange rate system, both have trended higher against the US dollar (and most other currencies). Expectations about the exchange rate are the primary motive and incentive behind speculative capital flow. This is a lesson that many economists have yet to learn, largely because many of their theoretical ideas of how exchange rates *should* behave do not work in practice.

Perception and outcome are intrinsically linked in the currency markets; they are both cause and effect. This creates a self-fulfilling and self-reinforcing phenomenon, which becomes more speculative the longer it lasts, until it becomes unsustainable and the bubble bursts.

Free floating exchange rates tend to trade and trend in cycles, and flows are both cause and effect in this regard. Such currency cycles are not of necessity timed with the economic cycle. It depends why they start. After the bubble bursts, there is usually a period of consolidation and reversal; the longer the initial trend or cycle, the longer in turn the reversal. Thus, we saw a weakening trend for the US dollar in the 1970s, followed by a strengthening in the early 1980s, followed by renewed weakening from 1985 to 1987, which again was reversed towards the end of that decade. The 1990s saw a similar pattern, with the US dollar weak from 1991 to 1995, which was followed by a broad strengthening trend that has lasted from 1995 through 2001. This suggests that at some point the US dollar strength cycle will end and be reversed. Trying to determine the top is for the most part impossible. It is more important to be able to understand the cyclical nature of the currency markets and to be able to plan accordingly ahead of that cycle ending. To prove the point, towards the end of 2001 the US dollar was continuing to strengthen despite the fact that the Fed funds' target interest rate was at 1.75%, while the European Central Bank's repo rate was at 3.25%. Nominal interest rates are not the primary incentive for speculative capital flow, never have been and never will be. The exchange rate itself is the incentive. This is an important realization.

3.3 SUMMARY

In this chapter, we have attempted to examine how "flows" interact with price action. The assumption of the efficient market hypothesis is that flows cannot affect price because of perfect information availability, yet as we have seen this assumption is clearly and manifestly wrong. Testimony to that fact is the subsequent growth of and interest in flow analysis, whether of the short-term kind as practiced by commercial and investment banks in looking at their own client flows, or of a more medium-term kind in the form of the US or Euro area capital flow reports. Just as flow analysis has become relatively sophisticated in analysing developed market exchange rate flow, so it is increasingly becoming so within the emerging markets. At this stage, data availability is the only thing holding it back, but this barrier will also fall in time. In sum, flow analysis is a very important and useful tool for currency market practitioners in the making of their currency investment or exposure decisions. The tracking of capital flows of necessity involves looking for apparent patterns in flow movement. Linked in with this idea is the discipline of tracking patterns in price. This discipline is that of technical analysis, which we shall look at in the next chapter.

4
Technical Analysis:
The Art of Charting

Technical analysis has much in common with the major principles at work in flow analysis. Both focus on behavioural patterns within financial markets. Both claim that market behaviour can indeed impact future prices. In addition, both reflect a belief that markets must move and traders must trade irrespective of whether or not there are changes in economic fundamentals. In this sense, if flow and technical analysis did not exist, they would have to be invented. Demand will eventually result in supply!

In this chapter, we take a look at the core ideas behind the fascinating and controversial field of technical analysis, its origins, how it works and its main analytical building blocks. For those looking to study this field in more depth, I provide useful references in the footnotes. Whereas flow analysis focuses on price trends that are created by order flow, technical analysis focuses on price patterns within those trends. Technical analysis remains a controversial subject for many people. Despite such controversy, its origins are rooted in mathematics and it has been around in one form or another for a very long time indeed.

4.1 ORIGINS AND BASIC CONCEPTS

At least in its modern version, technical analysis is generally seen as emanating from the "Dow Theory" established by Charles Dow at the start of the twentieth century. The core original ideas of technical analysis focused on the trending nature of prices, the idea of support and resistance and the concept of volume mirroring changes in price. Though we only touch on it here, the contribution of Charles Dow to modern-day technical analysis should not be underestimated. His focus on the basics of security price movement helped to give rise to a completely new method of analysing financial markets in general.

The basic premise behind this is that the price of a security represents a consensus. At the individual level, it is the price at which one person is willing to buy and another to sell. At the market level, it is the price at which the sum of market participants is willing to transact. The willingness to buy or sell depends on the price expectations of individual market participants. Because human expectations are relatively unpredictable, so the same must be said for their price expectations. If we were all totally logical and could separate our emotions from our investment decisions, one should assume that classic fundamental analysis would be a better predictor of future prices than it currently is. Prices would only reflect fundamental valuations. The fact that this is not the case suggests that other forces may be at work. Indeed, investor expectations also play a part, both at the individual level and also as a group.

Technical analysis is the process of analysing a currency or financial security's historical price in an attempt to determine its future price direction. It is founded in the belief that there are consistent patterns within price action, which in turn have predictable results in terms of future price action. In contrast to economics, technical analysis requires that financial markets are not perfectly efficient, that there is no such thing as perfect knowledge or perfect information availability or usage, and also that in the absence of other information market participants will look to past price action as a determinant of future prices. For precisely this reason, the economics profession generally has dismissed technical analysis as irrational. However, just as we have already seen that financial markets are not perfectly efficient, so substantial research has shown conclusively both that technical analysis is widely practiced by market participants and perhaps more importantly that it has yielded substantially positive results. Traders who have used technical analysis have frequently made consistently high excess returns. Furthermore, in the context of the currency markets, technical analysis has a particularly good track record in predicting short-term exchange rate moves. How can this be so? Simply put, nature abhors a vacuum and thus in the vacuum left by classic economic analysis, in its inability to predict exchange rates over the short term, came technical analysis.

4.2   THE CHALLENGE OF TECHNICAL ANALYSIS

Technical analysis has posed a challenge to economic analysis in its ability to predict exchange rates. As a result, considerable research has been undertaken by the economic community on how technical analysis works, both in practice and in theory. It is not for here to go through this research or literature in detail. Rather, we look at one such study as symptomatic of a general enquiry by the economics profession into the workings of technical analysis. More specifically, no less than the Federal Reserve undertook to examine this phenomenon, apparent confirmation of an ongoing change in the way both private and public institutions are approaching the field of technical analysis. Indeed, the reader can find no more useful and detailed investigation of the subject matter, starting from a macroeconomic perspective, than two reports by Carol L. Osler of the Federal Reserve Bank of New York, which examine how technical analysis is able to predict exchange rates.[1] These papers go a substantial way in explaining how technical analysis works and are particularly useful as they undertake this investigation from an economic perspective. In line with work done on studying order flow, which we looked at in Chapter 3, they suggest customer orders "cluster" around certain price levels and that such "clustering" creates specific price patterns depending on whether or not those levels hold. To a technician, this makes perfect sense given that a price represents the consensus of market supply and demand at any one time. Below the price, there should be "support" levels at which demand is expected to exceed supply and conversely above the price there may be "resistance" levels, where supply may exceed demand. From my perspective, I would suggest the following reasons why technical analysis has gradually taken on a more prominent and important role in predicting exchange rates:

• Over the short term, the currency market is essentially trend-following.
• The majority of market participants are speculative, that is they undertake currency transactions that have no underlying trade or investment transaction behind them.
• Nature abhors a vacuum — currency market participants have to trade off something whether or not there has been any change in macroeconomic fundamentals.
• Traditional exchange rate models have had relatively poor results, therefore another analytical discipline was needed that was able to achieve better results.
• Exchange rate supply and demand create price patterns, which in the absence of other stimulus may provide clues for future exchange rate moves.

---

[1]Carol L. Osler, *Currency Orders and Exchange Rate Dynamics: Explaining the Success of Technical Analysis*, Federal Reserve Bank of New York Staff Report No. 125, April 2001; "Support for resistance: technical analysis and intraday exchange rates", *Economic Policy Review*, 6(2) (July 2000).

There does appear to be a crucial self-fulfilling aspect to technical analysis, which is to say that because a large number of people see a particular price level as important, therefore *de facto* it becomes important. Needless to say, this is an aspect that critics of technical analysis regularly seize on. While this may be the case to an extent, it does not answer the obvious question of why such a number of people find those levels important in the first place. Technical analysis is the discovery of patterns within price action, patterns which can be used to predict future prices. The predictive results of technical analysis consistently exceed those suggested by a random walk theory.[2] Indeed, such have been the results achieved that there is now a sizeable and ever growing community of traders and leveraged funds that trade solely on the back of technical analysis signals. In short, technical analysis "works" to the extent that it produces results consistently for market participants who are trying to predict short-term exchange rate moves. If this is the case, what precisely is technical analysis and how can one use it?

4.3   THE ART OF CHARTING

Technical analysis is founded on the principle of "charting", which relates to creating charts to reflect price patterns. Once again, this is best explained by the use of a chart. In Figure 4.1, we are looking at the Euro–dollar exchange rate from April 1998 to October 2001. At this most basic stage, there are few clear patterns, apart from the one dominant pattern, which is that the Euro has been in a downtrend for some time! Clearly, in order to try and interpret this chart, we have to have a set of tools at our disposal, which provide some degree of unbiased, objective analysis as to likely trends and direction. To start this off, we look at the two most important building blocks of technical analysis:

- Support
- Resistance

4.3.1   Currency Order Dynamics and Technical Levels

Sceptics may suggest that **support** or **resistance** levels can just as easily be randomly picked. The evidence however does not support such scepticism. Indeed, on the contrary, both academic and institutional research suggests exchange rate trends are interrupted or reversed at published support and resistance levels much more frequently than is the case at randomly picked levels. Such levels are therefore seen as statistically important, most likely because of the clustering effect mentioned earlier. Customer orders are placed just above or just below previous highs or lows. As a result, this clustering can have the effect either of pausing or accelerating the short-term price trend at any one time. This link between capital flows and technical chart levels can be expressed in the following way:

- "Support" reflects a *concentration of demand* sufficient to pause the prevailing trend
- "Resistance" equally reflects a similar *concentration of supply*

---

[2]While there are a number of studies on the results achieved through technical analysis, readers may find particularly useful that done by Richard M. Levich and Lee R. Thomas, "The significance of technical trading-rule profits in the foreign exchange market: a bootstrap approach", as published in the *Journal of International Money and Finance*, October 1993 and also in Andrew W. Gitlin (editor), *Strategic Currency Investing: Trading and Hedging in the Foreign Exchange Market*, Probus Publishing Company, 1993.

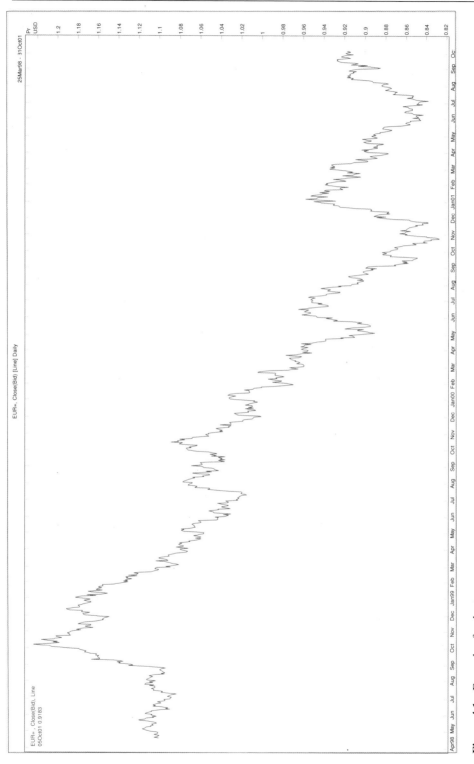

Figure 4.1   Example of a chart
Source: Reuters. Copyright Reuters Limited, 1999, 2002.

However, this clustering effect on prices can be further broken down into two specific types of customer order:

- Take profit
- Stop loss

There are important differences in the way that these two specific types of customer order tend to cluster. For instance, take profit orders tend to cluster *in front of* important support or resistance levels and thus tend to have the habit of causing the trend to reverse — thus reinforcing that support or resistance — if they are sufficient in number. By contrast, stop loss orders tend to be clustered *behind* important support or resistance levels, thus accelerating and intensifying the prevailing trend if triggered. Academic research has found that take profit and stop loss customer orders, which impose some degree of *conditionality* on the order, can make up between 10 and 15% of total order flow. As a result, they can have an important effect on trading conditions and therefore on price patterns. During calm market conditions, they can further restrict price action. Conversely, during volatile market conditions, they can exacerbate price volatility when such orders are triggered. Thus, both in calm and volatile market conditions, they re-emphasize the original importance of the support and resistance levels.

So far, we have been looking at "spot" foreign exchange orders, that is conditional customer orders to be executed for spot $(T + 2)$ delivery. However, conditional orders left in the options market can also impact spot currency price action. More specifically, "knock-in" and "knock-out" levels for exotic options, allowing a client to be knocked-in to the underlying structure or conversely knocked-out of it, can and do trigger specific spot currency price activity. Knock-in and knock-out levels are usually chosen based on previously important highs and lows. In other words, they are chosen based on technical support or resistance levels. As a result, there can be — and frequently is — both spot and option customer order clustering around such levels, further impacting price action.

It is not only customers that place conditional orders in the market. In order to limit a bank's balance sheet exposure to overnight price swings in exchange rates, interbank dealers either close out their positions at the end of the day or alternatively themselves leave take profit or stop loss orders with their dealing counterparts within the bank in the next time zone. Thus, a dealer in Singapore may pass on their customers' conditional orders as well as their own to London and London may in turn pass on such orders to New York and so on round the time zones, either until such orders are filled or conversely are cancelled. If there is a self-fulfilling aspect to this whole idea, it concerns therefore the very microstructure of the currency market itself. Broadly speaking, currency interbank dealers follow technical analysis more closely than the customer base of the bank, in part because they have a much shorter time frame than their customers and in part because they have to trade in order to make a living irrespective of whether or not there have been changes in economic fundamentals. Currency interbank dealers and short-term traders follow technical analysis, and because they make up the majority of currency market participants the levels and types of analysis that they follow automatically become important. Thus, structural aspects within the currency market may help explain to some degree the success of technical analysis. What it does not explain however is the superior degree of that success relative to classic economic analysis or alternatively to random walk theory in predicting short-term exchange rate moves. Given that take profit orders cause price trends to pause, while stop loss orders extend such trends, the logical conclusion is that the balance between such orders in the market place is an important real-time determinant of exchange rates.

4.3.2 The Study of Trends

At its heart, technical analysis represents the study of price trends (or anticipated trends). In price terms, at their most basic, these can be divided into uptrends and downtrends. Within such trends, we see points where little price action occurs and conversely other points reflecting substantial price action and market tension. The idea behind support and resistance is that if the price action fails to exceed a certain level, then that level becomes important. Thus, if a price fails to exceed a high and falls back, we call that high a resistance. Equally, if the price action fails to get below a low price level, then that low price level becomes support. Price trends reflecting a number of support and resistance levels are reflected by **trend-lines** (see Figure 4.2).

Resistance or support can be formed around such a trend-line. Note that at the bottom right of Figure 4.2, the price of the Euro–dollar exchange rate breaks up through the trend-line. From this, we can say that it has broken *trend-line resistance*. Thus, we can describe support and resistance levels as levels where a trend may be interrupted or reversed. Because such levels can determine the continuation or the cessation of a trend, they are seen as important by market participants. In this example, market participants may well have left stop loss orders to buy Euro and sell dollars above the trend-line resistance on the view that if such a level broke it would signal a short-term end to the downtrend. Of course, if enough people leave orders to buy (sell) above (below) trend-line resistance (support), then the reversal of the previous trend could well be accelerated. Furthermore, speculative elements could discover such orders and try to target them in order to cause what might become a self-fulfilling move, allowing for potential profits.

To identify support and resistance levels, technical analysts use a variety of information inputs, including but not exclusive to chart analysis and numerical rules based on previous price performance. The rule with support and resistance is that they are important until they are broken. This may seem like just stating the obvious, but the key thing to note is that there is no particular time limit to their importance.

4.3.3 Psychological Levels

In addition to the types of support and resistance that are identified by previous price action and thus previous lows and highs, there are also other sorts that focus instead on psychological factors or instead on flow dynamics specific to that particular exchange rate. In the first, market participants frequently focus on round numbers — such as 0.9400 for the Euro–dollar exchange rate — hence such levels are termed psychological support or resistance. They are important not because they represent of necessity a previous low or high, but instead because they reflect the expectation of a future move if they are breached. In the second, there can exist within specific exchange rates support or resistance levels reflecting anticipated flow dynamics. For instance, in the dollar–yen exchange rate, some Japanese exporters may prefer also to sell their receivables forward (selling dollars and buying yen) to achieve a round number. Thus, one anticipates this by adding the forward points. For instance, if the spot dollar–yen exchange rate is 120.45/55 and the three-month forward points are $-73/-72.5$, one might expect some exporter sales to occur at 120.73 (which would allow an outright level of 120.00 to be achieved). Consequently, one might see 120.73 as one type of resistance. Of course, the difficulty with this particular type of approach is that as the spot exchange rate and the interest rate differential move, so the forward resistance point moves.

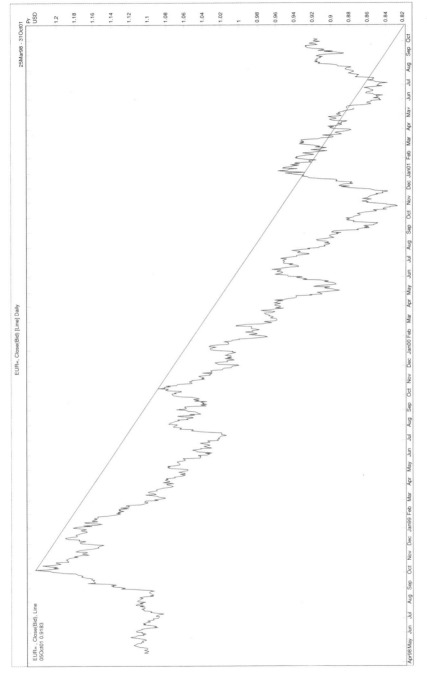

Figure 4.2 Example of a trend-line
Source: Reuters. Copyright Reuters Limited, 1999, 2002.

A further complication within technical analysis is that there are various ways in which charts can be drawn. In Figures 4.3–4.5, we look at the three main types:

- Line
- Candlestick
- Bar

The basic chart, which is a simple **line chart** (Figure 4.3), is as the title suggests formed from a single line. Of necessity that line must be formed by a series of highs, lows, open or closing levels. Thus, it is an approximation of the price action over a given time, reflecting more the overall trend rather than the intraday price action. Yet, highs and lows can be just as important as that trend, hence the **bar chart** (Figure 4.4) is also useful. Sometimes, for the same instrument, security or exchange rate, the line and bar charts can show quite different support and resistance levels. Yet, it can also be important when precisely those highs and lows occurred. For instance, the implication of price action on any given day may be quite different if the high in price action occurs at the start or at the end of a move. For this reason, analysis using a **candlestick chart** (Figure 4.5) can be useful.

These are the three most basic types of chart. For all three, we can use a number of technical tools and schools of thought to try and develop predictive knowledge from past price patterns. Before we go on to some of the more complex tools, it is probably worth having another look at support and resistance, accompanied by another building block — the **moving average**. As the name suggests, this is the average of the exchange rate values over a set time period. Because that exchange rate is constantly moving, so is the average rate of necessity. Moving averages can be studied according to periods of any length, but the most widely used and thus most important are the 20-, 55- and 200-day and the 55- and 200-week moving averages. Thus armed with the initial building blocks of support, resistance and moving averages, let's try to do some technical analysis, using the chart of the Euro–dollar exchange rate in Figure 4.6.

Here, we have our Euro–dollar exchange rate with the following technical tools:

- A trend-line
- A trend-channel (two parallel trend-lines)
- 55-day moving average
- 200-day moving average

So, what can we tell from this chart? A layman might not be able to tell much apart from the fact that Euro–dollar has been in a downtrend. Sometimes, such basic observations, made either by a layman or by a practising technical analyst, are the most important ones. However, a "technician" should be armed with a skill set that at least allows for the possibility of a more complex and sophisticated analysis. Looking at the chart again, we can identify the following points accordingly:

- Euro–dollar has traded within a long-term downward sloping trend-channel.
- It has only broken that channel on a sustained basis to the downside up until July of 2001 when it broke through and held above channel resistance.
- Before that, in December 2000, Euro–dollar briefly managed to exceed that trend-channel resistance and made a major high of 0.9595. Major highs and lows usually reflect the

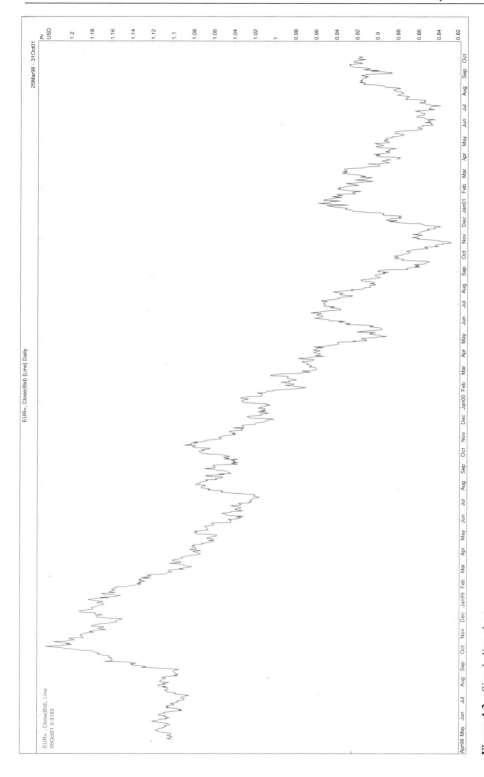

Figure 4.3   Simple line chart
Source: Reuters. Copyright Reuters Limited, 1999, 2002.

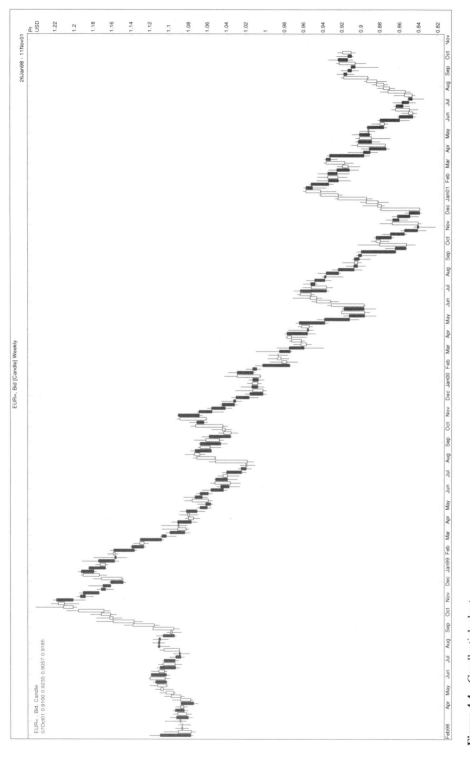

Figure 4.4 Candlestick chart
Source: Reuters. Copyright Reuters Limited. 1999, 2002.

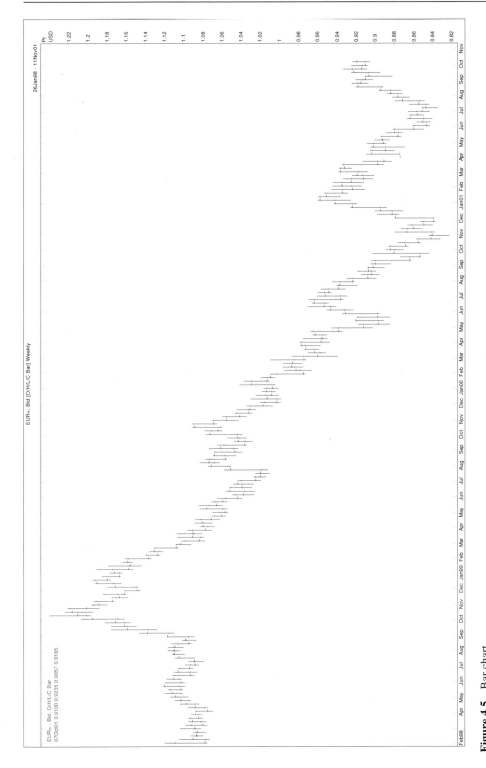

Figure 4.5 Bar chart
Source: Reuters. Copyright Reuters Limited, 1999, 2002.

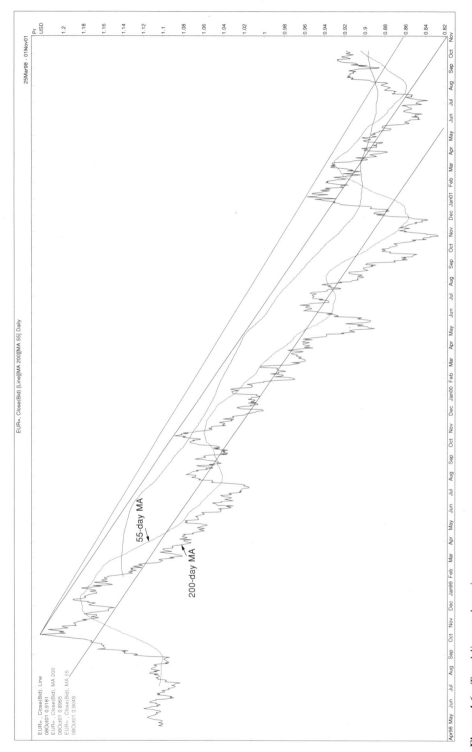

Figure 4.6 Trend-lines and moving averages
Source: Reuters. Copyright Reuters Limited, 1999, 2002.

ultimate extension of a trend reversal. Thus, 0.9595 needs to be exceeded for the medium-term downward trend to be negated.

- The fact that a shorter-term moving average has broken up through the longer-term counterpart would appear to validate the view that Euro–dollar trades higher in the short term, whether or not it actually manages to breach that level of 0.9595.
- More specifically, however, the fact that the 55-day moving average has broken up through the 200-day moving average is potentially very significant. Why? As we noted above, certain moving averages are seen as more equal than others. Notably, the break of a 200-day by a 55-day MA usually can potentially lead to impulsive moves and signal a short-term trend reversal. Here, the 55-day MA has broken up through the 200-day MA, which we call a "golden cross", arguing for potentially dramatic gains. Conversely, if the 55-day MA were to break down through the 200-day MA, that would be termed a "death cross" and be correspondingly bearish as the name might suggest.

One could go on, but I hope from this that the reader gets a picture of charts being able to reflect substantial amounts of potentially important information, information that in the absence of major changes in fundamentals may be the primary reason for subsequent, future price action. Along with support, resistance and moving averages, there is another technical tool that is useful in determining short-term moves in exchange rates — the **relative strength index (RSI)**. The aim of this indicator is to discover overbought or oversold levels, against which the index is measured. The time period for RSI is usually 14 days and overbought and oversold levels are usually taken as 70 and 30 for the index. Thus, we return to our Euro–dollar chart in Figure 4.7, including this time a reading of 14-day RSI.

The two dotted lines indicate the 30 and 70 oversold and overbought levels for 14-day RSI. Hence, we can note from this that according to the chart the RSI reading is currently roughly in the middle of its range. Combining this with the underlying chart, we note that at the same time as the RSI reading is in the middle of its bands, Euro–dollar has broken to the upside of a trend channel and the 55-day moving average has broken up through the 200-day moving average. We can potentially conclude from this that the benign RSI indicator may suggest there is more upside to come. Note that the RSI reading usually exceeds its 70 or 30 overbought or oversold levels *before* the peak or trough in the spot exchange rate. RSI analysis can be particularly useful when comparing divergences between it and the spot price action. For instance, if a spot exchange rate is making new highs while the RSI reading has already peaked, it may suggest that the spot exchange rate is itself about to peak and subsequently head lower.

RSI is one type of *technical indicator*. More generally, technical indicators reflect a mathematical calculation that can be applied to either an exchange rate's price or its volume. The result is of course a value, which is then used to try and predict future prices. By this definition, both RSI and moving averages are technical indicators. Another widely used technical indicator is the **moving average convergence divergence (MACD)** indicator. The MACD is usually calculated by subtracting a 26-day moving average of an exchange rate from its 12-day moving average. The result is an *oscillator* that reflects the convergence or divergence between these moving averages. In Figure 4.8, we again compare the standard Euro–dollar price chart with the 12/26-day MACD.

Here, we get a somewhat different picture than shown by the RSI comparison. While that appeared to suggest the Euro–dollar exchange rate may have been about to make further gains given the benign RSI reading relative to the move higher in price, this MACD comparison appears to be suggesting the opposite. For just at the time the Euro–dollar exchange rate is

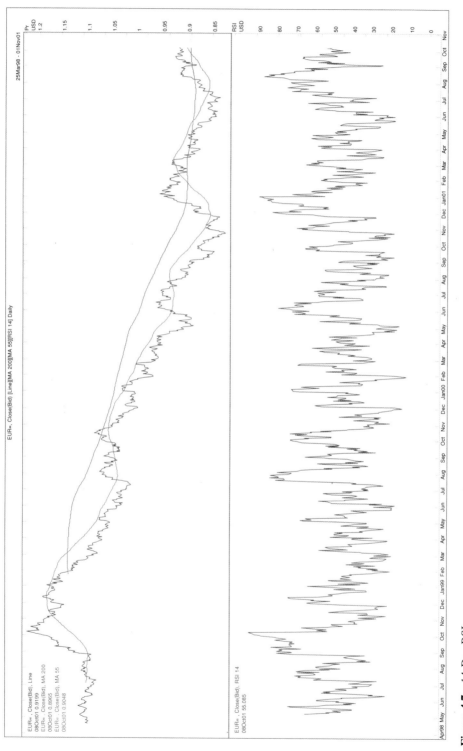

Figure 4.7 14-Day RSI
Source: Reuters. Copyright Reuters Limited, 1999, 2002.

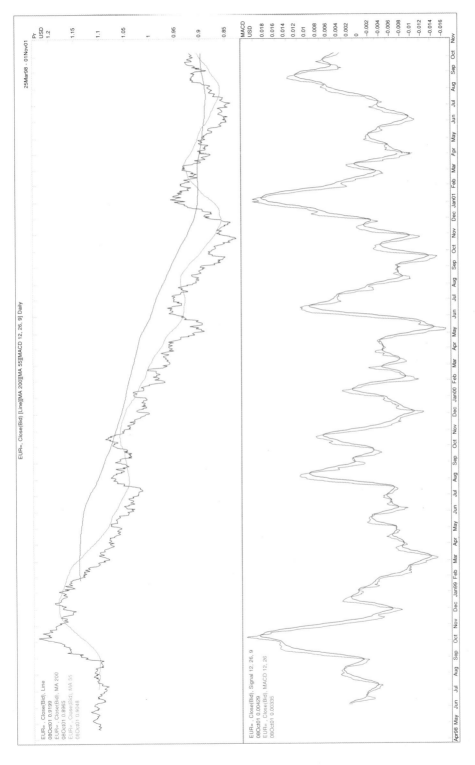

Figure 4.8 12/26-Day MACD
Source: Reuters. Copyright Reuters Limited, 1999, 2002.

making gains, the MACD reading has clearly failed well ahead of its previous high and is heading lower. This suggests *bearish divergence* on MACD and a potentially bearish signal as well for the Euro–dollar exchange rate. MACD oscillates above and below a zero level. When it is above zero, it means the 12-day moving average is higher than the 26-day moving average, which is potentially bullish as it suggests that "current" expectations (as reflected by the 12-day moving average) are more bullish than those expectations made prior to the 12-day moving average. Equally, when the MACD falls below zero, it suggests a bearish divergence between the moving averages. In our example, the MACD reading is still above zero, but it is heading lower towards that level.

Moving averages and MACD are examples of lagging technical indicators as they reflect previous price action and are particularly useful when an exchange rate trends over a long period of time. On the other hand, leading technical indicators give some indication of a price being overbought or oversold, thus RSI is an example of a leading indicator. *Divergence* occurs when the exchange rate trend does not agree with the trend of the technical indicator of that exchange rate. Hence, Figure 4.8 shows a clear example of *bearish divergence* using MACD.

4.4   SCHOOLS OF (TECHNICAL) THOUGHT

Having gone through the basic building blocks of technical analysis and the technical indicators that are used, we will now look at the major technical schools of thought that have dominated the way technical analysts and traders look at price patterns. The first one to focus on is the **Fibonacci** school of thought, named after Leonardo Fibonacci, an Italian mathematician born in 1170. Fibonacci discovered a series of numbers such that each number is the sum of the two previous numbers:

$$1, 1, 2, 3, 5, 8, 13, 21, 34, 55, 89, 144, 233 \text{ and so on} \ldots$$

To some, these numbers may seem more or less random. In fact, they are actually far from random, containing important interrelationships, and they are found in a surprising number of real-life examples. Indeed, it is not too much of an exaggeration to suggest that these numbers represent the mathematical building blocks of life. For a start, note that any given number is roughly 1.618 times the previous one. Equally, any number is 0.618 times the following number. As it stands, this does not answer the question of how Fibonacci happened to found, albeit inadvertently, a type of technical analysis. For this, we have to look first at Fibonacci's so-called "rabbit problem", which relates to his attempt to demonstrate the application of Hindu–Arabic numerals through the example of rabbits. The mathematical problem that Fibonacci posed is that if two rabbits were put in an isolated place, how many pairs of rabbits could be produced from that pair in a year if every month each pair produces a new pair, which itself from the second month also becomes reproductive? At the start of the first month, there would only be the first pair. By the start of the second month, there would be the original pair plus one new pair, resulting in two pairs of rabbits. However, during that second month, the original pair will again produce another pair while the second pair is maturing. Thus, at the start of the third month, there should be three pairs, which brings us back to the Fibonacci number series. In terms of a mathematical formula, this can be expressed as:

$$X_{n+1} = X_n + X_{n-1}$$

where X_n is the number of pairs of rabbits after n months.

This became known as the *Fibonacci sequence*, as coined by the French mathematician Edouard Lucas (1842–1891). As the Fibonacci sequence progresses, a clear relationship between the numbers becomes apparent, as reflected by the 0.618 and 1.618 ratios mentioned above. The very fact that there can be a consistent ratio between numbers is itself "statistically significant", confirming that there is more in this than just a random series of numbers. Note also that if you take any number and divide it by the number two higher in the sequence the ratio comes to 0.382. Not coincidentally, 38.2% and 61.8% are major Fibonacci retracement levels within the Fibonacci school of technical analysis.

While we look to Fibonacci and Lucas as the founders of modern-day Fibonacci analysis, it appears that long before them the importance of this sequence of numbers and ratios was well known and appreciated. Indeed, these ratios appear to have been used in the construction of both the Great Pyramid of Giza in Egypt and the Parthenon in Greece. The 0.618 or 1.618 ratio, also known as the *Golden ratio*, is commonly viewed in mathematics as one of the building blocks of natural growth patterns — in geometry as in life. Even the human body can be shown to contain elements of the Golden ratio, measuring the distance from the feet to the navel and in turn from the navel to the top of the head as a ratio. The basic building blocks of human beings, the DNA double helix, also contains the Golden ratio.

The link between Fibonacci and financial markets comes through another school of thought for technical analysis, **Elliott Wave Theory**, named after Ralph Nelson Elliott (1871–1948). Elliott first made the connection between his *Wave Theory* and the Fibonacci sequence of numbers in his book *Nature's Law — The Secret of the Universe* (1946). Elliott Wave Theory suggests financial markets move in five waves of *progression* followed by three waves *of regression*. As such a 5–3 wave move completes a wave cycle. The five "up" waves are labelled 1–5, while the three "down" waves are labelled a–c. Of necessity, waves 1, 3 and 5 are seen as *impulsive* waves while waves 2 and 4 are seen as *corrective*.

Remembering the Fibonacci sequence, it should be immediately obvious that 1, 3 and 5 are Fibonacci numbers. Furthermore, if we break each wave down into sub-waves, we notice two things, firstly that each sub-wave conforms to the 5–3 wave pattern and secondly that when we add up these sub-waves we come to 21 impulsive and 13 corrective waves, making 34 in total. Once again, 13, 21 and 34 are all Fibonacci sequence numbers.

Fibonacci sequence numbers are also used in other technical indicators, such as in moving averages — e.g. 5, 13 and 21 moving averages, 21, 34 and 55 or 31, 55 and 144. Within the financial markets, the most widely used application of the Golden ratio is through the *Fibonacci retracement*, which relates to the fact that corrective waves have retraced the previous wave by 38.2%, 50% or 61.8%. *Fibonacci fan lines* provide key support or resistance corresponding to the Fibonacci retracement levels. Once such a Fibonacci fan line support or resistance has been broken, this tends to suggest the extension of a correction and thus a potential wave reversal. In sum, Fibonacci levels can provide crucial tops and bottoms in the market and are widely watched by both short- and medium-term currency market participants.

A final school of thought is **Gann Theory**, created by W.D. Gann (1878–1955), which seeks to predict future prices using specific geometric angles. *Gann angles* or *Gann lines* can be created by graphing price against time. The basic Gann angle or line is created by assuming an increase in one unit for both price and time, resulting in a line which is at a 45° angle to both axes. Because of the price and time increases involved, this is called a 1 × 1 angle. Gann lines are drawn off major price tops and bottoms. If the price is above the 1 × 1 line, this signals a bullish trend and conversely if it breaks below the line this signals a bearish reversal. Including the 1 × 1 angle, Gann identified nine significant angles or lines relating to price and time:

- 1 × 8 — 82.5 degrees
- 1 × 4 — 75 degrees
- 1 × 3 — 71.25 degrees
- 1 × 2 — 63.75 degrees
- 1 × 1 — 45 degrees
- 2 × 1 — 26.25 degrees
- 3 × 1 — 18.75 degrees
- 4 × 1 — 15 degrees
- 8 × 1 — 7.5 degrees

Each of the angles or lines can provide a support or resistance depending on the trend. Generally speaking, the 1 × 1 angle as reflected by a trend-line is not sustainable given the steepness of the angle involved. Prices cannot continue appreciating at a 45° angle forever. The 3 × 1 angle is generally viewed as more sustainable in terms of price trends over the long term.

4.5   TECHNICAL ANALYSIS AND CURRENCY MARKET PRACTITIONERS

The various techniques of technical analysis, which we have only briefly touched on here, have been widely practiced by traders for a very long time — centuries rather than years. The first futures market was created in Japan in the early 1800s and the Japanese candlestick charting theory is seen as having emerged on the back of this. The very fact that we can chart US Treasuries back to the American Civil War confirms that the art of charting is also hardly a new phenomenon in the US either. While currency, equity and fixed income traders have long followed technical signals, corporations and asset managers have on the whole been somewhat more reticent to do so, either because of scepticism as to the merits of technical analysis or a lack of knowledge of how it works — or both. The best advance of any type of analytical discipline is that it actually works in practice; that it is capable of predicting exchange rates in this case and therefore using it one can generate excess returns. As Osler shows in her piece "Support for resistance: technical analysis and intraday exchange rates",[3] empirical evidence demonstrates that technical analysis can help in exchange rate prediction over and above the results available by simply using a random walk theory. Simply put, there is something to this.

Looking at a slightly longer time frame, can a corporate Treasurer or an investor use technical analysis as part of their currency risk decision? The answer in this case is also, yes they can. While the primary focus of technical analysis is short term, it is fully capable of predicting multi-month of even multi-year moves. As an example, at the end of 1999, when the dollar–rand exchange rate was trading at around 6, the CitiFX Technicals team put out a buy signal, based on a combination of Elliott Wave Theory and the "golden cross" between the 55- and 200-day moving averages, *with a multi-year target of 9.*[4] The exchange rate hit 9.00 on September 27, 2001. Again, the sceptical may see this as coincidence. However the fact is that skilful application of technical analysis principles correctly forecasts a move in the exchange rate that no interpretation of the "fundamentals" would have provided. At the very least, technical

[3]Carol L. Osler, "Support for resistance: technical analysis and intraday exchange rates", *Economic Policy Review*, 6(2) (July 2000). For other studies of technical analysis, look at Helen Allen and Mark Taylor, "The use of technical analysis in the foreign exchange market", *Journal of International Money and Finance*, June 1992; Kevin Chang and Carol Osler, "Methodical madness: technical analysis and the irrationality of exchange rate forecasts", *Economic Journal*, October 1998; John Murphy, *Technical Analysis of the Futures Market*: *A Comprehensive Guide to Trading Methods*, Prentice Hall, 1986.
[4]Martin Armitage-Smith/Tom Fitzpatrick, *CitiFX Technicals Bulletin*.

analysis should be a consideration for all types of currency market practitioner. Short-term traders are likely to use it as their primary analytical tool ahead of fundamental analysis because it is better suited to predicting short-term exchange rate moves than the traditional fundamental exchange rate models. Corporations and asset managers can use it as a cross-check of their fundamental views and also in terms of timing their hedging activity. The fact that traders watch technical levels and that traders make up the majority of currency market participants automatically makes those levels important.

What we have attempted in this chapter is to look at the basic principles and schools of thought within technical analysis, along with how and why it works. Having looked at pricing patterns, it is also important to look at the structural dynamics that determine that price. That is to say, one can look at a chart of an exchange rate, but it is also important to know how that price has been created and under what circumstances. Indeed, the type of exchange rate regime can render virtually worthless for periods of time most types of analysis, distorting both the fundamental and the technical signals that might otherwise be read. Thus, in the next chapter we take a look at the types of exchange rate regime and how each type might impact the exchange rate itself.

Part Two
Regimes and Crises

5
Exchange Rate Regimes:
Fixed or Floating?

To most modern-day readers, at least those within the developed markets, the exchange rate norm is and has always been freely floating. All sectors of society have become used to volatile exchange rates and have learned to plan accordingly. Individuals plan vacations when the currencies of their planned vacation destination are perceived as cheap. Businesses seek to hedge their transactional or translational risk according to a combination of their business needs and market conditions. Politicians have a mixed record with floating exchange rates, frequently viewing exchange rate strength as a sign of national economic virility — and exchange rate weakness consequently as a test of their own administration. Yet, it is not that long ago that such a test would have been inconceivable. Freely floating exchange rates are themselves a relatively recent phenomenon. Indeed, the period since 1973 and the break-up of the Bretton Woods exchange rate system has been the first sustained time in history in which the world's major currencies have not been pegged to some form or other of commodity. Such a world of freely floating exchange rates, massive private capital flows financing current account deficits and markets dictating government monetary and fiscal policies was completely inconceivable in 1944 when Bretton Woods was created. To recap, under this, member countries pledged to maintain their currencies within narrow bands against the US dollar, while the dollar itself was pegged to gold (at USD35 per ounce). Some degree of flexibility was allowed, but there was never any suggestion — or conception — that governments were not in charge. For 27 years, the Bretton Woods system held in place, helping to provide a foundation for economic growth in the 1950s and 1960s.

Then, as the value of the US dollar peg to gold came under ever increasing pressure, the US eventually scrapped its gold peg, trying in the process to create a slightly more flexible exchange rate system under the Smithsonian Agreement. In 1973, the effort to defend this too was exhausted and collapsed under the weight of its own contradictions. Thus, since 1973, we have had for the first time an international monetary system which has for the most part been characterized by freely floating exchange rates among the major industrial countries, free of official intervention or commodity-related pegs, with "the market" taking an increasingly important role, both relative to before 1973 and also to official government policy. Granted, since then, there have been several attempts, such as the Exchange Rate Mechanism (ERM), to shackle exchange rates within narrow bands. For the most part, such attempts to re-assert government control over the market have given way to some degree of accommodation between the two sides, with freely floating exchange rates allowed but official intervention seen as appropriate at times of extreme volatility or where prices have "overshot" economic fundamentals. This accommodation has resulted in specific victories of a sort for both sides. The ERM itself, having barely survived the 1992 crisis, was forced under extraordinary pressure in 1993 to widen its bands to ±15% from ±2.25%. However, since then, member countries have relinquished their national currencies in favour of the Euro, thus eliminating the question of fixed or floating at the national level. The Euro itself is still however a freely floating currency, as its volatile movements have born testimony.

Still, for the most part, the question of having a fixed or floating exchange rate regime has increasingly become a redundancy for the world's industrial countries, particularly as barriers to trade and capital have been broken down. The US dollar, Euro, yen, sterling and others all float against each other, for the most part without official interference. While there are still occasional bouts of intervention by the central bank, these are nowadays a relative rarity. What has become far more common is that central banks will attempt to guide the market through "verbal intervention". The extent of the accommodation arrived at by the market and the official community is such that this for the most part works well enough, though to be sure there are times when it is not enough and substantial foreign exchange intervention in the market has to be undertaken. For currency market practitioners in the industrial countries however, such as corporations or institutional investors, the question of the type of exchange rate regime is largely (though perhaps not completely) no longer relevant. National currencies may bind together to become regional currencies, but the bottom line is that they are still freely floating and not artificially pegged.

5.1   AN EMERGING WORLD

This is not the case in the "emerging markets" or "developing countries". While there has undoubtedly been a gradual trend towards freely floating exchange rates within the emerging markets, whether willingly or otherwise, many still have some form of peg arrangement, depending to some degree upon their state of development. Thus the question of the type of exchange rate system — fixed or floating — remains particularly pertinent for currency market practitioners who are involved in the emerging markets. In order to suggest how currency market practitioners might deal with exchange rate system issues, it might be useful to explain first why these exchange rate systems came about in the wake of the developments of 1973 and how each type works.

When — or if — one thinks about the 1970s, it is usually from a political perspective, as a time of war and revolt against war, as a time of political and social revolution. Nowadays, many of the protestors of that time are in business. Politically, much has changed. The economic world has also changed massively, to some extent in line with some of these political shifts. The decline of the Soviet Union coincided with the decline of the socialist attempt at economics. People who were finally able to turn on their television in the Warsaw Pact countries and tune them to Western stations found they had been lied to for a generation. The triumph of capitalism was confirmed. From that time, when West and East no longer glared down the barrel of a gun at each other (or more aptly the nose cone of an ICBM), such terms as "market economy" and "globalization" have developed. Just as we now take for granted floating exchange rates, so we also take for granted free trade and capital mobility, yet many of these were the direct result of the end of the Cold War.

With the decline of the Soviet Union and the end of the Cold War, emerging market countries have been able to move away from being mere chess pieces in a bi-polar world. Crucially, the breaking down of barriers to trade and capital, which began in the late 1980s and accelerated in the 1990s, has allowed them to participate to an increasing degree in the global economy. As the role of the emerging markets has increased within the global economy, and perhaps more specifically within global financial markets, so the pressure has grown on them over time to adopt more flexible exchange rate systems to be able to absorb the periodic shocks that free trade and free capital markets entail.

5.2   A BRIEF HISTORY OF EMERGING MARKET EXCHANGE RATES

The history of emerging market currencies and exchange rate systems can most usefully be divided into four main periods — 1973–1981, 1982–1990, 1991–1994 and 1995–2001.

1973–1981

For the most part, this period saw relative exchange rate stability, not least because most emerging market currencies were not freely convertible either on the current or capital accounts. There was a steady if modest capital outflow from the industrial countries to the emerging markets, which were mostly at that time dependent on commodities rather than the manufacturing bases they would become.

1982–1990

If the previous period was characterized by stability, that of 1982–1990 was one of anarchy followed by a gradual attempt at restructuring. Massive tightening of monetary policy in the US and a consequent dramatic rise in the US dollar, plunging commodity prices and a reversal in capital flows out of the emerging markets combined to trigger first emerging market currency devaluations and then defaults, most notably in Mexico and also elsewhere in Latin America. Given ensuing capital flight, many emerging market countries sought to impose capital controls, driving interest rates artificially low in response. The gradual debt restructuring process during 1985–1990 helped restore some stability to emerging markets, helped in part by lower interest rates in the US and a sharp fall in the value of the US dollar. The currency devaluations and then low nominal interest rates — and negative real rates — as capital controls were imposed, resulting in very poor returns for passive currency investors.

1991–1994

This was the heyday for the emerging markets. As the Berlin Wall was torn down, so the East was opened up to investment. Latin America had a slightly better time of it as economies gradually recovered in the wake of the Brady bond restructuring programme. Capital controls were lifted, largely as demanded by the IMF, and domestic interest rates, which had been kept artificially low, were set free to the whim of market forces. "Privatization" of state assets was greatly accelerated, supporting budget balances and helping to attract capital inflows. Rising interest and exchange rates greatly boosted total returns for currency investors during this period. In light of this, the Mexican peso devaluation of December 1994 came as rather a rude awakening.

1995–

This last period has been characterized above all by volatility, on the one hand by huge capital inflows and on the other hand by frequent currency devaluations. One by one, pegged exchange rate regimes tried to defend themselves, tried to delay the inevitable. However, capital mobility, coupled with pegged exchange rate regimes and in some cases a degree of monetary independence were a poor policy mix, forgetting the principles of Mundell–Fleming, and one by one they were forced off their pegs, to "float" (devalue) their currencies. Among those emerging market currencies forced to devalue during this time were:

- 1994/95 — Mexico
- 1996 — Czech Republic
- 1997/98 — Asian region (Thailand, Indonesia, Korea, Philippines)
- 1998 — Russia
- 1999 — Brazil
- 1999 — Ecuador
- 2000 — Colombia
- 2001 — Turkey

The year 2002 has brought with it so far the devaluation of the Argentine peso, the first "currency board" in history to be defeated, and also that of the Venezuelan bolivar. There have also been cases where emerging market countries have either had some success in fighting back or alternatively have de-pegged voluntarily during periods of exchange rate stability, rightly anticipating that a freely-floating exchange rate would provide a far more effective buffer for the economy during subsequent periods of market turbulence than the alternative, which would require defending an overvalued exchange rate. In the first camp, we have had countries such as Malaysia and also Hong Kong, which have tried various strategies to fight the market. Malaysia, for its part, in September 1998 banned offshore trading of the Malaysian ringgit and pegged it to the US dollar at 3.8 — where it has stayed ever since. Hong Kong, long the self-proclaimed bastion of the free market, intervened in the stock market, ostensibly to rid it of "manipulative, speculative elements". In the second camp, countries like Chile, Poland and Hungary have de-pegged their exchange rates voluntarily, under calm and stable market conditions. As a result, when market conditions became more volatile, the freely floating exchange rate was able to buffer or insulate the real economy from damaging imbalances or instability.

As the emerging markets became integrated into the global economy and particularly within the global financial system rather than just commercial trade, so the pressure became irresistible for them to move from a fixed or pegged exchange rate system to more flexible exchange rate arrangements, such as the free float — the reed that bends in the wind, rather than the pane of glass that shatters. Two major trends in terms of the liberalization of capital markets have played a major part in the development and history of exchange rate systems within the emerging markets — the rise of capital flows and the opening of the emerging markets to international trade.

5.2.1   The Rise of Capital Flows

A key reason for the move by emerging markets from pegged exchange rates to floating exchange rates has been the rise in the importance of global capital flows and the extent to which emerging markets have participated in and been integrated within those capital flows. As stated, the rise in the importance of capital flows since the early 1980s reflects the wave of capital account liberalization and capital market integration that has taken place since that time. As a proportion of GDP, capital inflows to the emerging markets rose six-fold in the 1990s relative to the 1970s and 1980s, only to fall back in 1998 in the wake of the Asian and

Russian crises. A similar trend has been seen in bank lending, which also fell back in the wake of these crises. The vulnerability of emerging markets to capital outflow and reversal has been a key focus for the emerging markets, and is likely to remain the case for some time to come. A key differentiation between the emerging markets and the industrial countries is the depth of their asset markets and their ability to absorb capital inflows and outflows without significant policy and economic distortion.

5.2.2   Openness to Trade

The degree of openness to commercial trade of goods and services is also an important consideration with regard to the exchange rate system, both how it has developed and where it is going. As with capital flows, emerging market participation in global trade has risen exponentially in the last two decades. The average share of external trade (measured by exports plus imports, divided by two) in GDP for emerging market countries rose from about 30% in the late 1960s to 40% in the late 1990s. Within this, the trend towards opening up to trade has been particularly marked in Asia. As trade makes up an increasingly large share of emerging market GDP, so changes in the exchange rate and in output and prices are increasingly interrelated. At the same time, the type of trade has changed significantly, moving away from a dependence on commodities towards manufacturing. This change appears to have helped stabilize the terms of trade of emerging market economies, as manufacturing prices change considerably more slowly than do commodities. However, it has also made the economy as a whole more sensitive to exchange rate fluctuations. Commodities are priced in US dollars and fluctuate for the most part independently of fluctuations in exchange rates. Conversely, supply and demand of manufactured trade is very sensitive to exchange rate fluctuations.

5.3   FIXED AND PEGGED EXCHANGE RATE REGIMES

These four periods have been characterized by a general — although not universal — move from fixed exchange rate systems to convertible pegs and finally to freely floating exchange rates. In the mid-1970s, almost 90% of emerging market countries had some form of fixed/pegged exchange rate. As of the end of 2001, this had fallen to 30%. It should be noted of course that this is still a high number and thus it remains important to examine the dynamics of fixed and pegged exchange rate systems, why they came about and their relevance in the modern world.

Fixed or pegged exchange rate systems made sense for emerging markets during the 1970s and 1980s. For the most part, their involvement in the global economy was still relatively limited, for both political and economic reasons. Their financial systems were still for the most part in their infancy and certainly not able to cope, at least early on, with the harsh disciplines imposed by global financial markets. A credible anchor was needed for monetary policy and it was found in the form of the US dollar. The pegged exchange rate value between the US dollar and the emerging market currency became the anchor of monetary credibility. Sometimes these were hard pegs to the US dollar, sometimes they were "crawling pegs", meaning that the peg value changed to reflect a gradual depreciation of the emerging market currency in line with its higher inflation rate. Others were pegged not to a single currency, but instead to a basket of currencies. In all cases, however, the exchange rate peg was the anchor of monetary credibility. What does this mean? A pegged exchange rate system implies a commitment by the financial authorities of a country to limit exchange rate fluctuation within the limits of the peg. At the macroeconomic level, the aim of this is to provide both stability and credibility. At the microeconomic level, it is to provide an implicit guarantee to the private sector of exchange rate stability.

5.3.1   The Currency Board

Aside from the complete adoption of another and more credible currency, such as the US dollar, the hardest form of currency peg is the currency board. Here, the central bank relinquishes theoretically all discretion over monetary policy. Capital inflows lead automatically to a proportional reduction in money supply by the "monetary authority", which replaces the job of the central bank, and vice versa. The monetary authority pledges to exchange the domestic currency for the peg currency, usually the US dollar, at the peg rate in any size. Needless to say, this means it has to have the foreign exchange reserves in order to be able to do so. This in turn has real impact on the economy. For a start, there has to be a strong degree of domestic price flexibility in order to ensure that domestic prices are able to adjust to changes in the economy since the external price — the exchange rate — cannot adjust because of its peg/currency board constraint.

Currency boards are no panacea. They imply and impose a very harsh policy discipline. A country has to be willing — and be seen to be willing — whatever economic pain is required in order to maintain the currency board. On the positive side, they should provide transparency and monetary credibility in addition to stability, which in turn should provide a medium-term foundation for growth, albeit at a cost. As the example of Argentina suggests, currency boards do not imply a guarantee of stability. They have tended however to be considerably more resistant to speculative attack than has been the case with the crawling peg, in large part because they have provided a greater degree of monetary credibility. Note that a currency board requires that the monetary authority's foreign exchange reserves more than cover the monetary base. They do not and are not able to cover the broad money definition, which means that they remain vulnerable in theory, particularly if locals abandon their own currency.

5.3.2   Fear and Floating

Many emerging market countries have chosen to float their currencies only as a last resort and only when they have been forced so to do. Even those who have eventually floated have still sought to manage or interfere in otherwise floating currency markets in some way. From this, we have the idea of "fear of floating", which Calvo and Reinhart set out in a major research paper.[1] While it is understandable that emerging economies fear — or at least are nervous about — the risks of allowing the market free rein, in my view this is like democracy — the worst option apart from all the rest. Government intervention in the economy inevitably creates economic distortions, which can have significant costs. Similarly, if intervention is anything other than occasional in order to smooth price action and correct market overshooting, it can create pricing distortions, which in any case will eventually be reversed.

This notwithstanding, the move from pegged to floating exchange rate regimes has frequently been done with considerable reluctance within the emerging markets, that is to say in many instances it has been forced by the market. Countries such as Mexico, much of Asia, the Czech Republic, Brazil and Turkey did not adopt floating exchange rates willingly. These were forced on them as a result of the breaking of currency pegs and maxi-devaluations that in many cases

---

[1] Guillermo A. Calvo and Carmen Reinhart, *Fear of Floating*, NBER Working Paper 7993, National Bureau of Economic Research, September 25, 2000.

resulted in catastrophic economic contractions. It should be no surprise therefore that the relationship between the emerging markets and the idea of freely floating exchange rates is an uneasy one. However, barring a major reversal in terms of trade or capital market deregulation and liberalization, there is no going back on this trend towards freely floating exchange rates. The question now is no longer whether emerging markets will choose freely floating exchange rates as one type of exchange rate regime, but when and how they will move to that.

5.3.3   The Monetary Anchor of Credibility

The discipline of floating exchange rates is quite different to that of a pegged exchange rate system. No longer is the exchange rate itself the anchor of monetary credibility. Instead, the conventional wisdom has moved towards inflation targeting through interest rate policy as the anchor of monetary credibility. As a result, the emphasis has shifted importantly away from the exchange rate regime and in favour of central banks in seeking to maintain both internal and external price stability. This move from the certainty of an exchange rate as the monetary anchor of credibility to the uncertainty of a central bank's monetary discipline is very much a leap of faith, and it can take a considerable period of time for a central bank to gain the respect needed of the global financial markets to pursue that discipline with the minimum of market instability. This is as true for the developed economies as it is for the emerging markets. For instance, it took the German central bank, the Bundesbank, over 30 years to achieve the revered status it had during the 1990s when German bond yields finally fell below those of the US for a sustained period of time. Further, a central bank's monetary credibility is hard won but easily lost.

In the emerging markets also, as with the broader trend, there has been a general move away from targeting the exchange rate towards targeting inflation. This is of course particularly evident within the EU accession candidates such as the Czech Republic, Poland and Hungary, which in any case have to adopt some form of inflation targeting to ensure that their inflation rates do not exceed EU/Euro entry rules. However, inflation targeting is also now present in Latin America and Asia.

The presumed premise behind this is that as the emerging markets continue to participate to an increasing degree in the global economy and in the global financial markets, so they will be increasingly judged by the most efficient economy of that global economy, the United States, and have to adopt its economic policies, such as inflation targeting. This is richly ironic since in fact the US has no formal inflation target. Indeed, it is not too much to suggest that the official community in Washington, led by the IMF, is in many cases demanding economic policies (as quid pro quos for new loans) that would simply not be acceptable in the industrial countries. Granted, this picture is not entirely negative. Inflation targeting frameworks are usually characterized also by a greater degree of policy transparency and accountability. Inflation targeting also allows some degree of discretion in the setting of the inflation target, but thereafter little latitude in missing it. Broadly put, financial markets "reward" administrations — through lower bond yields — that meet their inflation targets and punish those that do not. Any student of international economics knows the classical argument by Milton Friedman for price flexibility: if there is a change in economic conditions, the fastest and most efficient way of expressing this necessary adjustment is through the external price — the exchange rate — rather than through a large number of domestic prices. The analogy that Friedman used in 1953 to explain this was daylight saving time; that is, it is easier to move to daylight saving time than to coordinate a large number of people and move all activities one hour.

The basic argument in favour of flexible exchange rates is that it makes it easier for an economy to adjust to external shocks, such as a dramatic change in commodity prices which in turn triggers a change in the trade balance. A flexible exchange rate also allows the central bank to devote its energies to seeking to maintain domestic monetary stability rather than focusing on the external price. Of course, this is the theory. In practice, many central banks still try to focus on the exchange rate and not just to the extent that it affects domestic inflation. In principle, however, the central bank's focus on internal price stability frees it from the *obligation* of targeting the exchange rate.

Freely floating exchange rates also have a downside, most notably in that they can be volatile and also on occasion can significantly overshoot anything approximating fundamental value. This in turn can hurt the real economy. To return to Churchill's description of democracy, freely floating exchange rates are far from perfect, but they have so far proved better and more resilient than anything else on offer. That said, although a freely floating exchange rate system is probably the best and most flexible system on offer over the long term, there are specific economic factors that can determine which type of exchange rate system may be appropriate in the short to medium term:

- **Size/openness of the economy** — If an economy is very open to external trade, the economic costs of currency instability are likely to be a lot higher than if this is not the case. For instance, in the wake of the Asian crisis, the structural damage to the likes of India was far less than to Korea or Thailand, not least because trade is a far smaller proportion of the Indian economy. In turn, this may suggest that it may be appropriate over the short to medium term for small open economies, such as Hong Kong or Singapore, to have either fixed or managed exchange rate regimes.
- **Inflation** — If a country has a higher inflation rate than its trading partners, its exchange rate needs to be flexible (i.e. floating) in order to maintain trade competitiveness. Indeed, the law of PPP requires that its exchange rate depreciates to offset this higher inflation rate.
- **Labour market flexibility** — The more rigid the wage structure within the economy, the greater the need for exchange rate flexibility to act as a buffer against real economic shocks.
- **Capital mobility** — The general rule is that the more open an economy is to capital flow, the harder it is to sustain a fixed exchange rate system. The only exception to this is if a country adopts a currency board and relinquishes monetary independence.
- **Monetary credibility** — The stronger the credibility of a central bank, the less the need to peg or fix the exchange rate, and vice versa. The relationship between the monetary credibility of a central bank and the trust of the financial markets is very much a confidence game. As we saw earlier, it usually takes a considerable period of time for central banks to build that relationship and that trust with financial markets.
- **Financial development** — The degree of financial development, particularly with regard to the domestic financial system, may be a consideration when choosing a type of exchange rate regime. For instance, immature financial systems may not be able to withstand the volatility inherent in freely floating exchange rates.

5.4   EXCHANGE RATE REGIME SUSTAINABILITY — A BI-POLAR WORLD?

Within the emerging markets, there has been a gradual realization, particularly as barriers to trade and capital have come down, that fixed or pegged exchange rate regimes may no longer be appropriate in an economic world dominated by high capital mobility. Furthermore, there has been an equal realization that exchange rate pegs of one type or another inevitably increase "moral hazard", in that they are seen as an official guarantee of exchange rate stability and therefore serve to encourage the taking on of unnecessary and dangerous exchange rate risk. Pegging to an international currency such as the US dollar can provide substantial monetary credibility on the one hand, but on the other the fact that US dollar interest rates are likely to be substantially lower than those in the domestic market can encourage domestic corporations and finance companies to borrow in the pegged currency without hedging out the currency risk embedded in those liabilities. The Asian crisis was greatly exacerbated by the fact that Thai, Korean and Indonesian corporations borrowed heavily in US dollars, swapped back to domestic currency and lent that out at much higher rates or used it for investment purposes. Yet, the US dollar liability remained unhedged from a currency perspective. Consequently, when domestic currencies such as the Thai baht, Indonesian rupiah and Korean won devalued, the cost of paying those US dollar loans was multiplied proportionally in terms of the domestic currency. In practice, many corporations were bankrupted as a direct result, while others defaulted in such debts.

Gradually, emerging market countries have abandoned pegged exchange rates in favour of freely floating exchange rates, either willingly or otherwise, with this process being greatly accelerated in the wake of the emerging market crises of 1994–1999. With this process has come the realization that "soft" or "crawling" currency pegs are no longer sustainable in a world of high capital mobility. Either exchange rates should float freely or they should be constrained by the hardest of currency pegs. The middle ground of "intermediate" exchange rate regimes is no longer seen as tenable. This view of a *"bi-polar" world of exchange rates* was put most clearly and eloquently by the former IMF First Deputy Managing Director Stanley Fischer, reflecting a general move in favour of this view by the Washington official community. In several research pieces and speeches, Fischer noted that the currency pegs have been involved in just about every emerging market crisis during the 1990s, from Mexico in 1994 through to Turkey in 2001. Whether coincidence or not, emerging market countries that have not had pegged exchange rates have generally been able to avoid experiencing currency crises. Of the 33 leading countries classified as emerging market economies, the proportion with intermediate exchange rate regimes fell from 64% at the start of the 1990s to 42% at the end. By 1999, 16 of these countries had freely floating exchange rates, while three had hard currency pegs in the form of a currency board or dollarization. The remainder still had intermediate exchange rate regimes. Since then, the hollowing out of intermediate exchange rate regimes has continued, with Greece moving out of both emerging market status and a horizontal currency band into the Euro, while Turkey was forced off its crawling peg, floating its currency in the process.

This hollowing out process of intermediate exchange rate regimes has also happened with the so-called developed economies, a process dominated by the drive towards EMU and the creation of the Euro. The ERM crises of 1992 and 1993 were initially thought to have endangered if not ended the dream of EMU. Conversely, it appears they actually served to accelerate the momentum away from such an intermediate exchange rate regime to the hardest of pegs, the single currency. By the end of 1999, all but one developed economy had either hard pegs or freely floating exchange rates, with that one exception being Denmark.

As countries move from targeting the exchange rate, through intermediate exchange rate regimes, towards freely floating exchange rates, the monetary emphasis shifts towards targeting inflation as the monetary anchor of credibility. Whether a country chooses a hard currency peg or allows its currency to float freely may depend at least in part on its inflationary history. In theory, a hard currency peg makes sense for countries with long histories of high inflation and monetary instability. The peg imposes a harsh policy discipline, but it also acts as a straight jacket on inflationary pressure. Even if a currency has a hard peg regime, it is also important to have an exit strategy in case of a major change (deterioration) in economic conditions which requires a similar change in the exchange rate regime. A hard currency peg should not be seen as permanent. If a country chooses to de-peg, this is best done when the currency is under pressure to appreciate.

While this idea of a "bi-polar" world of exchange rates appeared to provide an answer to the vexing question of how countries could cope with increasingly mobile capital flow, the example of Argentina would appear to challenge this view. Not only was it the first currency board in history to be "defeated", but this example appears to prove that even the hardest pegs could be forced to de-peg. Certainly, the idea that a currency board cannot be defeated, once prevalent in the financial markets, has now gone. Going forward, it seems likely therefore that markets will charge a higher risk premium on currency board regimes than was previously the case as a result of this precedent. Not only is a hard currency peg no panacea, it can also be defeated. Countries are therefore left with the question of the most appropriate exchange rate regime in the face of a global market economy consisting of high capital mobility and instant information availability. For both developed and emerging market economies the choices left are:

- Freely floating exchange rates
- Adopt a base currency (US dollar or Euro)
- Adopt a regional currency

While some such as John Williamson of the Institute for International Economics have long argued that intermediate exchange rates are unjustly neglected and "corner solutions" are not immune to crisis—as the case of Argentina indeed proves—it remains to be seen whether financial markets will tolerate anything other than freely floating exchange rates or alternatively adopting a base or regional currency.

5.5   THE REAL WORLD RELEVANCE OF THE EXCHANGE RATE REGIME

Up to now, this chapter has largely focused on exchange rate regime theory. This section deals with how the choice of exchange rate regime actually affects currency market practitioners in practice. As the exchange rate regimes of both developed and emerging markets are still evolving, it is difficult to find definitive answers. That said, based on what we have already looked at we can draw some useful conclusions. For a start, "fixed" currency pegs are not necessarily fixed forever—if you get caught long a currency that has just devalued it can kill your balance sheet or portfolio. For instance, on February 19, 1982, the Mexican peso lost some 29% of its value. Some 15 years later, on July 2, 1997, the Thai baht lost 10% of its value in a single day. How do we avoid the kind of portfolio or balance sheet losses such disastrous events imply? Currency market practitioners within fixed or pegged exchange rate regimes need to consider the following points:

- **Does the currency peg contribute to economic stability or instability?** Currency pegs can provide monetary credibility by using the exchange rate to force inflation lower, but they can also attract substantial and potentially destabilizing capital flows.

- **To what extent is a country open to global capital flows?** If a country allows high capital mobility, a currency peg may not be appropriate unless it abandons monetary independence and adopts the hardest of pegs, such as a currency board. Capital flows are less easily anticipated than trade flows, but much more quickly reversed.
- **Is the currency pegged at the correct level?** This has been an important question not just for emerging but also for developed economies, notably with the ERM. Currency market practitioners should use the lessons learned in Chapters 1 and 2 to judge whether the currency peg level is appropriate. Corporations with subsidiaries in the countries concerned are well placed to do this given local pricing and demand knowledge.
- **Are there clear patterns of distress ahead of a peg's collapse?** Currency market practitioners can use the CEMC model (see Chapter 6) as a test of market conditions.
- **What do you do if a currency peg collapse appears imminent?** The trick of course is to try to anticipate this before the rest of the financial market does. Remember the lessons of the Asian crisis, where the preceding depreciations of the yen and yuan helped make Asian currencies uncompetitive. Remember also that PPP and REER may not be useful over the short term, but they are useful over a long-term horizon in suggesting currency over- or undervaluation. Also, don't ignore common sense! Did it make sense in 1998 for Russia, a country which was going cap in hand to the IMF for more money, to have some of the most expensive residential property in the world in Moscow? Every boom is characterized by incidents and anecdotes, which after the bubble bursts seem acts not of folly but of sheer lunacy. Look for signs of these.
- **Currency risk may not be the only consideration.** Within the emerging markets in particular, there may be other important considerations as well, such as convertibility and liquidity risk. Is a currency convertible on the capital account? Also, emerging market currencies are by nature much less liquid than those of developed economies. While USD200–300 billion may go through the Euro–dollar exchange rate every day (spot, forward, swaps and options), only USD10 billion goes through the South African rand, the second most liquid emerging market currency in the world behind the Singapore dollar. Finally, there is also political risk, which is a more important consideration in emerging markets.
- **Hedge when the market doesn't want to (and neither do you!).** When market conditions are benign is clearly when liquidity is best and pricing potentially most favourable. This is also the best time to hedge currency risk, particularly if one is potentially concerned about the sustainability of the currency regime. However, precisely because market conditions are benign this is not the time when markets are looking to hedge currency risk. The temptation to stay with the pack (or rather the flock!) should be strenuously avoided. If valuation considerations suggest a currency peg may be overvalued, hedging should be seriously considered. It is a question of cost vs. risk rather than risk vs. reward. For the cost of an option of around 1–2%, you hedge yourself against the potential risk of a devaluation of around 30–40%. Granted, options are not available in some markets, but in all markets there are benign and also malign market conditions and seasoned currency market practitioners should be able to tell the difference and take the opportunity when it is at hand.
- **When the market wants to hedge currency risk it is too late!** There is no use complaining about adverse pricing and liquidity developments when the market is scrambling to hedge currency risk. By that time, forwards have screamed higher and option risk reversals have blown out. Take the opportunity of favourable pricing and market conditions when it presents itself, based on valuation considerations.

Most of the ideas presented in the bullet points above focus largely on pegged or fixed exchange rate regimes. A different set of considerations may be required when looking at freely floating exchange rates:

- **Freely floating exchange rates imply high capital mobility.** The two tend to go together. The combination should mean in theory that capital flow reversals are transmitted through the exchange rate more efficiently and with less volatility.
- **Freely floating exchange rates can however still see major bouts of volatility.** While they tend to be rarer these days, particularly if there are no major economic imbalances involved, freely floating exchange rates can also see significant bouts of volatility. This is not just the case within the emerging but also within the developed markets. A case in point is the collapse in the dollar–yen exchange rate in the autumn of 1998 from around 135 to 114 in the space of 36 hours. Speculative trends always reverse and when they reverse they tend to do so violently.
- **As pegged exchange rates may be temporary, so freely floating rates are no panacea.** Freely floating exchange rates also exact costs and involve risks on the part of the currency market practitioner in seeking to manage currency risk.

5.6 SUMMARY

To sum up this chapter, we have looked at the various types of exchange rate regime, how they developed in the wake of the collapse of the Bretton Woods system, how they developed from fixed to pegged to floating, and in line with this looked at some of the major factors — such as capital and trade deregulation — that helped bring this transition about. The aim has been to acquaint currency market practitioners with the various issues involved with different exchange rate regimes and how they might deal with these in their business and investment decisions. In the wake of the emerging market crises of the 1990s, a conventional wisdom has developed suggesting only a "bi-polar" world of exchange rates, involving either freely floating exchange rates or the hardest of currency pegs, may be appropriate. If the history of economics or finance teaches us anything, it is that the conventional wisdom is frequently debunked. In this, exchange rates are no different. The Bretton Woods exchange rate system itself represented the conventional wisdom for almost 30 years, only to collapse under the weight of its own contradictions. Intermediate exchange rate regimes, in the form of soft or crawling pegs, were at one time the conventional wisdom only to be blown away by the irresistible force of capital flows. For centuries, the medium of exchange was not coloured paper but hard metal, in the form of either gold or silver. Who is to say this might not return? Granted, it seems extremely unlikely, but currency market practitioners should take nothing for granted. In this regard, the price not of democracy but of financial security is eternal vigilance. Equally, the price of a lack of vigilance is a balance sheet or a portfolio in tatters. The type of exchange rate regime is an extremely important consideration for currency market practitioners.

In this chapter, the focus has been on the type of regime rather than the extent of market conditions. The ultimate expression of market volatility however is the currency crisis, which as we have seen can occur frequently. To many these may seem chaotic and utterly unpredictable. This is however not necessarily the case. In the next chapter, we seek to build models to predict the exchange rate equivalent of the storm or the hurricane, the currency crisis.

6
Model Analysis:
Can Currency Crises be Predicted?

The type of exchange rate regime is important for normal market trading conditions, but it is especially important for abnormal periods of market stress that may lead ultimately to a "currency crisis". In this chapter, we look specifically at the phenomenon of currency crises and whether or not they can be predicted.

In the wake of the emerging market crises in Mexico (1994–1995), Asia (1997–1998), Russia (1998), Brazil (1999) and Turkey (2001), considerable effort has been made by the academic and financial communities to create models that might be able to predict such crises in the future. As with long-term valuation models aimed at finding a currency's "equilibrium" level, most of these are based on highly complex mathematical formulae and make certain key assumptions about human behaviour and psychology. Equally, like the equilibrium models, the results of these have been mixed at best to date. No-one has as yet come up with the definitive model capable of predicting currency crises ahead of time on a consistent basis. The best that has been achieved is some degree of success, albeit claimed after the fact.

For my part, I make no claim either as to a definitive breakthrough. What I would lay claim to however is having approached the issue of currency crisis from a different angle. Most of the existing models focus largely on the rationality of human behaviour. In a financial context, this implies rational investors investing where the best returns are to be found. If those returns diminish or if better returns are available elsewhere, it is assumed that they will leave. Such a rationally-dominated view does not allow for herd behaviour, that buying may continue long past the point at which *yield* returns have diminished significantly. There is an emotional hang-up, both within economic theory and within the official community, which labels buyers as investors and sellers as speculators. Yet, buyers can also be speculating. Indeed, some of the best examples of speculative excess gone mad have come from buying rather than selling, notably the internet bubble. Markets are ruled by such fundamental sentiments as greed and fear, and it is safe to say that in 1999–2000 greed was running rampant. Easy money was to be had — as it always is during such periods of market hysteria. The financial bubble got bigger and bigger and then burst spectacularly in mid-2000. We are still feeling the after-effects of the bursting of the economic bubble, that tidal wave of increasingly unprofitable investment. This is just one example of the "speculative" excess with which human history is littered.

In trying to create a model to predict currency crises, my aim has not been to fit economic theory around the facts, but rather to start the other way around, examining patterns within those facts and then aligning the theory to fit. The effort has been that of a forensic detective, rather than a psychic. Thus, the rather simple — though hopefully not simplistic — model that I created in 1998[1] is based not on complex mathematical formulae, but instead on the sum of those patterns that have been seen in the emerging market currency crises of the past 10 years. For want of a more pithy title, I called it the Classic Emerging Market Currency Crisis (CEMC)

---

[1] Callum Henderson, The Classic Emerging Market Currency Crisis model, 1998, as in *Asian Dawn: Recovery, Reform and Investing in the New Asia*, McGraw-Hill, 2000.

model, a title that is long-winded but hopefully captures the repetitious nature of currency crisis patterns. Our detective did find if not a smoking gun, then at least enough forensic evidence to discover the "how" and the "why".

The model focuses on emerging markets and more specifically the Asian currency crisis in large part because I witnessed the latter at first hand, having lived and been involved in the financial markets in Hong Kong during the second part of the 1990s. Because the model's initial aim was to discover patterns that specifically reflected the Asian crisis, *it was de facto a model that focused on fixed or pegged exchange rate regimes* and how those broke down. This is not to say it is only reflective of the Asian crisis. CEMC should be viewed as a template for emerging market currency pegged regimes generally. Indeed, it works remarkably well in explaining the key dynamics behind the currency crises in Mexico, Russia, Brazil and Turkey. The model is based on five key phases that appeared to take place during the Asian crisis, and were also mirrored in subsequent emerging market crises in Russia, Brazil and Turkey. Throughout, I use Thailand, seen as the catalyst for the Asian currency crisis, as an example of the general phenomenon at work. Outside of my work, I first expressed this model in published form in a previous book, *Asian Dawn — Recovery, Reform and Investing in the New Asia*. Here, I present the same CEMC model, albeit in a revised and expanded format.

6.1   A MODEL FOR PEGGED EXCHANGE RATES

6.1.1   Phase I: Capital Inflows and Real Exchange Rate Appreciation

Theory

The very purpose of having a local currency pegged to a base currency (usually the US dollar) is to provide a foundation for economic and financial stability. A currency peg reduces or even eliminates the issue of currency risk, and therefore attracts capital inflows. Those capital inflows become a self-fulfilling prophecy, since they help generate ever higher growth rates, which in turn attract further capital inflows. There are two monetary effects of these inflows. First, the local currency comes under mounting upward pressure. Second, interest rates paradoxically are forced lower. On the first of these, the currency is pegged so it cannot appreciate beyond a certain point. In order to maintain the peg, the central bank intervenes, selling its own currency for the base currency. In the money market, the central bank also conducts open market operations, sterilizing the effect of these inflows by withdrawing excess liquidity. Relative to the size of the inflows coming in, the ability of an emerging market central bank to conduct both of these monetary operations indefinitely is clearly limited. Meanwhile, precisely because interest rates are low and emerging market economies are not fully open, inflation rates are relatively high, higher that is than the inflation rate of the base currency. This should ordinarily mean that the local currency depreciates on a real basis in order to offset the higher inflation rate. The sheer weight of the capital inflows means this cannot happen. Indeed, the opposite happens. The local currency continues to appreciate on a real, inflation-adjusted basis. In turn, this causes widening external imbalances and loss of export competitiveness.

Practice

Asian countries pegged their currencies to the US dollar in order to provide a foundation for economic stability, while they got on with the job of growing their economies. In a sense these dollar pegs did their job too well. With Asian currencies pegged to the US dollar, it appeared that the idea of currency risk had been all but eliminated. Asia in the 1980s and early 1990s had been growing strongly in any case. Thus the Asian currency pegs together with strong domestic growth rates provided the platform for a veritable tidal wave of capital inflows to the region, both of the portfolio and foreign direct investment kind. The lack of currency volatility lulled investors into a false sense of security — though that false sense of security in some cases lasted for more than a decade.

Many Asian countries had relatively high inflation rates, higher than the US whose currency they were pegged to. Ordinarily, this should mean that a currency depreciates to offset its higher inflation rate, however in the case of Asia the sheer weight of massive capital inflows, combined with the currency pegs, meant that Asian currencies appreciated on a real (inflation-adjusted) basis, which was greatly exacerbated by the 35% devaluation of the Chinese yuan in 1994 and the depreciation of the Japanese yen from 1995. The result was widening Asian trade and current account deficits. Put simply, Asian countries were slowly but surely losing export competitiveness. High inflation and currency pegs meant high interest rates, despite the fact that most Asian countries ran healthy fiscal surpluses. This was not a problem for Asian governments since most were not seeking to expand domestic borrowing, but it was a problem for the private sector. Those currency pegs provided the illusion of exchange rate stability, encouraging corporations to borrow offshore at lower interest rates and swap back to domestic currency. As a result, significant external debt burdens were built up. Unlike in Latin America in the 1980s, this was private not public debt and went largely unnoticed in the more transparent public accounts. Thus, Asian corporate and bank balance sheets became increasingly exposed to external, US dollar-priced debt. While Asian currencies could not move, this was not an issue. Implicitly however, it meant if Asian currencies were ever allowed to depreciate, the capital base of those same corporate and banking sectors would be severely depleted if not eliminated. Asian currency devaluation would mean the cost of repaying that external debt would be multiplied by the extent of that devaluation.

By late 1996, real exchange rate appreciation had resulted in significant trade and current account balance deterioration. Thailand was running a current account deficit of some 8% of GDP. Assuming the balance of payments must indeed balance, the other side of a current account deficit must be a capital account surplus. This is indeed what happened in Asia. Massive capital inflows helped cause real currency appreciation, which in turn led to a rising current account deficit. To fund its widening current account deficit, Thailand had to attract an ever increasing amount of capital inflows. It did not get them. Instead, "fundamental" investors became increasingly wary and started if anything to reduce their exposure to Thailand in early 1997 due to a combination of increasing political and economic concerns and diminishing returns on their investments. As that capital fled — selling Thai baht in order to do so — so Thai domestic interest rates edged higher while the Thai baht itself came under increasing downward pressure.

6.1.2   Phase II: The Irresistible Force and the Moveable Object

Theory

As the capital account surplus is reduced while the current account deficit remains high, the pressure through the balance of payments is expressed through rising local interest rates and increasing downward pressure on the local currency. In order to maintain the peg, the central bank again intervenes, this time buying local currency (when capital was flowing in, it was forced to sell its own currency) and selling the base currency. In order to do so, it has to sell its foreign exchange reserves, which are denominated in that base currency. As local currency is bought from the market so supply is reduced and the interest rates attached to that local currency forced higher. The central bank has the unpalatable choice of sterilizing this effect by injecting liquidity back into the money market and thus effectively nullifying the effect of its foreign exchange intervention or allowing interest rates to rise and hurting the economy and asset markets in turn. As interest rates rise, so asset markets fall, forcing those investors who have stayed to cut their losses — and their positions — thus putting yet more pressure and so on and so forth. A vicious cycle develops, the length of which is decided only by the ability or the willingness of the central bank to expend its foreign exchange reserves. Eventually, one of two things happen, either the central bank runs out of reserves or the economic and financial cost of maintaining the currency peg becomes too great and the central bank scraps the peg and allows the currency to "float" (i.e. free-fall).

Practice

As Thailand's capital account came under increasing pressure so did the Thai baht as increasing numbers of foreign asset managers tried to get out while they could. Financial market volatility began to rise alarmingly. From the local perspective, Thai corporations and banks had up until then largely dismissed the idea of currency risk on the view the currency peg eliminated the need to hedge. Some not only borrowed in US dollars via the Bangkok International Banking Facility (BIBF) to reduce the corporation's interest rate bill but also to make what seemed a risk-free profit, borrowing those dollars, swapping back into Thai baht and then lending those baht onshore, making a very nice interest rate spread. The market volatility seen in the first quarter of 1997 made some of these Thai corporations re-think the issue of currency and interest rate risk (though clearly too few went through this re-thinking process given what transpired!). Perhaps currency risk should be a consideration after all. Thai corporations started to hedge, albeit selectively and cautiously, and certainly in small amounts compared to the size of their external debt exposure. Finally, some speculators arrived on the scene, attracted by the market volatility as a shark is attracted by the thrashing motion of a fish, and started to build up positions against several Asian currencies, including the Thai baht. Readers familiar with my work on the Asian crisis, *Asia Falling — Making Sense of the Asian Currency Crisis*, will be familiar with my view that if speculators can be accused of anything it is tardiness. Frankly, they were late on the scene. The situation had already deteriorated to the point of no return before they showed up. They were certainly not responsible for the subsequent currency devaluations. They may have added to the selling pressure, but they certainly did not cause it.

Whatever the case, the Bank of Thailand tried to respond vigorously to the rising selling pressure on the baht, intervening in the currency market and hiking official interest rates. Still the selling pressure increased, if anything it accelerated. In May 1997, the Bank of Thailand tried to ambush the market, stopping Thai banks from lending baht to the offshore market, hiking interest rates dramatically and intervening aggressively. The dollar collapsed against the baht and the Thai overnight borrowing rate skyrocketed to 3000%. It was a brave but ultimately unsuccessful attempt to defend the currency. Undoubtedly, many speculators were burned in the process, but so too were local market participants. Furthermore, it did nothing to stop the capital flight. The selling pressure on the Thai baht continued to intensify and the Bank of Thailand's foreign exchange reserves continued to fall. Eventually, it proved too much. If the Bank of Thailand did not scrap the peg and allow the currency to float freely it would simply run out of reserves with which to defend it within a matter of days. On July 2, 1997, the baht peg to the US dollar was scrapped and the currency allowed to float freely. It promptly collapsed in value, falling by some 10% on that day alone.

6.1.3   Phase III: The Liquidity Rally

Theory

A pegged currency that is allowed to float freely usually falls sharply for at least the first six months after the free float is put in place, overshooting any idea of fair value. The rule is the longer a central bank tries to defend it, the further the currency falls in the end. Currency market participants who earlier dismissed the idea of currency risk have to chase the market to put belated hedges in place. In addition, at the macroeconomic level inflation rises as the pass-through effect to the real economy of maxi-devaluation. The signal that the devaluation is at an end is when that inflation rate peaks. At that time, portfolio money starts to flow back into the country, attracted by high nominal interest rates. This in turn allows the local currency to recover potentially significant ground. In line with this, the trade account improves significantly as import demand collapses in the wake of economic contraction. Thus a liquidity-based rally in local asset markets and the local currency is created through lower interest rates and renewed portfolio inflows. This is different from Phase IV, which sees a fundamentally-based rally, as demand-side indicators continue to deteriorate during this period.

Practice

The collapse of the Thai baht extended well beyond levels seen on the first day of "flotation". Having been around THB25 to the US dollar before the "flotation" (devaluation), it subsequently fell to a low of 56.3 in the coming months, a decline in value of over 40%. In the case of the Indonesian rupiah, the fall was even more spectacular, plunging from IDR2,300 to the dollar to a low of 17,000, a devaluation of 85%! Asian countries generally tightened monetary policy in order to temper the threat of imported inflation from currency devaluations and in line with the IMF's initial call for tightening of both fiscal and monetary policy. Policy tightening in the face of maxi-devaluation of the currency tends to cause a slowdown in the economy to become a recession (if not a depression!), and in the cases of Thailand and Indonesia that is indeed what happened. In 1998, the Thai economy contracted 9.5%, while that of Indonesia contracted 13.2%. Whatever the merits of these policies, which were ostensibly aimed at providing long-term economic stability, there is no question that in the short term they severely exacerbated the regional economic slowdown. At street level, millions were forced into poverty. The World Bank estimated that half of Indonesia was living in a state of absolute poverty in 1998, defined as earning less than USD1 a day. Unemployment levels skyrocketed. Retail prices rose sharply to offset the free-falling currency in the likes of Indonesia, the Philippines and Thailand. Interest rates were tightened to offset this, compounding the misery.

In the wake of this, several leading commentators were heavily critical of the IMF policy response to the Asian crisis, saying the combination of tight fiscal and monetary policy represented a worse cure than the disease itself. While I have some sympathy with this view, particularly as public policy adjustment is not necessarily the appropriate policy response to private sector imbalance (too many Asian companies borrowing too much in dollars and speculating too much in their own stock and property markets), this still does not answer the question of how one stops a currency from free-falling. This is a key consideration bearing in mind that the collapse of the rupiah resulted in the bankruptcy of almost every company in Indonesia. Whether you favoured the argument of the IMF's Herbert Neiss or Harvard's Jeffrey Sachs, it is pretty irrelevant. By then, the damage was already done; the battle had already been lost. By then, it was a question only of damage limitation.

The example of the Brazilian crisis, however, suggests some refinements to the standard IMF policy response have been considered — not least at the IMF — in the wake of the Asian crisis. When the Brazilian real devalued in January 1999 and subsequently fell to a low of 2.2200 to the dollar from its 1.20 band level, many forecast 2.50 or even 3.00 and a similar type of recession to that Asia had experienced. In reality, neither of those two possibilities happened. Clearly, the appointment of Arminio Fraga as the new head of the Brazilian central bank was an important stabilizing measure, as Fraga was a widely respected figure in the financial markets. The maintenance of trade finance for Brazil was also a crucial difference.

Whatever the differences, the similarities between the crises in Asia and Brazil — and also with Mexico, Russia and Turkey — are clear. Most notably within this was the fact that once inflation peaked so too did local interest rates, allowing for a substantial rally in asset markets and the currencies themselves. In Indonesia, for example, this meant interest rates coming down from around 75–80% and the dollar–rupiah exchange rate falling back from around 17,000 to around 6500. Equally, in Thailand, the dollar–Thai baht exchange rate fell back from 56 to around 35. In the case of Brazil, the dollar–Brazilian real exchange rate fell back from 2.22 to 1.63. Fundamentally, during this period, the trade accounts in many Asian countries swung from significant deficits to massive trade and current account surpluses.

6.1.4   Phase IV: The Economy Hits Bottom

Theory

While Phase III remains ongoing, the economic patient is still showing no major sign of recovery. Inflation peaks, which in turn allows domestic interest rates to peak. The trade account swings hugely, in many cases from a deficit to a surplus as import demand collapses. This accelerates the recovery in liquidity, helping to force down interest rates and thus causing the liquidity-based rally which we talked about earlier. Eventually, the trade surplus, low interest rates and basing effects help support the economy. Put bluntly, the economy hits bottom and a period of stabilization ensues.

Readers should note that economic stabilization does not mean the same as recovery, in the same way that hitting the ground after a fall from some height does not entail recovery (indeed, if the height is sufficient there is unlikely to be any recovery!). Both processes usually entail a prolongation of pain, but at least the pain is not getting worse. Thankfully, economies are not as frail as the human body. They can indeed fall from great heights, smack down hard on the concrete with a sickening thud and yet still recover; the timing of that recovery depending crucially on the extent of the fall.

At the microeconomic level, companies are still continuing the process of de-stocking of inventory. Consumers remain very cautious and retail prices continue to decline to levels aimed at causing them to buy. That said, the fall in interest rates eventually provides crucial support for cash-strapped companies and banks. These hastily complete their inventory de-stocking process, switching most of that supply to export markets unaffected by the crisis, and start the process of re-stocking. At the international level, the reality of the economy hitting bottom, as evidenced by declining contractions in economic indicators, leads to the expectation of Phase V, economic recovery. Phase IV is not plain sailing for local currencies however. As domestic economies stabilize, so do imports. Indeed, year-on-year basing effects accelerate that process. Thus, what we usually see in Phase IV is those trade and current account surpluses peaking on a monthly basis. During Phase III and the initial part of Phase IV, trade flows are actually more important than capital flows — as most offshore investors have already left by then, taking their capital with them. Reduced trade surpluses thus have a greater effect on market movements than would otherwise be the case, serving to weaken the local currencies.

Practice

During Phase III, Asian currencies appreciated on the back of the liquidity-based rally. However, during Phase IV, trade and current account surpluses peak as import demand hits bottom. This is of course good news for the domestic economy, however it temporarily reduces the beneficial liquidity effect on local assets and local currencies. For this very reason, just as Asian economies bottomed around the turn of 1998/99, so Asian currencies started to weaken again, giving back some of the ground they had gained during the second half of 1998. More specifically, the Thai baht, which had risen to a high against the US dollar of THB35.65, fell back to around 38–39. The same kind of thing happened to the Indonesian rupiah, the Philippine peso and the Singapore dollar. The Malaysian ringgit was pegged to the dollar on September 1, 1998 at 3.80, hence it did not experience this renewed setback, nor for that matter did it experience the fundamental recovery which most Asian currencies subsequently enjoyed. In the case of Brazil, Phases III and IV happened much more quickly, partly because Brazil, unlike in Asia, was alone in its devaluation and not affected by region-wide devaluation. In addition, it continued to benefit from strong demand for its exports. Finally, at the corporate level, there was not nearly the same degree of structural dislocation, as Brazilian corporates were by then well aware of what had happened to their Thai and Indonesian counterparts and had already begun to hedge external liabilities long before the real's final devaluation in January 1999. The case of Russia is special for many reasons, not least because several key elements of the Russian government were not informed of the decision to devalue the rouble and default on the domestic debt market until the actual announcement was made. In addition, the size of the black market economy relative to the real economy, and the seemingly persistent state of chaos in the Russian government, has somewhat distorted price and economic development as anticipated by the model. Nonetheless, the key aspects of the model — the turnaround in the trade account, the defeat of inflation, the liquidity-based rally, still held true. So Phase IV sees a decidedly more bumpy ride for emerging market currencies than Phase III. Yet, economic stabilization, all else being equal, gradually becomes economic recovery — the person eventually picks him/herself off the floor after lying there in pain after the fall.

6.1.5 Phase V: The Fundamental Rally

Theory

What does economic recovery mean and how is it different from mere "stabilization"? It is the equivalent of the patient on the one hand getting back his/her vital signs but still remaining essentially horizontal, and on the other hand wandering around the ward. There is a clear difference! In economic terms, recovery means real economic indicators such as retail sales, industrial output and imports are no longer contracting, but actually rising. In particular, as imports start rising, first on a year-on-year basis due to basing effects and then on a month-on-month basis, this is the first real sign of fundamental recovery. At street level, more practically, the first sign of recovery is people back in the shops and retail prices making a bottom. During Phases III and IV, prices fall until such time as consumers are tempted back by bargain basement prices. Phase V is when that temptation produces results. The elimination of corporate de-stocking which had hitherto been a drag on growth, coupled with lower interest rates and looser fiscal policy which provide support for weak domestic demand, help boost economic growth. Corporate *re*-stocking of inventories gives a further lift to that growth take off. In terms of the trade balance, inventory re-stocking accelerates the recovery in imports, in turn accelerating the pullback in monthly recorded trade surpluses. However, by this time, capital flows have begun to offset and then exceed trade flows as investment returns to the region. Rising real economic indicators attract rising capital inflows, helping once again to produce a rally in the local currency. However, unlike in Phase III, this time the rally is fundamentally-based rather than just liquidity-based.

Practice

Fundamental rally was indeed the driving force for Asian currency strength in the second quarter of 1999. As the Asian economies showed increasing signs of recovery, so capital inflows resumed, more than offsetting renewed deterioration in their trade and current account balances. Asian currencies maintained their strength also for much of the third quarter before concerns over Y2K and specific microeconomic concerns in Korea and Thailand over Daewoo and Krung Thai Bank caused a retracement. In addition to these specific concerns, at the global level the US Federal Reserve changed the rules of the game. At its June 30 meeting of the Federal Open Market Committee, the US central bank raised interest rates for the first time since its March 25, 1997 meeting. The Fed hiked the Fed funds' target rate by 25 basis points to 5.00% from 4.75%, however it was not so much the degree of the move as what that move itself signified — the end of monetary easing.

Candidly, the problem with any economic model is that it does not, indeed cannot, take account of what we call "event risk". That is to say, it cannot by definition allow for events which occur unexpectedly and which can and often do cause temporary or even extended reversals in market sentiment. The CEMC model is no different in this. Its aim is to provide a framework for anticipating how emerging market currencies might perform, based on the phase in which they find themselves, *all other factors being equal*. Of course, in reality all factors are frequently not equal and event risk can play a part in distorting price action. A model aimed at targeting the various phases of emerging market currency crises cannot include external factors such as a change in Fed policy. That said, such external factors or event risk notwithstanding, CEMC is still a robust model in providing a predictive framework for emerging market pegged currencies.

This was not aimed at pegged currencies deliberately, but rather as a result of trying to provide an explanation for the Asian crisis and in turn link it to other emerging market currency crises — which also happened to involve currency pegs. The policy of pegging their currencies to the US dollar had provided substantial stability for the likes of Mexico, Asia, Brazil, Russia or Turkey. This had attracted significant capital inflows. In all cases however, those capital inflows caused real exchange rate appreciation and led to trade balance deterioration. The degree of that real exchange rate appreciation was much more significant in a fixed or pegged exchange rate regime. Equally, pegged currencies that experienced the greatest degree of real exchange rate appreciation also had the greatest degree of trade and current account deterioration. The one major exception was China, which in 1994–1995 experienced a real depreciation, thus cushioning the current account balance (a significant surplus) from the after-effects of the Asian crisis in 1997–1998. By early 1997, it was clear there were overvaluation concerns over several Asian currencies and that such overvaluation had been a major factor in current account deterioration. There were two possible macroeconomic responses. Either domestic prices collapsed to reduce the lost trade competitiveness as reflected by current account deterioration or the currency experienced a real depreciation to offset the previous appreciation. In the end, the currency took most of the burden of adjustment, and in spectacular fashion.

The lesson from this is that the type of exchange rate regime has a major influence on the real exchange rate performance and thus in turn on the trade balance. Indeed, the type of exchange rate regime coupled with an event — such as the US dollar's real exchange rate appreciation — led to a series of events. While the degree of eventual market reaction (the Asian currency crisis) could not have been and generally was not predicted, the series of events itself was predictable. For this very reason, we can deduce two things:

- The Asian currency crisis happened because of fundamental imbalances created by the exchange rate regime.
- A model can be created to reflect this series of events for the purpose of looking at other emerging and developed market currencies.

Thus, CEMC was created and can be used to watch the progress of the likes of Turkey, Argentina and Venezuela going forward.

Floating exchange rate regimes behave differently as the transmission mechanism from the exchange rate regime through the real exchange rate to the trade balance is also different. As an example, let's look again at the Polish zloty during 2001. During the first half of 2001, the zloty was one of the top performing currencies in the world against both the Euro and the dollar, supported by heavy capital inflows. Then, in early July 2001, it collapsed. What happened? In April 2000, the National Bank of Poland had made one of its smartest decisions, scrapping the zloty's crawl and peg regime and making the currency fully floating. Since the zloty was a floating currency how could it collapse? Economic theory suggests a floating currency will reflect economic deterioration gradually, thus militating against the worst effects of that deterioration. Economic theory suggests that economic deterioration through a widening current account deficit should lead to gradual real exchange rate depreciation in order to restore equilibrium. Yet, there is nothing gradual about a freely floating currency losing almost 10% of its value in a couple of days, as happened with the Polish zloty. Similarly, in the autumn of 1998 as noted earlier, the dollar–yen exchange rate collapsed from 135 to 114 in less than two days. So, what happened?

To answer this question, we have to refer back to the **speculative cycle of exchange rates** we first looked at in Chapter 2, which focuses specifically on speculative flow to explain moves and trends in freely floating exchange rates. To recap, the central idea behind this is that the longer an exchange rate trend develops, the inherently more speculative in nature it becomes. Eventually, speculative buying (selling) is overwhelmed by fundamental selling (buying) and the exchange rate trend reverses. Sometimes, this reversal is sudden and dramatic, as in the cases of the Polish zloty and the Japanese yen. Somewhat helpfully, ahead of that reversal, option volatility tends to start rising, which currency market practitioners should view as a warning of the reversal to come. This is indeed what happened with the zloty and the yen. We looked at this phenomenon briefly in Chapter 2. Here, in the context of a chapter devoted specifically to exchange rate models, we do so in considerably more detail. While this can be applied to developed market currencies, there are specific considerations with these such as "safe haven" and "reserve currency" status, which distort all models. This particular model is particularly effective with freely floating emerging market currencies, given how capital inflows influence nominal and real interest rates. In the case of the CEMC model, we used the example of Thailand to demonstrate it in practice. With the freely floating exchange rate model, specializing in emerging markets, we use the example of Poland.

6.2 A MODEL FOR FREELY FLOATING EXCHANGE RATES

6.2.1 Phase I: Capital Inflows and Real Exchange Rate Appreciation

Theory

Under a pegged exchange rate, capital flows are attracted by the perception of exchange rate stability created by the peg itself. Conversely, under freely floating exchange rates, such capital flows are attracted by the prospect of high returns, either of income or capital gain. Fundamental flows are attracted to a currency, attracted both by currency and underlying asset market-related valuation considerations. Such capital inflows force the currency to appreciate and simultaneously force nominal interest rates lower. As a result, during this period, the correlation between the asset markets and the currency increases. Capital flows lead to both nominal and real exchange rate appreciation.

Practice

During much of 2000, the National Bank of Poland tightened monetary policy by hiking interest rates to squash inflation. Towards the end of that year, with the NBP's 28-day intervention rate having peaked at around 19%, nominal and real interest rates peaked, as did inflation. The result was irresistible to fixed income investors, attracted both by extremely high interest yields and the prospect of capital gains. As the NBP began cautiously to relax its monetary policy, this triggered an increasing tide of capital inflows. Asset managers reduced or even eliminated their currency hedges. Dedicated emerging market investors raised their asset allocation in Polish bonds, while cross-over investors increased their exposure to what was an off-index investment.

6.2.2 Phase II: Speculators Join the Crowd — The Local Currency Continues to Rally

Theory

Most speculators, though admittedly not all, are trend-followers. Thus, the longer the fundamental trend continues, the more trend-following speculators are attracted to what seems risk-free profit and thus ultimately the more speculative the trend becomes. As the exchange rate continues to appreciate, nominal interest rates to decline and capital inflows to continue, so the other side of the balance of payments starts to deteriorate. The balance of payments must balance and therefore including errors and omissions, a rising capital account surplus must be offset by a widening current account deficit. Equally, real exchange rate appreciation must lead to external balance deterioration. For now, the deterioration is not sufficient to cause concern among fundamental investors and is more than offset by speculative inflows, thus the trend becomes self-fulfilling as more and more speculators join the trend.

Practice

From October 2000 through March 2001, Polish bonds roared higher, benefiting from cuts in official policy interest rates in response to clear signs of slowing economic activity within the Polish economy. The dollar–Polish zloty exchange rate, which at one time had been as high as 4.75 extended its downward trend, at one point breaking through the 4.00 barrier. More and more leveraged money funds sold US dollars or Euro and bought zloty on the back of this move. For a time, "real money" asset managers did the same, increasing their currency exposure as a result of their buying of Polish bonds. There was no incentive to hedge that currency risk. Indeed, there appeared to be every incentive not to hedge — the high cost, the appreciating trend in the zloty and the desire to keep the carry of the original investment (which hedging would reduce or even eliminate).

6.2.3   Phase III: Fundamental Deterioration — The Local Currency Becomes Volatile

Theory

Fundamental investors and speculators do not necessarily sit easily together. They have different investment aims and parameters, the first looking for regular investment capital gain or income over time, the latter looking frequently for short, quick moves. Granted, this is a gross exaggeration and generalization, but it gives at least something of a flavour for the different dynamics at work between the two investor types. The longer the trend continues the more speculative it becomes in a number of ways. In the first case more and more speculators join the trend, sure of easy money to be had. Equally, however, the longer this trend appreciation goes on, the more damage it does to the external balance and thus the more speculative it becomes in the sense of not being fundamentally justifiable. Real exchange rate appreciation must lead to external balance deterioration. Indeed, fundamental market participants, such as asset managers and corporations, increasingly reduce their currency risk for the very reason that there are such fundamental concerns. The ability of speculative inflows to offset fundamental outflows from the currency is increasingly reduced. Because of this increasing tension between fundamental and speculative flows, option implied volatility picks up in the face of increasingly choppy and volatile price action.

Practice

From March through mid-June 2001, the Polish zloty continued to appreciate, albeit in an increasingly erratic and volatile manner. Frequent sell offs would be followed by sharp rallies. Asset managers became increasingly aware of the degree of slowdown in the Polish economy. While this should conversely be good news for fixed income investors as it caused inflationary pressures to decline further, it was a source of increasing concern for equity investors. The market's overall appetite for risk remained relatively high, helped in large part by continued monetary easing by the Federal Reserve. Further, the National Bank of Poland was also cutting interest rates, albeit cautiously in the face of clear evidence of abating price pressures. However, both the pace and extent of zloty strength were a cause of concern to investors, and it seems also to the Polish government. Ahead of elections in September (in which it was subsequently routed by the opposition SLD party), the AWS-led government was increasingly desperate to boost the flagging economy, whether by interest rate cuts, fiscal expansion or a weaker zloty. Markets feared a change in exchange rate policy, either by the existing government or more likely by the opposition, which looked increasingly likely to win the election and in the end did indeed do so. Around June, given the gains seen by then in both Polish bonds and the currency, a combination of market concerns over fundamental deterioration in the economy, notably in the trade balance, and over the prospect of a likely SLD election victory in September triggered increasing interest by investors, particularly offshore investors, to take profit on those gains.

6.2.4 Phase IV: Speculative Flow Reverses — The Local Currency Collapses

Theory

The tension between speculative inflows and fundamental outflows continues to increase, causing violent price swings, until such point as those inflows are not sufficient to offset the rising tide of outflows. Like an inventory overhang that seems to appear out of nowhere in the wake of over-investment, the result is a supply–demand imbalance in the exchange rate. Demand collapses in order to restore equilibrium. In this case, that means a sharp reversal of speculative inflows, which are by nature more easily and more quickly reversed than their fundamental counterparts. Markets overshoot on both the upside and the downside, which means that the correction in the exchange rate to offset over-appreciation is likely to exceed what fundamentals suggest is required. Eventually it manages to stabilize again, starting off a new round of appreciation as fundamental inflows are attracted anew. The sharp correction in the exchange rate should help restore lost trade competitveness. Just as real exchange rate appreciation must lead to external balance deterioration, so the cure for the latter is real exchange rate depreciation. This can happen either through nominal exchange rate depreciation or through a sharp fall in inflation. The easiest and most efficient way for this to happen is through the former. Once that correction or nominal depreciation happens however, the external balance should respond positively.

Practice

At the June 27 FOMC meeting, the Federal Reserve cut interest rates by 25 basis points as expected. Notably, risk appetite indicators did not improve in the wake of this, the first time all year that Fed monetary easing had failed to boost risk appetite. In hindsight, this should have proved a major warning signal, and not just for the Polish zloty but for global financial markets as a whole. A week later, the tremors of the earthquake to come were starting to be felt. On the Thursday, the dollar–zloty exchange rate was already heading higher, boosted by profit-taksing on long zloty positions by asset managers and by a lack of fresh demand for zloty from this quarter. Having bottomed out at around 3.92, dollar–zloty broke back above the 4 level to retest 4.10. Come Friday morning, dollar–zloty broke above 4.20, then 4.25 and then it broke above 4.30. Speculative money that had been long zloty, both against the US dollar and the Euro, either decided to close out their long zloty positions or were stopped out of them. Despite fundamental outflows, there were still asset managers who had substantial positions in Polish bonds and most of these were unhedged from a currency perspective. The spike higher in Euro–zloty and dollar–zloty forced these to currency hedge their bond positions, in the process greatly accelerating the move. Dollar–zloty leapt forward, screaming through 4.40, 4.45, 4.50, only peaking out at around 4.55. In the first six months of 2001, the zloty appreciated by around 10% against its old basket value, only to lose that and more in two days in July. From a peak of around +15.5% against its basket, the zloty fell to as low as +2.5% before finally managing to stabilize. The fall provided a major competitiveness boost to Polish exporters, who quickly took advantage of the opportunity to hedge forward by selling US dollars and Euro against the zloty at such elevated levels. In this way, fundamental buyers returned to both the zloty and to the Polish asset markets, in the form of corporations on the one hand and investors on the other. The cycle began again. Over the next six months, the zloty appreciated from +2.5% to over +14% before again correcting, this time to around +6.8% before stabilizing.

Thus, where we have the **CEMC model** for pegged or fixed exchange rates, the **speculative cycle model** can be used for floating exchange rates. Readers will of course note that these two models have been used in the context of emerging markets. The dynamics of the developed currency markets are slightly different in so much as they are much more liquid and therefore the transmission from portfolio flows to currency strength is less immediate. Equally, very few developed market currencies are pegged — indeed one could argue that the very act of moving from a pegged to a floating currency is itself one necessary aspect of progression from emerging to developed country status. Thus, while the CEMC is not of much use for developed market exchange rates in this context, the speculative cycle model can be used for both emerging and developed exchange rates.

One should note however that the time period over which speculative cycles last in the developed exchange rate markets can be significantly longer — years rather than months — than is the case in the emerging markets. This is so because developed exchange rate markets are substantially more liquid, but more importantly because the size of capital flows has such a disproportionately larger impact on the real economy of emerging markets than is the case with developed economies. Capital flows that can have only a lasting impact on the real economy of a developed market after a substantial period of time are so large by comparison with the size of an emerging market economy that they have a much more significant impact.

If we look at what happens within the developed exchange rates, the speculative cycle of exchange rates also has major relevance, with the proviso that it takes place over a much longer period of time. The starting place for developed market exchange rates is of course the US dollar. If we examine the performance of the US dollar from 1991 to 2001, we can indeed see the speculative cycle of exchange rates at work. Roughly speaking, from 1991 to 1995, the US dollar was in a clear downtrend. Initially, this was due to fundamental concerns, both of valuation and of growth prospects. The Gulf War in 1990–1991 gave way to a deep if brief recession in 1991–1992. From 1993, this was exacerbated by the market's increasing view that the new Clinton administration had a deliberate policy of devaluing the US dollar in order to boost US export competitiveness and reduce the US trade and current account deficits, particularly against Japan. While US officials now say that this was never the case, at the time US officials made repeated statements that could easily have been interpreted as such, suggesting the US wanted a weaker currency. Fundamental investors increasingly sold their US assets during 1991–1993, and during 1993–1995 this process increased despite US economic recovery on the view that the US was deliberately devaluing the dollar. Eventually, as these things tend to do, this fundamental selling attracted the attention of the speculators, who also started to sell en masse. The speculative pressure grew and grew, causing the US dollar to fall in value against all of its major currency counterparts, such as the Japanese yen and the German Deutschmark. This increasingly happened as the fundamentals of the US were starting to improve, helped in large part by the dollar depreciation that had reduced that US trade deficit by making US exports more competitive. Fundamental investors started to get back into US assets, however the speculators, attracted even more by irresponsible US official comments on the currency, were still selling. Eventually, the patience of the US authorities snapped and the Federal Reserve intervened on several occasions in 1995 to stem the tide of speculative selling. The current Undersecretary of the US Treasury Peter Fisher was at the time the head of open market operations at the New York Fed and therefore responsible for the Fed's intervention in the foreign exchange markets. Fisher explained the Fed's aim not so much as to defend a specific currency level or to of necessity stop a currency from weakening, but rather to intervene in order to recreate a sense of two-way risk in the markets.[2] The Fed uses a number of market pricing indicators to tell whether or not two-way risk — the risk that a currency can go up or down — exists and most if not all of these were at the time suggesting that the market viewed all the US dollar risk as being to the downside. The Fed's intervention, carried out in conjunction with the Bank of Japan and also with monetary policy change by the BoJ, helped cause a sea-change in market sentiment. The US thus achieved what they were looking for, two-way risk in the dollar. In the wake of this, the fundamental buyers increased significantly in number and the speculators reversed and also started buying.

Thus, the speculative cycle worked, albeit with somewhat of a delay due to the view that the US was deliberately trying to devalue its own currency. From 1995, the US dollar thus has been on a trend of appreciation, more than reversing the weakness seen in 1991–1995. Readers will of course be aware that the speculative cycle works both ways, when a currency is appreciating and also when it is depreciating. Thus, the US dollar strength that we have seen since 1995 has indeed caused fundamental deterioration. If the speculative cycle holds up, the speculative buying will be overwhelmed by the fundamental selling by asset managers and the US dollar will reverse sharply lower. The warning sign for that to come will be when we see a sharp spike in options volatility without any major moves in the spot market, reflecting major flow disturbance in the market as the fundamental selling pressure intensifies.

In recent years, the economic community has developed a very large number of exchange rate models for analysing currency crises, and it is certainly not for here to repeat a list of them. That said, they can be classified into three broad categories of currency crisis model. **First-generation** crisis models focus on the "shadow price" of the exchange rate; that is the exchange rate value that would prevail if all the foreign exchange reserves were sold. These models generally view as doomed a central bank's efforts to defend a currency peg using reserves if the shadow price exchange rate is in a long-term uptrend. It is assumed that rational speculators will immediately eliminate a central bank's foreign exchange reserves as soon as the shadow price exceeds the peg level. A key feature of first-generation currency crisis models is that they generally see currency crises as being due to poor government economic policy; that there was a degree of *blame* involved, that poor government policy *caused* the currency crisis.

Unlike with the first-generation model, **second-generation** crisis models do not see a currency crisis as being due to poor government economic policy, but instead due to the currency peg being at an uncompetitive level. The main inspiration for second-generation crisis models

---

[2] As explained by Peter Fisher at the quarterly meetings at the New York Federal Reserve to discuss foreign exchange activity, 1995.

was the ERM crises of 1992–1993. In 1992, the UK was not willing to take the economic pain required to keep their peg of 2.7778 against the Deutschmark. In August 1993, most of continental Europe was forced to abandon their 2.25% bands. However, instead of allowing their currencies to float freely, they widened the 2.25% band to 15%, a compromise solution between a full flotation and a pegged exchange rate. In the cases of the UK and of continental Europe, the de-pegging of the exchange rate did not cause the much anticipated economic recession. Indeed, the cost of defending the peg was very high interest rates, thus hurting the economy. With the currency pegs gone, there was no longer any need for such high interest rates. Thus, the de-pegging of the exchange rate was on the one hand due to the government's unwillingness to take the economic pain needed to defend the peg, but on the other hand that pain was due to an uncompetitive exchange rate peg level. For the UK in particular, the de-pegging of sterling, which came to be known as "Black Wednesday", was the best thing that had happened to the UK economy for several years. Interest rates are lowered and exchange rates stabilize at a much more competitive and appropriate level when currency pegs are broken, according to second-generation models.

Third-generation currency crisis models, which developed in the wake of the Asian currency crisis, involved "moral hazard", that is the idea that private sector investment in a specific country will result if a sufficient number of investors anticipate that country will be bailed out by multinational organizations such as the IMF. Inward investment and external debt rise in parallel as a country continues to be bailed out until such time as the situation is untenable. The currency is one main expression of that situation's collapse.

With the first-generation currency crisis model, the focus is on blaming poor government economic policy, particularly poor fiscal policy. With the second-generation model, the issue of blame is less clear and the focus is more on an uncompetitive exchange rate rather than poor government economic policy. For its part, the third-generation model focuses not on the reason for the currency crisis but the result, or more specifically the massive real economic shock that came from "moral hazard" investment caused by the combination of currency devaluation and external debt. Put simply, second-generation models can be "good", but third-generation models are unequivocally "bad".

6.3 SUMMARY

In Chapter 5, we looked at how the type of exchange rate regime can affect currency market considerations. Here, in Chapter 6, we have tried to extrapolate this, looking at currency models for fixed and floating exchange rate regimes. While the aim of both chapters has been to show the practical aspects of these themes, the methodology has largely been theoretical rather than practical, that is the focus for the most part has been on the theory of how exchange rate regimes affect economic behaviour and equally the theory of how currency crises develop. In the next three chapters however, we take an entirely different line, focusing on practice rather than theory, looking at how the practitioners themselves can use currency analysis and strategy to conduct their business. We start this process by off by looking at how multinational corporations might seek to manage their currency risk.

Part Three
The Real World of the Currency Market Practitioner

7

Managing Currency Risk I — The Corporation: Advanced Approaches to Corporate Treasury FX Strategy

The management of currency risk by corporations has come a long way in the last three decades. Before the break-up of Bretton Woods currency risk was not a major consideration for corporate executives, nor did it have to be. Exchange rates were allowed to fluctuate, but only within reasonably tight bands, while the US dollar itself was pegged to that most solid of commodities, gold. The responsibility for managing currency risk, or rather maintaining currency stability, was largely that of governments. Needless to say, that burden, that responsibility has now passed from the public to the private sector.

This chapter deals with the corporate world, how a corporation is affected by and how corporate Treasury deals with the issue of currency or exchange rate risk. More specifically, this chapter will look at:

- Currency risk — defining and managing currency risk
- Core principles for managing currency risk
- Corporate Treasury strategy and currency risk
- The issue of hedging — management reluctance and internal hedging
- Advanced tools for hedging
- Hedging using a corporate risk optimizer
- Advanced approaches to hedging transactional and balance sheet currency risk
- Hedging emerging market currency risk
- Benchmarks for currency risk management
- Setting budget rates
- Corporations and predicting exchange rates
- VaR and beyond
- Treasury strategy in the overall context of the corporation

In short, there is a lot to cover. This chapter is aimed first and foremost at corporate Finance Directors, Treasurers and their teams. In addition, it attempts to give corporate executives outside of the Treasury a greater understanding of the complexity and difficulty entailed and the effort required in managing a corporation's exchange rate or currency risk. As we shall see later in the chapter, many leading multinationals have set up oversight or risk committees to oversee the Treasury strategy in managing currency and interest rate risk. This is an important counter-balance for the corporation as a whole, but of course it requires that the committee itself is as up-to-date with the latest risk management ideas and techniques as are the Treasury personnel themselves.

The way the corporation has dealt with currency risk has changed substantially over time. Corporations, many of which were reluctant to touch anything but the most vanilla of hedging structures, have now greatly increased the sophistication of their currency risk management and hedging strategies, particularly over the last decade. In this regard, two developments have helped greatly — the centralizing of Treasury operations, particularly within large multinationals, and the focus put on hiring specifically experienced and qualified personnel to manage the day-to-day operations of risk management.

Before going on I would point out that perhaps to some reading this, it may seem strange and slightly out of touch to be examining advanced approaches to the management of currency risk at a time when the number of currencies worldwide seems to be rapidly diminishing. The creation of the Euro-zone has eliminated a large number of western European currencies, with the prospect that many countries within eastern Europe will enter it from 2004–5 onwards, giving up their own currencies in the process. In the Americas, the creation of the North American Free Trade Area has created a *de facto* US dollar bloc. Though some may not like to see it that way, that is surely the reality and on the whole it has been a positive development. As yet, the talk that there may be a unification of the US and Canadian dollars is just that, talk, but who knows for the future? There is no such talk about unification with the Mexican peso, as it is doubtful whether any Mexican administration that suggested any such would survive. That said, there is little question that the economic impact of NAFTA appears to have added greatly to the stability of the Mexican peso, rendering the question redundant for now. In Asia, there are occasional mutterings that there could be a single currency, either in Asia as a whole (i.e. the Japanese yen) or more specifically within the ASEAN region of countries. On the first, any prospect of a pan-Asian currency seems far off, not least because a number of Asian countries, notably China, would not accept the dominant role that any such currency would automatically give Japan. In addition, given Japan's slow economic descent in the 1990s, it is questionable whether anyone in their right mind would want to unify their currencies with the yen and thus by doing so import deflation. The more specific idea of an ASEAN currency is a greater possibility, at least in relative terms, though it has not yet been raised to any serious extent. Moreover, the idea of the Asian Free Trade Area (AFTA) has yet to see fruition. It would probably be best to focus on that first, before considering a single currency area.

There is no question however that the number of national currencies is on a downtrend. This may cause some to assume that the need for currency risk management should similarly be on a downtrend. In fact, quite the opposite is the case. The desire of corporate executives "just to be able to get on with the company's underlying business" is a natural one, but it will be some time — if ever — before they will be able to ignore currency risk. There may be a single currency in the Euro-zone, but there is not worldwide — whatever we think of the role of the US dollar — and there is unlikely to be any time soon. Even in the brave new world of the Euro-zone, where currency risk should in theory be a thing of the past, it remains an important consideration. To use John Donne, just as no man is an island, the same is true for the corporation. Within the Euro-zone, currency translation and therefore direct currency risk has been eliminated. However, corporations are still exposed to competitive threats from exchange rate movements between the Euro-zone and the rest of the world. A single currency area such as the Euro-zone can eliminate only one form of currency risk, that is the direct kind. However, it cannot eliminate indirect currency risk for the very reason that the Euro-zone is but one area, albeit an important one, within the global economy. National currencies still have to be dealt with and that is unlikely to change near term.

7.1 CURRENCY RISK

So, what precisely is currency risk? There is no point in focusing on an issue if one cannot first define it. Although definitions vary within the academic community, a practical description of currency risk would be:

The impact that unexpected exchange rate changes have on the value of the corporation

Currency risk is very important to a corporation as it can have a major impact on its cash flows, assets and liabilities, net profit and ultimately its stock market value. Assuming the corporation has accepted that currency risk needs to be managed specifically and separately, it has three initial priorities:

1. Define what kinds of currency risk the corporation is exposed to
2. Define a corporate Treasury strategy to deal with these currency risks
3. Define what financial instruments it allows itself to use for this purpose

Currency risk is simple in concept, but complex in reality. At its most basic, it is the possible gain or loss resulting from an exchange rate move. It can affect the value of a corporation directly as a result of an unhedged exposure or more indirectly.

Different types of currency risk can also offset each other. For instance, take a US citizen who owns stock in a German auto manufacturer and exporter to the US. If the Euro falls against the US dollar, the US dollar value of the Euro-denominated stock falls and therefore on the face of it the individual sees the US dollar value of their holding decline. However, the German auto exporter should in fact benefit from a weaker Euro as this makes the company's exports to the US cheaper, allowing them the choice of either maintaining US prices to maintain margin or cutting them further to boost market share. Sooner or later, the stock market will realize this and mark up the stock price of the auto exporter. Thus, the stock owner may lose on the currency translation, but gain on the higher stock price.

This is of course a very simple example and life unfortunately is rarely that simple. For just as a weaker Euro makes exports from the Euro-zone cheaper, so it makes imports more expensive. Thus, an exporter may not in fact feel the benefit of the currency translation through to market share because higher import prices force it to raise export prices from where they would otherwise would be according to the exchange rate.

The first step in successfully managing currency risk is to acknowledge that such risk actually exists and that it has to be managed in the general interest of the corporation and the corporation's shareholders. For some, this is of itself a difficult hurdle as there is still major reluctance within corporate management to undertake what they see as straying from their core, underlying business into the speculative world of currency markets. The truth however is that the corporation is a participant in the currency market whether it likes it or not; if it has foreign currency-denominated exposure, that exposure should be managed. To do anything else is irresponsible. The general trend within the corporate world has however been in favour of recognizing the existence of and the need to manage currency risk. That recognition does not of itself entail speculation. Indeed, at its best, prudent currency hedging can be defined as the elimination of speculation:

The real speculation is in fact not managing currency risk

The next step, however, is slightly more complex and that is to identify the nature and extent of the currency risk or exposure. It should be noted that the emphasis here is for the most part on non-financial corporations, on manufacturers and service providers rather than on banks or other types of financial institutions. Non-financial corporations generally have only a small amount of their total assets in the form of receivables and other types of transaction. Most of their assets are made up of inventory, buildings, equipment and other forms of tangible "real" assets. In order to measure the effect of exchange rate moves on a corporation, one first has to define the type and then the amount of risk involved, or the "value at risk" (VaR). There are three main types of currency risk that a multinational corporation is exposed to and has to manage.

7.2   TYPES OF CURRENCY RISK

1. Transaction risk (receivables, dividends, etc.)
2. Translation risk (balance sheet)
3. Economic risk (present value of future operating cash flows)

7.2.1   Transaction Risk

Transaction currency risk is essentially cash flow risk and relates to any transaction, such as receivables, payables or dividends. The most common type of transaction risk relates to export or import contracts. When there is an exchange rate move involving the currencies of such a contract, this represents a direct transactional currency risk to the corporation. This is the most basic type of currency risk which a corporation faces.

7.2.2   Translation Risk

Translation risk is slightly more complex and is the result of the consolidation of parent company and foreign subsidiary financial statements. This consolidation means that exchange rate impact on the balance sheet of the foreign subsidiaries is transmitted or *translated* to the parent company's balance. *Translation risk is thus balance sheet currency risk.* While most large multinational corporations actively manage their transaction currency risk, many are less aware of the potential dangers of translation risk.

The actual translation process in consolidating financial statements is done either at the average exchange rate of the period or at the exchange rate at the period end, depending on the specific accounting regulations affecting the parent company. As a direct result, the consolidated results will vary as either the average or the end-of-period exchange rate varies. Thus, all foreign currency-denominated profit is exposed to translation currency risk as exchange rates vary. In addition, the foreign currency value of foreign subsidiaries is also consolidated on the parent company's balance sheet, and that value will vary accordingly. Translation risk for a foreign subsidiary is usually measured by the net assets (assets less liabilities) that are exposed to potential exchange rate moves.

Problems can occur with regard to translation risk if a corporation has subsidiaries whose accounting books are local currency-denominated. For consolidation purposes, these books must of course be translated into the currency of the parent company, but at what exchange rate? Income statements are usually translated at the average exchange rate over the period. However, deciding at what exchange rate to translate the balance sheet is slightly more tricky. There are generally three methods used by major multinational corporations for translating balance sheet risk, varying in how they separate assets and liabilities between those that need to be translated at the "current" exchange rate at the time of consolidation and those that are translated at the historical exchange rate:

- The all current (closing rate) method
- The monetary/non-monetary method
- The temporal method

As the name might suggest, the all current (closing rate) method translates all foreign currency exposures at the closing exchange rate of the period concerned. Under this method, translation risk relates to net assets or shareholder funds. This has become the most popular method of translating balance exposure of foreign subsidiaries, both in the US and worldwide. On the other hand, the monetary/non-monetary method translates monetary items such as assets, liabilities and capital at the closing rate and non-monetary items at the historical rate. Finally, the temporal method breaks balance sheet items down in terms of whether they are firstly stated at replacement cost, realizable value, market value or expected future value, or secondly stated at historic cost. For the first group, these are translated at the closing exchange rate of the period concerned, for the second, at the historical exchange rate.

The US accounting standard FAS 52 and the UK's SSAP 20 apply to translation risk. Under FAS 52, the translation of foreign currency revenues and costs is made at the average exchange rate of the period. FAS 52 generally uses the all current method for translation purposes, though it does have several important provisions, notably regarding the treatment of currency hedging contracts. Under SSAP 20, the corporation can use either the current or average rate. Generally, there has been a shift among multinational corporations towards using the average rather than the closing rate because this is seen as a truer reflection of the translation risk faced by the corporation during the period.

Translation risk is a crucial issue for corporations. Later in this chapter, we will look at methods of hedging it. For now, it is important to get an idea of how it can affect the company's overall value.

Example

Take an example of a Euro-based manufacturer which has bought a factory in Poland. Needless to say, the cost base in Poland is substantially below that of the parent company, one of several major reasons why the acquisition was made in the first place. From 1999 to 2001, the Euro was on a major downtrend, not just against its major currency counterparts but also against most currencies of the Central and East European area, such as the Polish zloty. Thus we get the following simple model:

$$\text{EUR–USD} \downarrow = \text{EUR–PLN} \downarrow$$

where:

EUR–USD = The Euro–US dollar exchange rate
EUR–PLN = The Euro–Polish zloty exchange rate

This is an over-simplification to be sure. For one thing, the Polish zloty was pegged to a basket of Euro (55%) and US dollar (45%) with a crawl and trading bands up until 2000, and thus was unable to appreciate despite the ongoing decline in the value of the Euro across the board. For another, it does not take account of EUR–PLN volatility. That said, general Euro weakness has clearly been an important factor in the depreciation of the Euro–zloty exchange rate. Note however that as the Euro–zloty exchange rate has depreciated for this and other reasons so the value of the original investment in the Polish factory has increased in Euro terms. Thus:

$$\text{EUR–PLN} \downarrow = \text{EUR } \textit{translation} \text{ value of Polish subsidiary} \uparrow$$

Whatever our Euro-based manufacturer may think of Euro weakness, it is entirely beneficial for the manufacturer's translation value of the Polish factory/subsidiary when the financial statements are consolidated at the end of the accounting period. The translation benefit to the balance sheet will depend on the accounting method of translation. Conversely, were the Euro ever to rally on a sustained basis, this might cause the Euro–zloty exchange rate to rally, thus in turn reducing the translation value of the corporation's Polish subsidiary. The consolidation of financial statements would mean that this not only has an impact on the Euro value of the Polish subsidiary but also on the balance sheet of the parent, Euro-based manufacturer. The risk of a sudden balance sheet deterioration of this kind is not negligible where corporations have a broad range of foreign subsidiaries, with accompanying transactional and translational currency risk.

7.2.3 Economic Risk

The translation of foreign subsidiaries concerns the consolidated group balance sheet. However, this does not affect the real "economic" value or exposure of the subsidiary. Economic risk focuses on how exchange rate moves change the real economic value of the corporation, focusing on the present value of future operating cash flows and how this changes in line with exchange rate changes. More specifically, the economic risk of a corporation reflects the effect of exchange rate changes on items such as export and domestic sales, and the cost of domestic and imported inputs. As with translation risk, calculating economic risk is complex, but clearly necessary to be able to assess how exchange rate changes can affect the present value of foreign subsidiaries. Economic risk is usually applied to the present value of future operating cash flows of a corporation's foreign subsidiaries. However, it can also be applied to the parent company's operations and how the present value of those change in line with exchange rate changes.

Summarizing this part, transaction risk deals with the effect of exchange rate moves on transactional exposure such as accounts receivable/payable or dividends. Translation risk focuses on how exchange rate moves can affect foreign subsidiary valuation and therefore the valuation of the consolidated group balance sheet. Finally, economic risk deals with the effect of exchange rate changes to the present value of future operating cash flows, focusing on the "currency of determination" of revenues and operating expenses. Here it is important to differentiate between the currency in which cash flows are denominated and the currency that may determine the nature and size of those cash flows. The two are not necessarily the same. To complicate the issue further, there is the small matter of the parent company's currency, which is used to consolidate the financial statements. If a parent company has foreign currency-denominated debt, this is recorded in the parent company's currency, but the value of its legal obligation remains in the currency denomination of the debt. In sum, transaction risk is just the tip of the iceberg!

Of necessity, the reality of currency risk is very case-specific. That said, there has been an attempt by the academic and economic communities to apply the traditional exchange rate models to the corporate world for the purpose of demonstrating how exchange rates impact a corporation. More specifically, the models typically used for this purpose have been those of PPP, the international Fisher effect and the unbiased forward rate theory, which we looked at in Chapter 1. To recap:

- PPP (or the law of one price) suggests that price differentials of the same good in different countries require an exchange rate adjustment to offset them.
- The international Fisher effect suggests that the expected change in the exchange rate is equal to the interest rate differential.
- The unbiased forward rate theory suggests that the forward exchange rate is equal to the expected exchange rate.

Generally, these theories arc grounded in the efficient market hypothesis and therefore flawed at best. Over the long term, these traditional "rules" of exchange rate theory suggest that competition and arbitrage should neutralize the effect of exchange rate changes on returns and on the valuation of the corporation. Equally, locking into the forward rate should, according to the unbiased forward rate theory, offer the same return as remaining exposed to currency risk, as this theory suggests that the distribution of probability should be equal on either side of the forward rate.

The unfortunate thing about such models, however worthy the attempt, is that they do not and cannot deal with the practical realities of managing currency risk. What academics regard as "temporary deviations" from where the model suggests the exchange rate should bc can be sufficient and substantial enough to cause painful and intolerable deterioration to both the P&L and the balance sheet.

To conclude this part, a corporation should define and seek to quantify the types of currency risk to which it is exposed in order then to be able to go about creating a strategy for managing that currency risk.

7.3 MANAGING CURRENCY RISK

Transactional currency risk can be hedged tactically or strategically by the corporate Treasury to preserve cash flow and earnings, depending on their currency view.

Translational currency risk is usually hedged opportunistically rather than systematically, notably to try to avoid emerging market-related shocks to net assets, usually focusing on either long-term foreign investment or debt structure.

Hedging economic risk is complex, requiring the corporation to forecast its revenue and cost streams over a given period and then to analyse the potential impact on these of an exchange rate deviation from the rate used in calculating revenue and cost. For the debt structure, the currency of denomination must be chosen, the amount of debt estimated in that currency and the average interest period determined. The effect on cash flow should be netted out over product lines and across markets. What's left from this process is the economic risk that has to be managed. For large multinationals, the net economic risk may in fact be quite small because of offsetting effects. However, economic risk can be substantial for corporations that have invested in only one or two foreign markets.

The first two steps of this process appear to have been accomplished. Firstly, we have defined very specifically the types of currency risk that a corporation is exposed to. Secondly, we have looked at broad strategy, the brushstrokes of managing that currency risk. Yet, while this currency risk may be defined, it must also be quantified. Quantifying an amount of currency may be easy for transaction risk, but for translation or economic risk it is no easy task. Just as with other types of risk management, the most popular way of doing this is to use a "VaR" model.

7.4 MEASURING CURRENCY RISK — VaR AND BEYOND

Value at risk is defined as:

The maximum loss for a given exposure over a given time horizon with x% confidence

VaR helps a user to define the maximum loss on an exposure for a given confidence level and has helped investors and corporations in managing their risk. VaR is on the face of it an excellent risk management tool, which can be used to measure a variety of risk types.

However, it should be noted that:

VaR does not define the worst case scenario

It may give the maximum loss for an exposure with 99% confidence using a 3000-iteration Monte Carlo simulation. The question remains however, what happens to the exposure for that 1% point of confidence? The frank truth is a VaR model is incapable of answering that question. Thus, a degree of both care and common sense is needed. The more sophisticated corporate Treasuries frequently seek to refine their VaR model to go beyond the natural confidence level limit to try and define the maximum loss with 100% confidence. A practical way of trying to achieve this is to impose operational limits (such as in terms of number of contracts, nominal amount, sensitivities or stop loss orders) in addition to VaR limits. That relates to the aspect of care. The common sense aspect relates to never trusting your risk to a computer model alone. If you cannot quantify it itself without use of the model, you have a problem.

7.5   CORE PRINCIPLES FOR MANAGING CURRENCY RISK

So far we have examined currency risk, how to manage and quantify it. Before we go on from theory into practice, it may well be useful to establish a framework, a reference for corporate Treasury of core principles of managing currency risk. There have been several notable efforts along these lines, most notably of course the "Core Principles of Managing Currency Risk" set out by the Group of 31 (US multinational corporations) and Greenwich Treasury Advisors.

Clearly, there is a danger in attempting anything even approaching best practice for corporate Treasury as corporations vary so significantly in terms of their exposures, requirements and focus. Such concerns notwithstanding, the importance of the issue equally requires that the attempt be made to create a reference from which individual corporations can perhaps take what might be appropriate to them. Thus, what follows is my own tentative suggestion of what any such list of core principles of managing currency risk should contain:

1. **Determine the types of currency risk to which the corporation is exposed** — Break these down into transaction, translation and economic risk, making specific reference to what currencies are related to each type of currency risk.
2. **Establish a strategic currency risk management policy** — Once currency risk types have been agreed on, corporate Treasury should establish and document a strategic currency risk management policy to deal with these types of risks. This policy should include the corporation's general approach to currency risk, whether it wants to hedge or trade that risk and its core hedging objectives.
3. **Create a mission statement for Treasury** — It is crucial to create a set of values and principles which embody the specific approach taken by the Treasury towards managing currency risk, agreed upon by senior management at the time of establishing and documenting the risk management policy.
4. **Detail currency hedging approach** — Having established the overall currency risk management policy, the corporation should detail how that policy is to be executed in practice, including the types of financial instruments that could be used for hedging, the process by which currency hedging would be executed and monitored and procedures for monitoring and reviewing existing currency hedges.

5. **Centralizing Treasury operations as a single centre of excellence** — Treasury operations can be more effectively and efficiently managed if they are centralized. This makes it easier to ensure all personnel are clear about the Treasury's mission statement and hedging approach. Thus, the Treasury can be run as a single centre of excellence within the corporation, ensuring the quality of individual members. Large multinational corporations should consider creating a position of chief dealer to manage the dealing team, as the demands of a Treasurer often exceed the ability to manage all positions and exposures on a real-time basis. The currency dealing team must have the same level of expertise as their counterparty banks.

6. **Adopt uniform standards for accounting for currency risk** — In line with the centralizing of Treasury operations, uniform accounting procedures with regard to currency risk should be adopted, creating and ensuring transparency of risk. Create benchmarks for measuring the performance of currency hedging.

7. **Have in-house modelling and forecasting capacity** — Currency forecasting is as important as execution. While Treasury may rely on its core banks for forecasting exchange rates relative to its needs, it should also have its own forecasting ability, linked in with its operational observations which are frequently more real time than any bank is capable of. Treasury should also be able to model all its hedging positions using VaR and other sophisticated modelling systems.

8. **Create a risk oversight committee** — In addition to the safeguard of a chief dealer position for larger multinational corporations, a risk oversight committee should be established to approve position taking above established thresholds and review the risk management policy on a regular basis.

Clearly, this list of core principles of managing currency risk is aimed at the larger multinational corporations that have the means and the business requirements for such a sophisticated Treasury operation. That said, such a list can also be used as a benchmark for those who, while they cannot or do not need to comply with all elements, can still find some useful. Corporations of whatever size and sophistication must balance the real cost of implementing such an approach to managing currency risk against the possible cost of not doing so. The first cost is tangible, the second intangible — but by the time the second becomes tangible it is too late! That is precisely what we are trying to avoid.

It may be useful for a corporation to split currency risk management into two parts — the first part focusing on the overall approach towards managing of currency risk, the second dealing with the actual execution of currency risk management. Many corporations have this kind of division of labour, whether or not they formalize it. However rigorous a currency risk management policy is, it still runs the risk of being bypassed by events, technology and innovation. Thus, it is very important to have a regular review process to ensure the currency risk management policy remains up-to-date and in line with the corporation's needs. In this review process, important questions to be raised may include:

- Do the currency risk management policy and the Treasury's mission statement still represent the corporation's business needs? Should the corporation maintain or change its approach towards managing currency risk?
- How has currency hedging performed relative to the established benchmarks? How can the costs of currency hedging be reduced?
- Are VaR or credit limits, or the financial instruments relating to currency risk management, still appropriate?

7.6 HEDGING — MANAGEMENT RELUCTANCE
AND INTERNAL METHODS

Having looked in detail at the issue of managing currency risk, we should now be looking at the specifics of how to hedge that risk. Before we do that, we first have to examine the issue of management reluctance to hedge a risk many see as merely an operational hazard of international investment. Some may dismiss this section, either because it is irrelevant to them or because they view any such approach as inappropriate. While I too share the view that currency risk should be managed, such management reluctance should not be ignored, but instead should be understood and thereafter combated. Three key reasons for this reluctance which come up time and again are the following:

- Management does not understand active currency management methods
- Management thinks currency risk cannot be measured accurately
- Management sees active currency management as outside of core business

Some of these points are reasonable. Currency forwards and options may well be outside the field of expertise of a corporation's management, and will certainly be outside the core business operations. Many managements consider such financial instruments as speculative. However, it is the job of Treasury to explain that not managing currency risk actively leaves the corporation vulnerable to major exchange rate movements, which can cause substantial swings in the company's value. Using forwards or options may indeed be speculative, depending on what they are used for. However, not hedging currency risk may be even more speculative. Active currency management is a necessary byproduct of a corporation's overseas investments and operations. Again, it is the job of the Treasury to educate the management and ultimately the board on the need for active currency management, not least to maintain and ensure the corporation's equity market value. A corporation may not be able to boost shareholder value significantly through active currency risk management, but it can certainly damage it by not managing currency risk.

When management says it is difficult to measure currency risk it is correct, but that does not mean such risk cannot be quantified. Imprecision is not an excuse for indecision in the corporation's underlying business. Neither should it be tolerated with regard to currency risk management.

Even if a management is willing to consider currency hedging, there are ways of "natural" or internal hedging that it may consider first, such as:

- Netting (debt, receivables and payables are netted out between group companies)
- Matching (intragroup foreign currency inflows and outflows)
- Leading and lagging (adjustment of credit terms before and after due date)
- Price adjustment (raising/lowering selling prices to counter exchange rate moves)
- Invoicing in foreign currency (this cuts out transactional exposure)
- Asset/liability management (for balance sheet, income or cash flow exposure)

Netting involves the settling of intragroup debt, receivables and payables for the net amount. The simplest form of this is bilateral netting between two affiliates.

Matching is similar but can be applied both to intragroup and third-party flows. Here, a corporation "matches" its foreign currency inflows and outflows with respect to amount and timing.

Leading and lagging refer to adjusting credit terms between group companies, where "leading" means paying an obligation in advance of the due date and "lagging" means after the due date. This is a tactic aimed at capturing expected currency appreciation or depreciation.

Price adjustment involves increasing selling prices to counter exchange rate moves.

Invoicing in foreign currency reduces transaction risk relating specifically to exports and imports.

Asset and liability management can be used to manage the balance sheet, income statement or cash flow exposure. Corporations can adopt either an active or a passive approach to asset and liability management, depending on their currency and interest rate risk management policy.

Finally one can hedge internally by increasing corporate gearing. Leverage shields corporations from taxes because interest is tax-deductible whereas dividends are not. However, the extent to which one can increase gearing or leverage is limited by costs. That said, if currency hedging reduces taxes, shareholders benefit.

For practical purposes, three questions capture the extent of a corporation's currency risk:

1. How quickly can a corporation adjust prices to offset exchange rate impact on profit margins?
2. How quickly can a corporation adjust sources for inputs and markets for outputs?
3. To what extent do exchange rate moves have an impact on the value of assets?

Within a corporation, it is usually the case that those who can come up with the best answers to these questions are directly involved in such tasks as purchasing and production. Thus, finance executives who focus exclusively on the credit and currency markets can in fact miss the real essence of a corporation's currency risk. Furthermore, the exact answers to these questions need to be known not only by the oversight or risk committee, but preferably by the CEO as well. If they don't, they effectively don't know both the value and the exposure of the corporation.

7.7   KEY OPERATIONAL CONTROLS FOR TREASURY

Assuming the corporation has accepted the need to manage currency risk, appointed a risk or oversight committee and in the case of large multinational corporations a chief dealer as well, it needs then to establish a set of operational controls in order to be able to monitor that risk and ensure inappropriate positions are not being taken. The importance of doing this is underlined every time the news headlines show another corporation has lost millions of pounds, dollars or yen by not putting such controls in place, or rather by not ensuring their enforcement. There are other operational controls that are important, but among the key ones to put in place are the following:

- Position limits — Positions above a certain limit or threshold should not be undertaken without the written authorization of the chief dealer, Treasurer, oversight committee and the board.
- Position monitoring — Treasury must have the technological and manpower capability to monitor and mark-to-market all the currency and interest rate positions it has taken on at any one time.
- Performance benchmarks should be established — For corporations that only participate in the currency market for hedging purposes, currency hedging benchmarks should be

established. For those that are allowed to trade in the currency market, a trading budget should be established at the start of the year and the performance monitored on a monthly or quarterly basis.

7.8   TOOLS FOR MANAGING CURRENCY RISK

The board has given Treasury free rein to manage the corporation's currency risk within the parameters set out in the currency risk management policy. Within that policy, there should be a section on what financial instruments can be used for this purpose. Hedging currency risk in no longer a simple matter of using vanilla forwards and options. As the needs of the modern corporation have changed, so the tools or structures for hedging that risk have changed accordingly, consisting of ever greater specificity and flexibility to meet those needs. Most of the development within this field has happened in financial options, given the more flexible nature of the option instrument relative to the forward. Thus, I present a pair of tables looking for the most part at the types of option structures that corporations are using today, breaking these down into "traditional" (Table 7.1) and "enhanced" (Table 7.2) structures, relating to their degree of sophistication.

Table 7.1   Traditional hedging structures

Instrument	Definition	Advantages	Disadvantages
Plain vanilla call	Buy an upside strike in an exchange rate with no obligation to exercise	Simplicity, cheaper than the forward and the maximum loss is the premium	Higher cost than more sophisticated structures
Plain vanilla forward	Buy a currency contract for future delivery at a price set today	You are 100% hedged	High cost and risk of the exchange rate moving against you
Call spread	Buy an at-the-money call (ATMF) and sell a low delta call	Lower cost than a vanilla call	Allows cover only for modest exchange rate appreciation as dictated by strikes
Calendar spread	Buy a 3M call and sell a 1M call (of the same delta)	Allows you to capture a timing view on FX moves	Leaves you vulnerable to adverse moves in one of the legs
Risk reversal	Buy a 25 delta call, sell a 25 delta put	Risk reversals capture the market's "skew" thus they offer buying/ selling opportunity relative to historical risk reversals; can be structured to be low or zero cost	Writing the 25 delta put leaves you vulnerable to an adverse move in spot which may cause a spike higher in vol not offset by the higher vol in the call
"Seagull"	Buy an ATMF call, sell a low delta call and sell a downside put	Can be structured to be zero cost	Unless structured in a ratio, leaves you net short vol; not covered against a major spot move

Table 7.2   Enhanced hedging structures

Instrument	Definition	Advantages	Disadvantages
Knock-out	Buy a 30 delta call with a downside knockout (down-and-out)	Reduces cost of call; lets you re-hedge lower down in the exchange rate	If knocked-out you are not hedged and vulnerable to an adverse FX move
Knock-in	Buy a 30 delta call with upside knock-in (up-and-in)	Reduces the cost; you are not hedged until knocked-in	If knocked-in, you are then vulnerable to a spot reversal
Range binary	Buy a double knock-out	Gives you leverage premium, expecting range trading	If knocked-out, you will have to re-hedge
Window option	Buy the right to buy a 30 delta call in a given number of periods	Lets your currency view be "wrong" a number of times	Higher cost than the vanilla call
Fade-in option	Buy a 30 delta call and fade into the call incrementally over a given period of time	Allows you to "fade in" to the call for a period, thus giving you more cost and time flexibility	If spot moves while you are fading in, you do not capture as much of the move as with a vanilla call
Convertible forward	Buy a call, sell a down-and-in put	Converts to forward at agreed rate; client can take advantage of a contrarian move in spot up to the KI	The strike is more expensive than the forward and must be paid if structure is knocked-in
Enhanced forward	Buy an up-and-in–down-and-in call/sell an up-and-in–down-and-in put; buy an up-and-out–down-and-out call/buy an up-and-out–down-and-out put	If the currency stays within an agreed range, the rate is significantly improved relative the vanilla forward	If spot goes outside of the range, the forward rate to be paid becomes more expensive
Cross-currency coupon swap	Buy a currency swap and at the same time pay fixed and receive floating	Lets you manage FX and interest rate risk in markets suited to the corporation	Leaves the buyer vulnerable to both currency and interest rate risk
Cross-currency basis swap	Buy a currency swap, at the same time pay floating interest in a currency and receive floating in another	Currency risk is the same as a standard currency swap, but the basis currency swap allows you to capture interest rate differentials	The risk in this structure is interest rate risk rather than currency risk

7.9   HEDGING STRATEGIES

7.9.1   Hedging Transaction Risk

The unbiased forward rate theory suggests the expected spot exchange rate is the forward rate. If this worked, it would mean that failing to hedge currency risk would yield similar results in the long run to hedging. There are two problems with this. First, the Treasurer would probably be fired before the "long run" arrived. Second, the unbiased forward rate theory is a poor predictor of future exchange rates in practice. Basically it does not work. Therefore, a corporation should use market-based currency forecasting in addition to the forward rate to predict future exchange rates. The discretionary aspect to the currency forecast means the corporation has the choice of hedging:

- Tactically and selectively
- Strategically
- Passively

Corporations vary in their attitude towards transaction hedging. Some hedge passively, that is to say they maintain the same hedging structure and execute over regular periods during the financial year. This type of transaction hedging does not involve the corporation "taking a (currency) view". The other two types of hedging strategy do indeed involve taking a currency view. Strategic hedging involves the corporation taking a view for a longer period than immediate transaction receivables and payables might require. In January 1999, I remember wave after wave of European corporations hedging both developed and emerging market currency risk as far out as one year. Corporations who usually called in USD20–30 million to hedge very short-term receivables were calling for prices in a number of emerging market currency pairs in USD200–300 million. The Russian crisis of August 1998 and the collapse of LTCM had clearly scared global financial markets. With the threat looming of devaluation in Brazil (which indeed happened in January 1999), many European corporations were apparently taking advantage of the relaxation in global market tensions and reduced risk premiums in the market in the wake of the Fed's extraordinary monetary easing of August and September, with three interest rate cuts in quick succession to hedge their transactional currency risk as far out as they could go. That is an example of strategic hedging. Finally, tactical and selective hedging of transactional currency risk is the usual business that a corporate dealing desk does with its clients. A bank's clients may choose to allow certain currency exposures to be translated at the period end, and others they may choose to hedge, depending crucially on their currency view. Typically, it makes sense for a corporation to use the tactical and selective approach for most transactional currency risks and only occasionally to pull the trigger on strategic hedging should the need arise. While passive hedging may appeal to some, it hurts flexibility, not only with regard to the hedging strategy but also with regard to domestic pricing.

7.9.2   Hedging the Balance Sheet

While corporate Treasury is usually active in hedging transaction currency risk, it rarely considers translation risk — or hedging the balance sheet. This is largely because balance sheet risk is largely made up of foreign direct investment or the debt structure of the corporation. In the first case, the management has a natural and instinctive objection to the idea of hedging the balance sheet risk, involving a direct investment abroad, since that would seem to negate the reason for the initial investment. For this very reason, many corporations do not hedge translation or balance sheet risk because of:

- The long-term nature of their investments in subsidiaries
- The perceived zero-sum nature of currency risk over the long term
- Accounting and tax issues
- Cash flow impacts

A further disincentive is that currency translation affects the balance sheet rather than the income statement, which may make it less of an immediate priority for management. Equity analysts tend to focus on EBIT (or EBITDA) before debt/equity ratios. Eventually, however, the deterioration in balance sheet ratios can impact the corporation's average cost of capital and ultimately its valuation in the market place.

Example

European exporters with US subsidiaries have seen two major benefits as a result of the Euro's weakness against the US dollar over the last two years. Firstly, at the direct level, this Euro weakness has made their exports cheaper to the US, allowing them to lower export prices and thus gain market share. Secondly, Euro weakness has, just as we saw with the previous Polish example, boosted the Euro value of their US subsidiaries. At some stage, the Euro's decline against the dollar may reverse. How would the corporate Treasury best cope with this? The export question concerns transaction exposure. The question of the subsidiary's value when translated back into Euros is one of *translation* currency risk or exposure. In this case, both types of "polar" hedge — zero or 100% hedged — seem inappropriate. The risk of the Euro rallying on a sustained basis against the dollar may be seen by many as small, but it is not zero. Therefore it would be inappropriate to have a zero-rate balance sheet hedge to cover the risk of valuation loss in the subsidiary. On the other hand, it would also seem extreme to hedge 100% of the subsidiary's value. A neat way round this dilemma might be to use a variable hedge ratio for net balance sheet exposures, which are triggered by the interest rate differential. Remember that when hedging balance sheet risk, what you are hedging is the net assets (gross assets less liabilities) of the subsidiary or subsidiaries that may be affected by an adverse exchange rate move. Thus, important considerations are the financing, net cash flows and intangibles relating to those subsidiaries. The corporation's debt structure is also an important consideration. Corporations with higher local tax rates tend to debt finance their investments in order to reduce their average cost of capital.

There are two parts to this issue however. Up to now, we have looked at the idea of hedging the risk within the consolidated balance sheet relating to foreign investment. The other part of this issue relates to the corporation's debt profile. The risk this represents is broadly affected by the debt's currency and maturity composition. The corporation can change this currency and maturity composition to reduce the degree to which exchange rates are able to cause volatility in net equity and earnings. Optimization can be used for this purpose, though this will not completely eliminate currency risk and tactical hedging may be needed in addition.

There is no question that hedging balance sheet risk is more easily quantifiable than is the case with economic risk. That said, hedging the remaining currency exposure after you optimize the debt composition remains a controversial subject because it can be expensive, the corporation may regret the decision to hedge if exchange rates do not move in the anticipated direction and balance sheet hedging may cause either cash flow or earnings volatility, which is in fact what you are trying to avoid. Ultimately, the decision whether or not to hedge balance sheet risk must be a function of weighing the real costs of hedging against the intangible costs of not hedging. This is certainly not science. That should not be an excuse however for ignoring balance sheet risk.

7.9.3 Hedging Economic Exposure

Economic risk or exposure reflects the degree to which the present value of future cash flows may be affected by exchange rate moves. However, exchange rate moves are themselves related through PPP to differences in inflation rates. A corporation whose foreign subsidiary experiences cost inflation exactly in line with the general inflation rate should see its original value restored by exchange rate moves in line with PPP. In that case, some may argue economic exposure does not matter. However, most corporations experience cost inflation that differs from the general inflation rate, which in turn affects their competitiveness relative to competitors. In this case, economic exposure clearly does matter and the best way to hedge it is to finance operations in the currency to which the corporation's value is sensitive.

7.10   OPTIMIZATION

As with investors, corporations can use an "optimization" model to create an "efficient frontier" of hedging strategies to manage their currency risk. This measures the cost of the hedge against the degree of risk hedged. Thus, the most efficient hedging strategy is that which is the cheapest for the most risk hedged. This is a very efficient and useful tool for hedging currency risk in a more sophisticated way than just buying a vanilla hedge and "hoping" it is the appropriate strategy. Hedging optimizers frequently compare the following strategies to find the optimal one for the given currency view and exposure:

- 100% hedged using vanilla forwards
- 100% unhedged
- Option risk reversal
- Option call spread
- Option low-delta call

While such an approach to managing risk is extremely helpful in providing the cheapest hedging structure for a given risk profile, it is not perfect and relies on a discretionary exchange rate view. Further research needs to be done in turning a corporation's risk profile into a mathematical answer rather than a discretionary view. A starting point for this may be found in the type of equity market profile the corporation wants to create — value, income, defensive and so forth. From this, it may be possible to suggest an optimal profit stream the corporation should generate according to this profile and from this in turn we may be able to extrapolate a more exact hedging strategy to maintain that profit stream than simply a discretionary view might give.

As it is, optimization, using a corporate risk optimizer (CROP), can be undertaken for transaction, translation or economic currency risk as long as one knows the risks entailed and gives a specific currency view within that. For example, if a corporation is looking for the best and most efficient hedging strategy in emerging market currencies, a CROP model can integrate the specific characteristics of those currencies together with the size of the exposure and hedging objectives (efficient frontier, performance maximization, risk minimization).

Performance can be measured as P&L, an effective hedging rate or a distance to a given budget rate. The risk embedded in the hedge is expressed as a VaR number that will be consistent with the performance measure. While most CROP models do not provide a hedging process for basket currency hedging, they are very useful for finding the most efficient hedge for individual currency exposures. A CROP model is thus a tool for optimizing hedging strategies for currency-denominated cash flows.

Users of a CROP model are able to define the nature of their specific exposure and hedging objectives. The model also allows for scenario building, whether it be a neutral market view, the incorporation of budget/benchmark rates or the jump risk associated with emerging market currencies. If the objective is risk reduction, an efficient frontier can be created to find the most efficient hedge, which incorporates the cheapest hedge which offsets the most risk. Both performance and VaR are measured as effective rates.

Emerging markets are an example where corporate hedging used to adopt a binary approach — that is, to hedge or not to hedge. Options are a perfect tool for hedging, taking account of long periods when emerging market currencies do nothing and also capturing dramatic moves when they occur. They are cheaper and leave the corporation less exposed to an adverse exchange rate move. Furthermore, a CROP model can give the optimal hedging strategy using options or forwards for a given currency view and a given currency exposure. The way this works is as follows:

- Determine a possible exchange rate scenario over a specified time period, say six months.
- Run a random distribution within the scenario specified.
- Calculate the effective hedge rate for each hedging instrument used and the risk in local currency points.
- Solve to find the hedging strategy with the lowest possible effective hedge rate for various accepted levels of uncertainty.

It should of course be noted that it is not possible to choose a single optimal hedging strategy without defining the risk one is allowed or willing to take. In scenarios reflecting a perception of volatility or jump risk, options will always produce a better or similar effective hedge rate at lower uncertainty than the unhedged position. Where the local currency has a relatively high yield and low volatility, options will almost always produce a better effective hedging rate than forward hedging.

7.11   HEDGING EMERGING MARKET CURRENCY RISK

Emerging market currencies have important characteristics which a corporation needs to take account of with specific regard to a currency hedging programme:

- Liquidity risk,
- Convertibility risk,
- Event risk,
- Jump risk.
- Discontinuous price action.
- Implied volatility is a very poor guide to future spot price action.
- In emerging market currency crises, the exchange rate weakens in at least two waves after an event, with the maximum devaluation usually found in the first nine months (and this period seems to be decreasing, that is the market "learns").

- Interest rates often peak just prior to such an event unless a new exchange rate regime has been attempted or the spot move is really large.
- Interest rates become an estimate of the size of the final event, making short-term interest rates the most volatile.
- Whenever the implied emerging market volatility is below the implied vol of a major (i.e. when the Euro–zloty implied is below Euro–dollar) this has proven to be unsustainable in the past and a very good level to buy.
- Besides range trading, emerging market implied vol tends to fall only when the emerging market currency is strengthening.
- Implied vol always increases on emerging market currency weakness.

7.12   BENCHMARKS FOR CURRENCY RISK MANAGEMENT

Corporations can use a variety of hedging benchmarks to manage their hedging strategies more rigorously. Aside from the hedging level as the benchmark (e.g. 75%), corporations which want to limit fluctuation in net equity use the reporting period as the benchmark for forward hedging. Typically, US companies hedge quarterly whereas European corporations use 12-month benchmarks given different disclosure requirements. Accounting rules have a major impact on what hedging benchmarks corporations use. Budget rates are also used to define the benchmark hedging performance and tenor of a hedge, as these would generally match cash flow requirements.

Using a benchmark enables the performance of an individual hedge to be measured against the standard set for the company as a whole, which should be set out within the currency risk management policy.

7.13   BUDGET RATES

The setting of budget rates is crucially important for a corporation as it can drive not only the corporation's hedging but also its pricing strategy as well. Budget exchange rates can be set in several ways. The benchmark or budget rate for an investment in a foreign subsidiary should normally be the exchange rate at the close of the previous fiscal period, often referred to as the accounting rate. On the other hand, when dealing with forecasted cash flows, the issue becomes more complex. Theoretically, the budget exchange rate should be derived from the domestic sales price, which is the operating cost plus the desired profit margin, as an expression of the foreign subsidiary sales price. Thus, if the parent sales price for a good is USD10 and the Euro area sales price is EUR15, the budget rate should be 0.67. The actual exchange rate for Euro–dollar may be some way away from that. Thus, the corporation needs to evaluate the degree of demand for its product relative to changes in the product's Euro price to see whether or not it has leeway to cut its Euro price without also reducing margin substantially in order to set a budget rate that is closer to the spot exchange rate. If there is a major difference between the spot and budget exchange rates, either the hedging or the pricing strategy may have to be reconsidered.

Corporations can also set the budget rate so as to link in with their sales calendar and thus their hedging strategy. If a corporation has a quarterly sales calendar it may want to hedge in such a way that its foreign currency sales in one quarter is no less than that of the same quarter one year before, implying that it should make four hedges per year, each of one-year tenor. Alternatively, instead of hedging at the end of a period, thus using the end-of-period exchange rate as its budget rate, the corporation may choose to set a daily average rate as its budget rate. In this case, if the corporation chooses as its budget rate the daily average rate for the previous fiscal year, it only needs to execute one hedge. It stands to reason that the best way of achieving this in the market place is to use an average-based instrument such as an option or a synthetic forward, entered into on the last day of the previous fiscal year, with its starting day being the first day of the new fiscal year. Of late, an option structure known as a double average rate option (DARO) has become increasingly popular among multinational corporations. This allows a corporation to protect the average value of a foreign currency cash flow over a specified time period relative to another period. This is a simple way of passive currency hedging, taking out discretionary uncertainties and instead putting the hedging programme on auto pilot where it can be more easily monitored.

Whether a corporation hedges currency risk passively or actively, once the budget rate is set the Treasury is responsible for securing an appropriate hedge rate and ensuring there is minimal slippage relative to that hedge rate. Timing and the instruments used are key to being able to achieve that. The last point to make on budget rates is that they flow naturally from relative price differentials. This however is also the heart of the concept of PPP, which states that exchange rates should adjust for relative price differentials of the same good between two countries. While PPP models are of relatively little use in forecasting short-term exchange rate moves, they have a substantially better record in forecasting exchange rates over the long term. Thus, a corporation could do worse than setting the budget rate with a PPP model in mind, albeit with the realization that tactical hedging may be necessary either side of that budget rate over the short term in order to capture exchange rate deviation from where PPP suggests it should be. Finally, it is important to underline that budget rates can provide companies with one thing only: a level of reference. Set up randomly, they are of very little use. And at some point, prolonged currency moves against the functional currency must be passed on, or strategic positioning and hedging must be addressed; in any case two topics well beyond our budget rates discussion. In the end, while the process of setting budget rates cannot resolve all of a corporation's issues, it can be dramatically improved by clearly defining the company's sensitivities and benchmarking priorities. The hedging frequency as well as the choice of the hedge instrument will naturally flow from this process.

7.14   THE CORPORATION AND PREDICTING EXCHANGE RATES

A key aspect of corporate pricing strategy is forecasting future exchange rates. Aside from using banks to help them do this, the internal models corporations use are typically one or more of the following kinds:

- Political event analysis
- Fundamental
- Technical

For the reasons we have mentioned earlier in this chapter, it is not a good idea for corporations to use the forward rate as a predictor of the future spot rate because of "forward rate bias" — the idea that the unbiased forward rate theory does not in fact work. Academics argue that markets are efficient and therefore there is no point in corporations trying to "beat the market" by forecasting future exchange rates. This supposition is premised on a falsehood — markets may be efficient over the long term, but they are inherently inefficient over short time periods. The latter can be substantial enough to make a material impact on the corporation's income statement were it to assume a perfectly efficient market and use unbiased forward rate theory accordingly.

The importance of market-based forecasts for the corporation is derived from comparing these to anticipated net cash flows. For the corporation, the crucial question is how will these cash flows respond if the future spot exchange rate is not equal to the forecast? The nature of this kind of forecast is completely different from trying to outguess the foreign exchange markets.

7.15 SUMMARY

In this chapter, we have taken a detailed look at some of the advanced approaches to corporate strategy with regard to exchange rates. Managing currency risk is not a luxury but a necessity for multinational corporations. That said, just realizing it is a necessity does not make the practical reality of hedging any easier. The field of how corporations hedge specific types of currency risk has become increasingly sophisticated in the last few years. The issue of transaction risk hedging is merely the tip of the iceberg! Below the water line, translation and economic currency risk are real issues which ultimately can affect the profitability and the market's valuation of the corporation. Boards ignore these issues at their peril.

Having taken a look at the corporate world, we switch now to that of the institutional investor. Just as with corporations, there is a reluctance within some investors to hedge or manage currency risk and for the same reasons, not least that participating in the currency market is seen as being outside of the investor's core competence. This may well be so, but the reality is that the investor is a participant in the currency market whether they like it or not. Moreover, currency risk can make up a significant portion of the investor's portfolio volatility and return. It is to this world of the investor that we now turn.

8

Managing Currency Risk II — The Investor: Currency Exposure within the Investment Decision

Investors and corporations face similar types of risk on foreign currency exposure. For instance, investors face *transaction risk* when they invest abroad. They also face *translation risk* on assets and liabilities if they spread their operations overseas. For its part, the corporate sector clearly seems to have moved to a view that currency risk is an unavoidable issue that has to be managed independently from the underlying business. Within the investor world, the battle for hearts and minds on this issue is ongoing. There remain specific types of investor who are ideologically opposed to the idea of managing currency risk. However, here too, there are signs of a gradual shift towards the view that currencies are an asset class in their own right and therefore currency risk should be managed separately and independently from the underlying assets, as the continuing rise in the number of currency overlay mandates would appear to confirm.

8.1 INVESTORS AND CURRENCY RISK

The relationship between institutional investors and the idea of currency risk has been an uneasy one. For a start, there remain an overly large number of investors who are either unwilling or unable, due to the specific regulations of their fund, to consider currency risk as separate and independent from the underlying risk of their investment. Such a view is particularly prevalent among equity, although it is also present to a smaller extent with fixed income fund managers.

The aim of this chapter is to err on the practical, to take the ideological out of the equation and seek to demonstrate empirically and theoretically that managing currency risk can consistently boost a portfolio's return.

On the face of it, this chapter may seem targeted at only those who manage currency risk on an active basis. This is not the case. Rather, it is aimed at any institutional investor who faces in the course of their "underlying business" exposure to a foreign currency, whether or not they are in fact allowed to carry out some of the ideas and strategies presented herein. Let us start then with two core principles on the issue of currency risk:

1. Investing in a country is not the same as investing in that country's currency.
2. Currency is not the same as cash; the incentive for currency investment is primarily capital gain rather than income.

Almost before we have started, some may view the above as controversial. In my career, I have come up against not infrequent opposition to these principles, albeit for varying reasons. The answer I have given back has always been the same:

The dynamics that drive a currency are not the same as those that drive asset markets

8.2   CURRENCY MARKETS ARE DIFFERENT

Throughout this book, we have looked, albeit from varying perspectives, at the governing dynamics that drive the global currency markets. If we have learned one thing, it is surely this, that the currency markets are by their nature predominantly *"speculative"*. That is to say, the majority of currency market participants are what we would define as "speculators", using the definition of this book for currency speculation as the trading or investing in currencies without any underlying, attached asset. The predominance of speculation within currency markets is neither a good nor a bad thing. On the one hand, it provides needed liquidity for those aspects of the economy deemed productive rather than speculative. On the other hand, it can and frequently does lead to overshooting relative to perceived economic fundamentals.

The speculative nature of the currency markets may be an important reason why most long-term fundamental equilibrium models work poorly in trying to forecast exchange rates. At the least, it serves as an excellent excuse for those who otherwise are unable to forecast exchange rates using the traditional methods. All of this may be true, and all of it makes for a very different world from those of the equity or fixed income, markets. By necessity, these are not speculative by nature since they are themselves underlying assets relating to the economy in some way. This is not at all to suggest that speculation does not occur in equities or fixed income, for any such suggestion would clearly be foolish. The recent bubble in the NASDAQ should serve as an excellent warning for any who think these markets are always fundamentally-driven and incapable of speculative excess. That said, this same example is surely notable by its rarity. Throughout history, there have indeed been examples of speculative excess across all markets. In equity and fixed income markets, relative to "normal" conditions however, these are the exception rather than the rule. This is not the case in currency markets, where traditional economic theory has all but given up trying to explain short-term moves and longer-term exchange rate models have far from perfect results.

The dynamics of the asset and currency markets are "fundamentally" different. Therefore these risks should be dealt with separately and independently from one another. For the international equity fund manager, investing in a country is not the same and should not be the same decision as investing in a country's currency. Eventually, they may have the same risk profile over a long period of time. However it is questionable whether the investor's tracking error and Sharpe ratio, not to say the investor themselves, should have to go through that degree of stress!

Equally, currency is not the same as cash. An individual investor may treat currency as cash from a relative performance perspective. Unfortunately, however, such a comparison provides a false picture. Most currency market participants, and therefore the currency market as a whole, do not buy or sell currencies for the income that a "cash" description would of necessity entail. On the contrary, they do so for anticipated directional or capital gain. In other words, they are seeking to profit from precisely the risk that the investor is not hedging! It is a generalization, but nevertheless true that the reluctance to manage currency risk is far more predominant among equity fund managers than fixed income fund managers. That may have something to do with the intended tenor of the investment, suggesting fixed income fund managers may be more short-term in investment strategy than their equity counterparts. Any such view seems greatly oversimplistic, and would require a study on its own to verify or otherwise. Many cannot manage currency risk simply because the rules of their fund do not allow them so to do. There remains however a substantial community of institutional investors who apparently have yet to be convinced by either the merits or the need to manage currency risk separately. By the end of this chapter, it is my hope that I will have caused many within this community to at least reconsider their view as regards currency risk. To summarize this part, the way currencies and underlying assets are analysed and the way they trade are both different from each other. Consequently, the way they should be managed should also be different.

8.3   TO HEDGE OR NOT TO HEDGE — THAT IS THE QUESTION!

Central to the idea of managing currency risk separately and independently from the risk represented by the underlying asset is the issue of whether or not to hedge that currency risk. Just as the idea of separating currency risk continues to attract much debate, so the more specific issue of hedging out that currency risk remains a topic of much controversy and discussion, both within the academic world and within the financial markets themselves. Indeed, while there may be some who take a pragmatic view of compromise, approaching this from the perspective of a case-by-case basis, the majority seem polarized between two opposite and opposing camps. Within the academic world, this is expressed at opposite ends of the spectrum by Perold and Schulman (1988) and by Froot and Thaler (1990, 1993), who advocated on the one hand full hedging of currency risk and on the other leaving currency risk unhedged.

There is a clear division of opinion within the financial markets as well, if perhaps marginally less pronounced and polarized. Within the institutional investor community, international equity funds are generally known for taking a view of either not hedging currency risk or adopting an unhedged currency benchmark. Fixed income funds are clearly more tolerant of the idea of hedging currency risk, frequently adopting a currency hedging benchmark that reflects such a view. We will go through the range of possible currency hedging benchmarks shortly, but for now suffice to say that they vary at the most basic level, being hedged (partially or fully) and unhedged. The "sell side", which is used to selling foreign exchange-type products, is well versed in the need for hedging availability. Conversely, the fixed income sell side within the financial industry in general appears to focus more on selling the core product rather than on its denomination, or the potential need to separate and hedge out that corresponding currency risk.

In response, the majority of rigorous studies have distilled this debate down to an elegant compromise between risk and reward, focusing less on an absolute answer to the question than the need to account for the individual investor's requirements and the portfolio variance across the spectrum of hedging strategies. The debate between hedging or not hedging thus remains unresolved, and there appears little prospect on the horizon of that changing. There is no one answer to the question of whether or not to hedge currency risk, nor perhaps should there be. Any such answer depends crucially on the specifics of the investor's portfolio aims and constraints. The assumption might on the face of it be that one's approach to managing currency risk can be broken down simply into active or passive — or alternatively not to manage currency risk! At a slightly more sophisticated level however, the focus should be on the type of returns targeted; that is absolute vs. relative returns.

8.4   ABSOLUTE RETURNS — RISK REDUCTION

Just as a corporation has to decide whether to run their Treasury operation as a profit or as a risk reduction centre, so a portfolio manager has to make the same kind of choice. While one can theoretically change one's core approach to managing the portfolio at any time, it is usually better to make that choice right at the start. In the process, the portfolio manager should decide what style of portfolio management is to be adopted as regards the underlying investments, the desired return profile of the portfolio and also the style of currency management to be used.

In the case of a portfolio manager who is focusing on absolute returns, the currency risk management style that is synonymous with this focuses on reducing the risk of the overall portfolio. This in turn usually means adopting a passive style of currency risk management.

8.4.1   Passive Currency Management

Passive currency hedging or currency management involves the creation of a currency hedging benchmark and sticking to that benchmark come what may, avoiding any slippage. As a result, it involves the taking of standard currency hedges and then continuing to roll those for the life of the investment. The two obvious ways of establishing a passive hedging strategy are for instance:

- Three-month forward (rolled continuously)
- Three-month at-the-money forward call (rolled continuously)

The advantage of passive currency management is that it reduces or eliminates the currency risk (depending on whether the benchmark is fully or partially hedged). The disadvantage is that it does not incorporate any flexibility and therefore cannot respond to changes in market dynamics and conditions. Passive currency management can be done either by the portfolio manager themselves or by a currency overlay manager, and focuses on reducing the overall risk profile of the portfolio.

8.4.2   Risk Reduction

The emphasis on risk reduction within a passive currency management style deals with the basic idea that the portfolio's return in the base currency is equal to:

The return of foreign assets invested in + the return of the foreign currency

This is a simple, but hopefully effective way of expressing the view that there are two separate and distinct risks present within the decision to invest outside of the base currency. The motive of risk reduction is therefore to hedge to whatever extent decided upon the return of the foreign currency. From this basic premise, we can extrapolate the following:

$$\text{Return (unhedged)} = \text{Return (asset)} + \text{Return (currency)}$$

and

$$\text{Return (hedged)} = \text{Return (asset)} + \text{Return (hedge currency)}$$

The overall aim remains the same, and that is to reduce the overall risk of the portfolio, maximizing the total or absolute return in the process. In other words, it is to boost the portfolio's Sharpe ratio, which is usually defined as the (annual) excess return as a proportion of the (annual) standard deviation or risk involved.

It should be noted from this formula however that some investors balk at the idea of hedging on the simplistic view that the hedge cost automatically reduces not just the hedged return of the asset but the asset's total return in base currency terms. This is not necessarily the case. Actually, the converse can be argued, namely that the hedge reduces or eliminates any

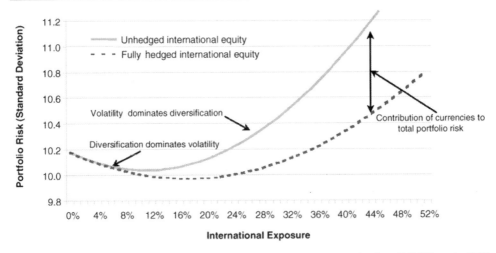

Figure 8.1   USD balanced investor, 1973–1999: EAFE + Canada combined to 60% US equity/40% US bond portfolio

possible currency loss. Whether or not the investor hedges, there is the foreign currency return to be considered. That may add or detract from the asset return in foreign currency terms, and therefore may in turn boost or reduce the asset return in domestic currency terms. The hedging cost component will clearly depend on a number of variables, including the currency hedging benchmark and the financial instruments that can be used, but has clear parameters. The potential unhedged currency loss is theoretically limitless.

Example

As an example of risk reduction, we will take an average balanced investor with international exposure. As Figure 8.1 shows, looking from 1973 to 1999, currency hedging can significantly reduce the overall risk profile of the portfolio.

8.5   SELECTING THE CURRENCY HEDGING BENCHMARK

A crucial decision for portfolio managers who want to manage their currency risk, whether actively or passively, is the selection of their currency hedging benchmark. After all, when we are talking about managing currency risk, we are really talking about establishing whether or not there may be a need to hedge out that currency risk. Using a currency hedging benchmark is a more disciplined and rigorous way of managing currency risk than either not hedging or at the other extreme conducting all currency hedging on a discretionary and "gut feel" basis.

There are four main currency hedging benchmarks used by institutional investors, which can be divided into:

- 100% hedged benchmark
- 100% unhedged benchmark
- Partially hedged benchmark
- Option hedged benchmark

Being 100% hedged is usually not the optimal strategy, apart from in exceptional cases. Equally, using a currency hedging benchmark of 100% unhedged would seem to defeat the purpose of managing currency risk, again apart from in exceptional cases. A further consideration is that many funds are not allowed to use options as they are viewed as a speculative financial instrument, ironically in the same way that some corporations are also not allowed to use them. This still leaves them however with the choice of three possible currency hedging benchmarks of 100% hedged, 100% unhedged or partially hedged. The primary instrument for such hedging would be the forward for passive currency management, though active currency managers would no doubt have greater flexibility, both in the currencies in which they can operate and the financial instruments they can use.

Currency hedging benchmarks of 0% or 100% are known as asymmetrical or polar benchmarks and have obvious limitations. With a polar benchmark, an active currency manager is able to take positions only in one direction. As a result, their ability to add value is also limited. For example, it is extremely difficult for a currency manager to be able to add value operating under an unhedged currency benchmark when foreign currencies are appreciating because the manager is generally unable to take on additional foreign currency exposure. The best the manager can do is to mimic the benchmark by holding the unhedged benchmark exposure and avoiding hedging. Similarly, when operating under a fully hedged benchmark, it is difficult for a manager to add value when foreign currencies are falling.

Adoption and use of benchmarks depends critically on the currency risk management style, for which the type of fund is clearly a key determinant. For instance, a pension fund manager may use a fully hedged or alternatively unhedged currency benchmark to either reduce risk on the one hand or minimize transaction costs on the other. Meanwhile, the active currency manager will seek a partially hedged benchmark, preferably 50%, to give them as much flexibility and room as possible with which to be able to add value. With such a symmetrical benchmark, active currency managers can take advantage of both bull and bear markets in their currencies. In the context of *relative returns*, it should therefore be of no surprise that there is good evidence to suggest that symmetrical benchmarks have consistently added more "*alpha*" than their asymmetrical counterparts.

Example

A classic example of a group of international investors that typically use one specific type of currency hedging benchmark is that of **international equity funds**, which generally either do not hedge or adopt unhedged benchmarks. Though the technical details are different between these two approaches, they amount to the same thing. There may be some debate as to what should be the optimum currency benchmark for an international equity fund in terms of the hedging ratio. However, what is clear is that the hedging ratio for these should in theory be higher than for those funds with only a small portion of international equity risk, on the simple premise that the higher the currency risk the higher the required hedge ratio. Despite this, unhedged currency benchmarks remain very popular among this group of investors. In part, this is because many fund managers still suggest that the long-term expected return of currencies is zero and in addition that currency hedging generates unnecessary transaction costs. Furthermore, the idea that investing in a country means investing in the currency remains prevalent within international equity funds.

For the reasons that we have already outlined earlier in this chapter, we would dispute both these views. The very idea of long term is subjective for one thing. For another, currency weakness in the short term may lead to intolerable mark-to-market and tracking error deterioration. Finally, the trading and analytical dynamics of currency and asset markets are as we suggested different from one another, ergo the two risks they represent should be treated and managed separately and independently from one another. Generally speaking therefore, we would suggest having an unhedged currency benchmark would be inappropriate, even supposing the currency risk management motive was for risk reduction rather than adding alpha. Using a partially hedged benchmark can undoubtedly reduce the portfolio's overall risk and thus boost its Sharpe and information ratios.

A possible exception to this broad disagreement with the general idea of using unhedged benchmarks is where the fund has only a small portion of its assets in international as opposed to domestic equities. Indeed, if the international allocation of an equity fund is below 10–15%, it may not make sense to have a hedging benchmark above that allocation as that might in fact add to the portfolio's risk while detracting from the return. In other words, under certain circumstances it may make sense to use an unhedged benchmark for those equity funds with only a small international allocation. Generally however, if an international equity fund has an international allocation that significantly exceeds its benchmark weight, this represents unnecessary currency risk that should be managed.

8.6 RELATIVE RETURNS — ADDING ALPHA

Asset managers who are focused on absolute returns when managing their currency risk tend to use strategies that are characterized by risk reduction, adopting a passive currency management approach in order to achieve this. By contrast, funds that are focused on relative returns tend to manage currency risk more actively. Their aim is after all to outperform an unhedged position, or in some cases the hedged benchmark, in other words to "*add alpha*". In this, there is no "right" and "wrong". It depends completely on the risk management style of the fund and what risk approach it takes towards both the underlying assets and also the embedded currency risk.

8.6.1 Active Currency Management

Active currency management around a currency benchmark means the fund has given either the asset manager or a professional currency overlay manager the mandate to "trade" the currency around the currency hedging benchmark for the explicit purpose of adding alpha to the total return of the portfolio.

With active currency management, the emphasis should be on flexibility, both in terms of the availability of financial instruments one can use to add alpha and also in terms of the currency hedging benchmark. On the first of these, an active currency manager should have access to a broad spectrum of currency instruments in order to boost their chance of adding value. Similarly, their ability to add value is significantly increased by the adoption of a 50% or symmetrical currency hedging benchmark rather than by a 100% hedged or 100% unhedged benchmark.

8.6.2 Adding "Alpha"

The motive of risk reduction is primarily defensive, in that it seeks to defend or maintain the portfolio's return within a given tolerance of overall risk. That for adding "alpha" on the other hand is quite different, in so much as "alpha" refers to the excess return generated by an active currency manager relative to a passive hedging programme.

Economic theory suggests that the long-term return of a currency is zero, so how can an active currency manager add value or "alpha"? There appear to be two aspects to this question. Firstly, currency markets are dominated by short-term movement. Thus, while their long-term return may be zero, their short-term returns (and losses!) may be significant. Secondly, it should be remembered that the same theory that suggested there were fundamental equilibrium levels for currencies also suggests that their long-term returns are zero. While not rejecting such a theory outright, it should surely be treated with some care, put in this context.

Indeed, there is a fine — and increasing — body of academic work that suggests that contrary to theory, managing currency risk can indeed add "alpha". Among these, I will draw out several notable examples. Firstly, while formulating his "Universal Hedging Policy" in 1989, Fisher Black suggested that currency was, contrary to theory, not a zero sum game and investors could indeed increase their returns by holding currency inventories. Needless to say, this contradicted the widely held view that currencies could not provide added value because currency markets were perfectly efficient. A relatively short time after that, Mark Kritzman put forward the view that active currency managers could take advantage of the apparent serial correlation in currency returns. Subsequent research by Taylor (1990) and Silber (1994) targeted market trends as being behind persistent positive returns from currency managers.

Two further research reports that should be mentioned are those by Strange (1998, updated 2001) and The Frank Russell Company (2000). In the first case, the survey by Brian Strange, as published in *Pensions and Investment* (15/6/98), entitled "Do Currency Managers Add Value?" stated that of the 152 individual currency overlay programmes managed by 11 firms, these produced an average of 1.9% per year over a 10-year review period from 1988 to 1998, while simultaneously reducing the risk of the portfolio. In other words, not only did currency managers consistently add value, but their action of seeking to manage currency risk also helped lower the overall risk profile of the portfolio, thus boosting the Sharpe ratio from both sides! The second example is that of the Frank Russell study of May 2000 entitled "Capturing Alpha through Active Currency Overlay", which analysed the historical performance of currency overlay mandates and confirmed the view that managing currency risk does indeed add value or "alpha".

As noted above, a host of empirical studies have proven conclusively that active currency management can indeed boost the portfolio's return, both on an absolute basis and in this context relative to not hedging, in contrast to classical exchange rate theory. In line with this, a number of studies have been published suggesting clear market inefficiencies, which might therefore be taken advantage of by active currency managers. For instance, the 1993 study by Kritzman, suggesting that the discount/premium of the currency forward contract "systematically and significantly overestimated the subsequent change in the spot rate". Kritzman also introduced the concept of so-called "bilateral asymmetry", referring to a bias by risk-averse investors for the perceived predictable returns of the interest rate differential as opposed to the unpredictable returns of the currency. Work by Choie (1993) supported these findings. Overall, a body of informed opinion has developed, supportive of the view that active currency management can add value.

After finally admitting that currency markets may offer profit potential, whether over the short or long term, academic theorists have suggested that such profit opportunities may exist in currency markets because there are some currency market participants that are not solely or even mainly motivated by profit. Classical theory suggests rational currency market participants are solely profit-seeking and moreover offset each other, with the result that any outstanding profit opportunities are instantly arbitraged away. Thus, from this, they seek to explain the existence of sustained profit opportunities within currency markets by suggesting that non-profit-seeking currency market participants such as central banks, tourists and national or corporate Treasuries effectively distort pricing. To me, such a view appears more reflective of the guesswork of someone who does not actually know the answer but is afraid to own up. Currency markets generate profits because it is the theory that they should not that is wrong rather than the currency market itself.

Active currency management can add value because there is value to be had in currency markets, plain and simple. Within this, an active currency manager will clearly favour the most flexibility possible to add that value, both in terms of the currency benchmark that they have to operate under and the currencies and financial instruments with which they are allowed to trade. For the active currency manager, the foreign currency return is not just a matter of currency translation of the underlying asset, but also of the excess return or alpha that the currency manager is able to add. The alpha an active currency manager generates is usually measured against an unhedged position. However, probably a truer idea of the alpha the active currency manager generates would come from comparing their returns to those of a passive currency management strategy of maintaining the benchmark hedge ratio. Historically, the typical mandate has allowed managers to vary the hedge ratio between 0 and 100% regardless of the benchmark.

8.6.3 Tracking Error

Just as corporations have to deal with "forecasting error" in terms of the deviation of forecast exchange rates relative to the actual future rate, so investors have to deal with "tracking error" within their portfolios, which is the return of the portfolio relative to the investment benchmark index being used. Within this, there is "expected" and "realized" tracking error. Expected tracking error is as the name suggests determined before the fact — ex ante — whereas the realized tracking error is determined after the fact.

Determining the relevance of tracking error is also a function of comparing the portfolio's hedging strategy with a random strategy, which creates hedge/don't hedge signals with equal probability on a regular basis. Using polar benchmarks — i.e. 0% or 100% hedged — the equal probability of the outcome of the random strategy suggests that hedge deviations will be zero in half the cases and 100% in half the cases. However, with a partially hedged currency benchmark, the deviations will vary in direct proportion to the ratio of the benchmark. For instance, for a symmetrical or 50% hedged currency benchmark, the deviations will be 50% from each side of the benchmark.

From this, we can gather two things, firstly that the tracking error — or the deviation — is a function of the hedged ratio used for benchmarking and secondly that the tracking error for a partially hedged benchmark should be less than that for a polar benchmark. Indeed, generally, the tracking error for a symmetrical or 50% currency hedging benchmark should be around 70% of the tracking error using polar benchmarks. Expressed differently, the tracking error of a polar benchmark should be 1.41 (square root of 2) times higher than that of a 50% hedged benchmark.

The advantage of a symmetrical or 50% currency hedged benchmark for a portfolio manager is that it reduces the tracking error of the portfolio and also enables them to participate in both bull and bear markets compared to the polar benchmark where the participation is limited to either/or.

Tracking error can be further reduced by a technique known as "matched hedging", which increases or decreases the hedge ratio relative to the change in asset allocation. Historically, the act of asset allocation itself within fixed income portfolios has been a major and seemingly unavoidable factor in increasing a portfolio's tracking error. Matched hedging can reduce though clearly not eliminate this.

Tracking error can also occur under passive currency management. This is because in order to implement a passive currency hedging programme a portfolio manager still has to adjust the amount of the currency hedge relative to the value of the underlying as it changes on a regular basis — i.e. once a month. In reality, many portfolio managers don't bother to do this. As a result, the residual that is left over- or under-hedged contributes to the tracking error. In this, the portfolio manager has to balance the transaction costs of re-balancing the currency hedges against the negative effect on tracking error.

8.7   EXAMPLES OF ACTIVE CURRENCY MANAGEMENT STRATEGIES

There are a wide variety of active currency management strategies that are used in the market, varying at one end of the spectrum from entirely discretionary-based trading to strict rule-based strategies. Three prominent strategies that we will look at in this section are closer to the latter rather than the former end of this spectrum:

- Differential forward strategy
- Simple trend-following strategy
- Optimization of the carry trade

All three of these strategies have consistently added alpha to a portfolio if followed rigorously and interestingly have also proven to be risk reducing compared to unhedged benchmarks. Thus, they also help to boost significantly the portfolio's Sharpe ratio. With what follows, the contributions and advice of Henrik Pedersen of the CitiFX Risk Advisory Group and Emmanuel Acar of Bank of America's Risk Management Advisory Group are gratefully acknowledged.

8.7.1   Differential Forward Strategy

The core idea behind this is that of "forward rate bias", or the reality that forward rates are poor predictors of future spot exchange rates, in contrast to the theories of covered interest rate parity and unbiased forward parity. We have looked at some of the academic backing for this admission earlier in this chapter, notably by Fama (1984), Kritzman (1993) and finally Bansal and Dahlquist (2000), who suggested that the negative correlation presented by Fama between future exchange rate changes and current interest rate differentials is crucially linked to changes in macroeconomic variables.

As outlined by Acar and Maitra (2000), the differential forward strategy seeks to take advantage of the apparent market inefficiencies as represented by "forward rate bias" by hedging the currency risk only when the interest rate differential is in favour of the hedger. That is to say, only when the forward points are at a discount. Conversely, the currency manager should not hedge currency risk when the forward points are at a premium and consequently the interest rate differential would reflect a cost. More specifically, when the interest rate differential pays the investor to hedge, the currency manager should have a hedge ratio of 100%. Conversely, when the interest rate differential costs the investor to hedge, the hedge ratio should be zero. Thus, if the currency manager is operating under a symmetrical benchmark, the manager would go overweight the hedge by 50% when the interest rate differential is in their favour and underweight by 50% when it represents a cost.

The results of this strategy have proved to be extremely robust and have been tested across some 91 currency pairs. For the sake of simplicity and clarity, only seven of these are shown in Figure 8.2.

Of necessity, when the interest rate differential is favourable, the differential forward strategy will have the same returns as a full forward hedge. Equally, when the interest rate differential represents a cost, the differential forward strategy will have the same returns as an unhedged strategy. Thus, overall, the returns of the differential forward strategy will be a function of both fully hedged and fully unhedged strategies. The advantages of such a strategy are the following:

- As established, it has consistently added alpha for active currency managers.
- Equally, it has also reduced risk relative to benchmarks.
- The strategy combines the decisiveness of a full hedge with significant flexibility when used with a symmetrical benchmark.
- The expected returns of the differential forward strategy are a function both of the expected returns of the fully hedged and fully unhedged strategies.

Given that the differential forward strategy is based on exploiting the principle of "forward rate bias", it must follow to an extent that its expected returns are also a function in turn of the extent of that forward rate bias and thus of the interest rate differential relative to the expected future interest rate differential. For any given interest rate differential, the hedging strategy will perform best when the correlation between the hedged and unhedged returns is more negative.

8.7.2   Trend-Following Strategy

A second popular strategy for active currency managers is the "trend-following" strategy, which involves using several technical moving averages to provide trading or hedging signals. Active currency managers can use this strategy to either trade around their benchmark in order to add alpha, or alternatively to provide a hedging signal. The academic backing for trend-following strategies is as deep as that for the differential forward strategy, including works by Bilson (1990, 1993), Taylor (1990), LeBaron (1991) and Levich and Thomas (1993), which showed that these strategies can indeed produce consistent excess returns over sustained periods of time. I would suggest however that the seminal breakthrough in this area came in the form of the note by Lequeux and Acar (1998), which gave the strategy more specific properties by suggesting that in order to be representative of the various durations followed by investors an equally weighted portfolio based on three moving averages of 32, 61 and 117 days would be most appropriate. Simply put, the core idea behind this strategy is to go long the currency pair when the price is above a moving average of a given length and to go short the currency pair when it is below. More specifically, if the spot exchange rate is above all three moving averages, hedge the foreign currency exposure 100%. If it is above only two out of the three moving averages, hedge one-third of the position. In all other cases, leave the position unhedged.

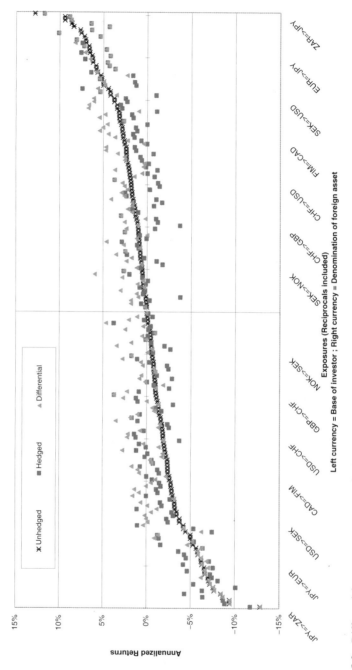

Figure 8.2 Differential strategy returns tested over 91 currency pairs and reciprocals: May 1990–April 2000 (x-axis labels have been limited to seven of the currency pairs for increased clarity)

Example

For instance, consider the example of a Euro-based portfolio manager who invests in US equities and fixed income. In order to allow the potential for adding alpha, the portfolio manager has given a mandate to an active currency overlay manager, who is allowed to operate under a symmetrical currency hedging benchmark which gives the most flexibility for providing that alpha. Using a trend-following strategy, the currency overlay manager would hedge 100% of the underlying US exposure if spot Euro–dollar broke above all three of the 32-, 61- and 117-day moving averages. If Euro–dollar was only able to break above two out of the three moving averages, the currency overlay manager would hedge only one-third of the underlying. In all other cases, they would remain unhedged.

As with the differential forward strategy, the trend-following strategy may involve numerous transactions and thus may cause potential concern for investors with regard to transaction costs. However, such costs have historically been small relative both to the consistent returns that have been provided by such strategies and also to the potential losses of not hedging. Figure 8.3 looks at the dollar–mark exchange rate from 1975 to 2000, showing clearly that there were definite and sustained trends, both in the exchange rate and in interest rate differentials which could have been — and were — exploited to varying degrees by the differential forward and trend-following strategies.

8.7.3 Optimization of the Carry Trade

The final strategy example that we will look at for active currency managers is that of optimizing the carry trade. We looked at the carry trade idea initially in Chapter 2 and will do so again in Chapter 9 in the context of an appropriate strategy for currency speculators, when using a risk appetite indicator, for the purpose of gauging when are the best and worst times to buy higher carry currencies (and thus go short the lower carry currencies).

This combination of a risk appetite indicator and a basket of higher carry currencies can also be used for the purpose of currency hedging by an active currency manager who trades and hedges currency risk around their benchmark. For a currency speculator, the principle of the risk appetite/carry trade combination is that the basket of higher carry currencies should be bought when the risk appetite indicator is in either risk-seeking or risk-neutral mode and should be shorted when it is in risk-aversion mode. Similarly, the currency hedger could use this combination of indicators to go underweight the hedge relative to the benchmark in higher carry currencies when the risk appetite indicator is benign and overweight when the indicator moves into risk aversion. Such a strategy should reduce transaction costs relative to a passive currency management programme, while also reducing the portfolio's overall risk and adding alpha.

Yet, we can fine tune this strategy still further using a portfolio optimizer to take into account the volatility and correlation of currencies in addition to their yield differentials alone. This should both in theory and practice produce better returns than the simple carry trade strategy. The carry trade can be an excellent strategy by itself for adding alpha, however it can also exhibit substantial volatility at times. A fine example of this was when the dollar–yen exchange rate fell by around 15% in the space of a few days in October 1998. By comparison, the optimized carry trade would in the case of the currency speculator represent the buying of higher carry currencies with low volatility and the selling of low carry currencies with high volatility. For the currency hedger, this would in turn mean going underweight the hedge relative to the

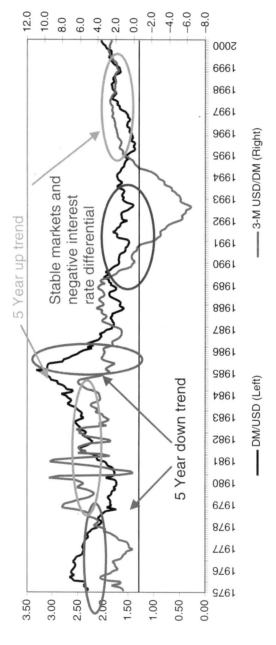

Figure 8.3   DEM/USD and a three-month rate differential

benchmark on higher carry currencies with low volatility and overweight the hedge on lower carry currencies with higher volatility.

For both a portfolio manager who is looking to hedge currency risk and an active currency manager who can trade that currency risk, optimizing the carry trade can be a useful and productive way both to reduce risk and to add alpha. Indeed, it is an improvement on the differential forward strategy in so much as that is another expression of a basic carry trade strategy. The optimized carry trade strategy has consistently produced good returns with of necessity less volatility, resulting in higher Sharpe and information ratios.

It should of course be noted that just as one can optimize the carry trade for improved performance over the simple carry trade, so one can do exactly the same thing for either the differential forward strategy or the trend-following strategy. One does this by looking at volatility-adjusted exposure rather than the simple exposure per se. Thus, for example in the case of the differential forward strategy, one can over an extended period of time look at the relationship between implied volatility and historical volatility of the underlying exchange rate. Optimizing for volatility-adjusted exposure, the active currency manager would increase the leverage of the forward hedge when implied vol is below a predetermined threshold relative to historic vol at the same time as the forward points are in favour of the hedger, and conversely lower it when implied vol is above. The extent to which this generally improves performance far exceeds any concerns about increased transaction costs. One thing which may have to be taken into account however is the likelihood that raising or lowering the leverage of a differential forward strategy, both on an absolute basis and relative to the benchmark, may have an impact on the volatility of the tracking error.

Similarly, one can seek to optimize through volatility-adjusted exposure the trend-following strategy. Again, this should improve on the alpha provided by the basic strategy. A final point on these active currency strategies is that they are obviously not dependent on the base currency for adding alpha given that the total portfolio weighting and risk remains the same whatever the base currency.

8.8   EMERGING MARKETS AND CURRENCY HEDGING

It has been noted that emerging markets have different market properties to those of the developed markets. Here, it is important to sell these out and then in turn relate them to the considerations of passive and active currency risk management. First off, let us look at the major differences that appear present in emerging markets:

- **Liquidity risk** — Emerging market currencies are less liquid than their developed counterparts. For instance, every day some USD300 billion goes through EUR–USD. This compares with around USD10 billion daily in the South African rand. Needless to say, this lower liquidity affects pricing and price action.
- **Convertibility risk** — Even less than liquidity risk, convertibility risk is not a consideration for developed currency markets as all major currencies are freely floating and fully convertible. A number of emerging market currencies however are still not convertible on the capital account, and indeed a few are still not fully convertible on the current account.
- **Exchange controls** — In line with this, several emerging market currencies still have varying degrees of exchange rate controls, which also distort exchange rate pricing and economic activity. Exchange controls create "black market" activity and paradoxically can lead to capital flight.

- **Emerging markets have structurally high levels of inflation** — Stronger growth levels and economic inefficiencies are important reasons behind structurally high levels of inflation relative to developed markets. This in turn means that policy interest rates are in most cases substantially higher in emerging markets than in developed markets, resulting in high forward premiums.
- **Capital inflows however can depress market interest rates** — The size of global capital flows relative to the size of local capital markets in most emerging markets can mean that the latter are swamped by a relatively small portfolio shift in assets either into the market or out of it. As a result, interest rate volatility is a lot higher.
- **Forward rate bias is lower in emerging markets** — While forward exchange rates are poor predictors of future spot exchange rates in the developed markets, this is less so in many emerging markets. The exhaustive 2000 study by Bansal and Dahlquist tested the presence of forward rate bias and found emerging market currencies show significantly less correlation between current interest rate differentials and subsequent spot returns than those in the developed markets. That said, emerging market currencies tend to appreciate on a real basis and then collapse to adjust for the trade balance deterioration caused by that real exchange rate appreciation.
- **Implied emerging market volatility below developed market volatility is a buy signal** — Historically, lower levels of implied volatility in emerging market currencies than the corresponding developed market currencies has proven a good buy signal for the former. Intuitively, emerging market volatility should be higher, though there are periods when the sheer weight of capital inflows forces it artificially lower. Note that emerging market implied volatility is skewed in that it tends to fall only when the emerging market currency is strengthening, but always rises when the currency weakens.
- **Implied emerging market volatility is a very poor predictor of future exchange rates** — Looking at previous emerging market crises, the options market has usually got it "wrong" in the sense that such crises have never been priced in ahead of time by the options market. Thus, we can say that the options market is a poor predictor of future exchange rate levels in the emerging markets, though measured against historic volatility levels it may well be a much better indicator of relative value.

What we find in the emerging markets is that shifts in global capital flows have major domestic interest rate implications. For instance, high inflation and therefore interest rate differentials should, according to classical economic theory, suggest a depreciation of the local currency in proportion to that interest rate differential or forward premium. However, this may not occur due to heavy capital inflows, which swamp the domestic market's ability to cope with these without economic distortion. As a result of this, the currency may experience significant nominal and real appreciation, in seeming violation of the international Fisher effect and covered interest rate parity. Real currency appreciation however leads to a real economic shock, and more specifically real trade and current account balance deterioration. Eventually, this has to be reversed and not too surprisingly through real currency depreciation. The longer and more powerful the real appreciation, the potentially more violent the subsequent depreciation. Emerging market currencies trade in these types of cycles, in line with the "speculative cycle" that we looked at earlier in the book. As a result, we can tell from this that the forward rate bias is extreme for emerging market currencies on both sides of the forward. In line with this, some caution is needed in using the differential forward strategy in the emerging markets. Emerging market interest rate differentials would mean theoretically that an investor never hedged emerging market currency risk using the differential forward strategy, yet this is clearly not the appropriate strategy in some cases.

For similar reasons, the carry trade has provided significant alpha for active currency managers, both in the basic and in the optimized version. However, the distortion to interest and exchange rates that capital inflows provide in emerging markets means that a significantly higher degree of both care and discretion is needed in picking higher carry currencies to either invest in or hedge depending upon the reading of the risk appetite indicator.

8.9 SUMMARY

In conclusion, when portfolio managers are taking a risk reduction approach, there is a strong incentive to be fully hedged, particularly for fixed income fund managers who generally have less opposition to such an idea than their equity counterparts. This is consistent with the fact that a significant part of a fixed income portfolio's risk is the currency risk. On the other hand, if the portfolio manager is adopting a performance approach, an active currency risk management approach for the purpose of adding alpha is clearly more important.

In Chapters 7 and 8, we have looked at the "fundamental" world of corporations on the one hand and "real money" or institutional investors on the other, and how they deal respectively with the issue of currency risk. For the most part, their approach to currency risk is that of the hedger. On the other hand, the vast majority of currency market participants are speculators, that is people who trade currencies without an underlying attached asset. While many who focus on the currency markets put the emphasis on so-called "real" flow, the reality is in fact that this makes up the minority of overall flow relative to speculation. It is to this speculative — and misunderstood — world that we now turn.

REFERENCES

Acar, E. and Maitra, B. (2000/2001). Optimal portfolio selection and the impact of currency hedging. *The Journal of Performance Measurement* Winter.

Bansal, R. and Dahlquist, M. (2000). The forward premium puzzle: different tales from developed and emerging economies. *Journal of International Economics* 51.

Bilson, J. (1990, 1993). Value, yield and trend: a composite forecasting approach to foreign exchange trading. In A. Gitlin (ed.), *Strategic Currency Investing: Trading and Hedging in the Foreign Exchange Market*, Probus Publishing.

Black, F. (1989). Universal hedging: optimising currency risk and reward in international equity portfolios. *Financial Analysts Journal* July/August.

Choie, K. (1993). Currency exchange rate forecast and interest rate differential. *Journal of Portfolio Management* Winter.

Fama, E.F. (1984). Forward and spot exchanges. *Journal of Monetary Economics* 14, 319–338.

Froot, K. and Thaler, R. (1990, 1993). Anomalies: foreign exchange. *Journal of Economic Perspectives* 4 (3).

Kritzman, M. (1989). Serial dependence in currency returns: investment implications. *Journal of Portfolio Management* Fall.

Kritzman, M. (1993). The optimal currency hedging policy with biased forward rates. *Journal of Portfolio Management* Summer.

Lequeux, P. and Acar, E. (1998). A dynamic benchmark for managed currency funds. *European Journal of Finance* 4, 311–330.

Levich, R. and Thomas, L. (1993). Internationally diversified bond portfolios: the merits of active currency risk management. In A. Gitlin (ed.), *Strategic Currency Investing: Trading and Hedging in the Foreign Exchange Market*, Probus Publishing.

Perold, A. and Schulman, E. (1988). The free lunch in currency hedging: implications for investment policy and performance standards. *Financial Analysts Journal.*

Silber, L.W. (1994). Technical trading: when it works and when it doesn't. *The Journal of Derivatives* Spring.

Strange, B. (1998, updated 2001). Currency matters. *European Pension News* 28 May (Currency Overlay Supplement), 19–21.

Taylor, S.J. (1990). Profitable currency futures trading: a comparison to technical and time-series trading rules. In L.R. Thomas (ed.), *The Currency Hedging Debate*, IFR Publishing Ltd.

The Frank Russell Company (2000). Capturing alpha through active currency overlay, May.

9

Managing Currency Risk III — The Speculator: Myths, Realities and How to be a Better Currency Speculator

After looking at the different worlds of the corporation and the "real money" institutional investor, it would be remiss of us if we did not also look at that of the "speculator". Few subjects related to currency markets cause more discussion, debate or emotion for that matter than currency "speculation". Indeed, in the last few years, currency speculators have undergone a notable deterioration in the way they are regarded by a substantial proportion of the academic and official community.

It used to be the case in standard economic text books that "speculators" were widely viewed as a benign force, providing liquidity to the productive areas of the economy such as manufacturing and services, thus lowering the cost of production. Speculation was seen as a necessary balancing force in the overall economy, which provided the liquidity not found elsewhere. Those economists who acknowledged that in the currency markets there could be periodic if brief divergence from fundamental equilibrium also saw currency speculators as benign in that they worked to eliminate the divergence quickly and efficiently, more or less under the efficient market hypothesis.

9.1 THE SPECULATOR — FROM BENIGN TO MALIGN

In the last decade however, some have increasingly taken a different view in the wake of one currency "crisis" after another. The first real currency crisis of the decade came not in the emerging markets but in the developed world. The ERM crisis of 1992 was a wake-up call to countries in a number of ways. On the face of it, it was manifested in the form of Scandinavian currencies breaking their pegs to the Deutschmark and ERM countries such as the UK and Italy being forced out of the system. Inevitably in the chaos of that time, many wrong lessons were learned. It appeared that the liberalization of the currency markets had allowed currency speculators to become such a huge force that they were now capable of dismantling exchange rate systems and causing the downfall of governments — or at least Prime Ministers. The UK Chancellor of the Exchequer Norman Lamont may have been said to have sung in his bath after sterling was expelled from the ERM, but Prime Minister John Major was not singing the same tune a few years later when his government was routed more completely than any government this century at the 1997 general elections. Headlines reporting that George Soros' famous Quantum "hedge fund" made around USD1 billion by speculating against sterling only served to reinforce the misconception that currency speculators alone forced sterling out of the ERM, that they were indeed large enough to accomplish such a feat.

A year later and currency speculators were again on the attack, this time against the ERM system itself. Under enormous pressure, after having resisted through intervention for months, in August 1993 the governments of the ERM countries gave in and widened the ERM currency trading bands to ±15% from ±2.25%, thus *de facto* allowing a depreciation of their currencies against the ERM anchor, the Deutschmark. The idea of recrimination after a currency crisis is thought of these days as a feature of the emerging markets, indeed currency crises themselves are thought of as an emerging market phenomenon. Thus, it is important to remember the sense of outrage, fury and a desire almost for vengeance that permeated official Europe in the wake of that exchange rate band widening. The enemy of the European project, of the European dream of integration and eventual unification was clear, and it was "Anglo-Saxon" speculators.

After the ERM crises of 1992–1993 however, it was indeed the turn of the emerging markets to see one currency crisis after another. Here the sense of betrayal at the hands of the "market" was particularly acute because many emerging market countries had adopted free market practices precisely to progress economically and eventually bridge the perceived gap between the emerging and developed worlds. Thus, the 1994–1995 currency crisis in Mexico was a very rude awakening indeed, not just for Mexico and its neighbours but also for the emerging market countries as a whole. After that, came the Czech koruna currency crisis in 1996–1997. Like the Mexican peso, it was pegged to a base currency. In the Czech case this was the Deutschemark, and like the Mexican peso it eventually was forced to de-peg from that base currency and promptly collapsed.

In 1997–1998, the Asian currency crisis exploded on the international scene. I remember it in the context that I was living and working in Hong Kong when it took place. It is an important realization in discussing the subject of currency speculation that countries facing a currency crisis experience a stage of siege followed by something very akin to bitter defeat. Blame is sought, or more accurately in some cases scapegoats are found. It is easy to forget in the 24/7 information society that we now live in just how that time was. It was a time of high drama and higher emotion. In September of 1997, the IMF held its annual meetings in Hong Kong (for the most part in the huge, new exhibition and conference centre made famous by the signing of the Handover of Hong Kong from the UK to China in that same year). The Thai baht had devalued on July 2 of that year and thereafter most Asian currency counterparts followed suit, albeit unwillingly. Answers to this crisis were sought and not surprisingly many were found, of varying accuracy. At those meetings, in front of a packed audience, the Malaysian Prime Minister Dr. Mahathir Mohammed, in all else a most erudite and educated man, thundered that currency trading was "unnecessary, unproductive and immoral", that it should be "banned . . . it should be made illegal", that the profits of currency speculation "came from the impoverishing of others".

It should be reiterated that it was a time of high emotion, a keen sense of betrayal and great pain. Asian economies up until then had been viewed as the model for emerging markets generally within the official community. The World Bank itself coined the phrase the "Asian miracle" — as close as the official community has ever come to verbal irrational exuberance — to define the Asian boom from 1985 to 1996. Asia was a success story for other regions within the emerging markets to only hope of emulating. Indeed, the Asian-related optimism, both within and without, went so far as to have the western media suggest that the economic centre of power was shifting from the West to the East. Given all the fundamental progress made and the resulting praise globally, how else to explain Asia's collapse in 1997–1998 other than by malign, almost "terrorist" means? Indeed, the terrorist analogy was used specifically at the height of the crisis to describe the suspected hand of unnamed evil forces at work. While the remarks by Dr. Mahathir were undoubtedly the most prominent in reflecting the backlash within Asian countries against the perceived evil of currency speculation, they were by no means the only example of this backlash. In Thailand, there was talk that the Bank of Thailand was keeping a "black book" of suspected foreign banks which had speculated against the Thai baht, though the Bank of Thailand denied the existence of such a list. In Indonesia, the Indonesian Justice Minister was reported as considering that currency speculators could face subversion charges if their activities were found to damage the economy, and that the ultimate penalty for economic or political subversion was death. At around the same time, the Indonesian *Republika* newspaper published a public service announcement featuring a westerner (presumably a currency speculator) wearing a terrorist mask and *keffiyah* in the form of US 100 dollar bills, with an underlying question "Are you a terrorist of this country?" Indonesians were exhorted to "Defend the *Rupiah*, defend the nation". Even in the Philippines, where the authorities had traditionally taken a benign view of market forces, there was some suggestion of blaming foreign speculators.

The effort to find blame for the calamities which befell the region in 1997–1998 reflected not only the political desire to find convenient scapegoats and lay the blame on others, but also a deep sense of injustice and anger at the way Asia had been treated and abused by financial markets, at the way much of Asia's economic progress over decades had been destroyed so savagely in so little time. Initially, it was more expedient to blame foreign speculators for the Asian currency crisis than to try to discover the fundamental economic reasons why the crisis should have happened, since the latter might have involved laying some of the blame at the feet of the Asian governments themselves. This was not only for politically pragmatic reasons, but also more seriously for reasons of political survival. It should be seen as no coincidence that the dictator Soeharto was overthrown in the aftermath of the Asian crisis. Equally, in Thailand, a series of corrupt governments gave way to significant political reform and the administration of Chuan Leepkai. Needless to say, there may have been some Asian governments opposed to such ideas of change, preferring the old social pact of stability and prosperity. The only problem with this was that there was no longer any prosperity. Whoever was to blame for it, the Asian currency crisis impoverished millions. After the crisis, it was said that in Indonesia the economic work of three decades had been all but wiped out, and that as a result half the country lived in a state of absolute poverty as defined by the World Bank, living on USD1 a day.

An official backlash against currency speculation was certainly not limited to the Asian crisis or to the emerging markets as a whole. Following sterling's ejection from the ERM in September 1992, the UK government's first public reaction was to blame the German central bank for either not coming to the aid of the UK in defending the ERM parity, or in fact deliberately seeking its ejection. There was talk that the Bank of England was drawing up a list of banks which had played a part in speculating against sterling — a ridiculous measure given that the whole market had been selling sterling and the Bank of England had effectively been the only buyer. Equally, after the forced widening of the ERM bands to 15% on August 1, 1993, the hysterical reaction by officials within the French and German governments, lambasting the implied devaluation of the ERM currencies as the result of nefarious activities by heinous "Anglo-Saxon speculators" — presumably the German officials simultaneously forgetting their own ethnic origins — would have made Asian government comments seem tentative by comparison. Europe's best and brightest didn't only talk either. Some of them sought to punish those who had dared go against their precious plans for currency union, by keeping interest rates at punitive levels subsequent to the band widening — in the process, hurting the "innocent" along with the "guilty".

In Asia, the response was also not just verbal. Thailand created a two-tier foreign exchange and interest rate system, while the Philippines and Indonesia slapped on limits to swap market trading and Malaysia went so far as to ban offshore trading in the ringgit and peg it at MYR3.80

to the US dollar. While the dividing line is somewhat thin, these measures were not so much aimed at punishing speculators after the fact as they were efforts at self-defence during the climax of the speculation and panic. The reaction to the Asian crisis by governments was initially in many cases one of recrimination, however with one notable exception that eventually turned to one of pragmatism and the realization of a need for accelerated reform. The essence of Asia's official protest at its rough handling was two-fold: firstly, a natural reaction to such treatment whatever the reasons, and secondly an issue of control — the authorities had lost control, or at least a high degree of it, and the market had gained it. Of necessity, control is a subject close to the heart of any government or central bank. This was the case in Europe after the two ERM crises, and it was also the case with Asia. Control was relevant not only for economic reasons but also because the previously strong growth had masked or postponed underlying political and social problems.

The Asian currency crisis was followed swiftly by the Russian currency crisis of August 1998. It is interesting if not amusing to remember now that a high-ranking Russian official said at the 1997 IMF annual meetings in Hong Kong (which I attended) that the Asian crisis had prompted a re-think of currency policies generally, and of Russia's in particular. That Russia would not act immediately but would *clearly have to reconsider their exchange rate policy in the face of such events.* Politicians say a lot of things, but that is not to say that they actually do them. In the case of Russia, clearly the process of reconsideration was neither speedy nor decisive enough. In August 1998, the Russian rouble de-pegged from the US dollar and collapsed, and Russia defaulted on its domestic debt. This was followed shortly by a currency crisis on the other side of the world, in Brazil. In January of 1999, the Brazilian real also de-pegged and collapsed in value. It seemed to some almost as if some immense and malign force was at work, triggering currency crises and devaluations and in the process setting these countries back years if not decades in terms of economic progress. Just to bring this book up-to-date, in February of 2001, the Turkish lira experienced the same fate, de-pegging against the US dollar from 600,000 and falling to a low of around 1.65 million in October of that year.

It is without doubt that these experiences over the last 10 years have coloured our judgement and opinion on the subject of currency speculation. It would be difficult for that not to happen. The aim here, in this chapter, is therefore to attempt a difficult task, namely that of looking at the issue of currency speculation from a fair and unbiased perspective. At the offset, I must say if it is not already clear, that as a currency strategist in a global investment bank I am obviously (to a limited extent!) a participant in the currency market. My own experience should also be taken into account. That said, I am no more biased than anyone in the official community on this issue. They have their (biased) perspective, a currency strategist has his/her own. Moreover I have considerably more experience of seeing currency speculation than many, certainly most within the official community. With that in mind, the aim here is neither to see currency speculation as a benign or as a malign force. Rather, it is first to draw the fangs of emotion and morality from the debate and then to seek a balanced, unemotional and practical perspective of this issue of currency speculation. The very first thing one has to do in this regard is to seek some sort of definition for what one is talking about. There are probably as many definitions of this issue as there are people on the planet, however clearly that is not helpful. The broad definition I have used so far in the book is the following:

Currency speculation is the trading in currencies with no underlying attached asset

This is of course far from a perfect definition. However, any weakness of this definition does not detract from our essential need to have a definition in order to put this whole debate — and indeed this chapter — in context. This is clearly not the only kind of currency speculation, but it is a useful reference, not least for the *incentive* of a currency speculator. Their main aim has nothing to do with an underlying, attached asset such as an equity or fixed income product. Their aim is purely to achieve what academic text books suggest is impossible — consistent excess returns from currency directional trading.

9.2   SIZE MATTERS

So armed with this definition, however inadequate, let us now look at the issue of currency speculation in more depth. The second aspect of currency speculation to realize is its size. On the face of it, it is immense. The global currency markets turn over some USD1.2 trillion in daily volume, according to the 2001 report by the Bank of International Settlements. That is the rough equivalent of world trade in global goods and services *every day*. In the last two decades, as barriers to capital have broken down and capital markets become liberalized, in line with the move to liberalize trade in goods and services, capital flows have played an increasingly important role in global currency markets. By comparison, world trade has seen its role diminish proportionally as a determining factor in exchange rate movement. Trying to work out the percentages of global currency volume is very far from an exact science given that one is faced with issues such as double counting and so forth. Nevertheless, it is possible to get a rough idea of the relative flow importance of the different sectors of the market. Put together, and being generous rather than conservative in one's estimation, world trade and investment (portfolio and direct) makes up around 30% of currency market volume. The rest, using our definition, is currency speculation, with no underlying asset behind it. I have not the slightest doubt that these figures will cause debate, if not outright rejection. The truth however is that I have been charitable and generous with the first half of the equation, that of trade and investment. The imbalance in favour of currency speculation should actually not be that surprising. If one thinks about it, the economic text book definition of a currency speculator as a liquidity provider to the productive areas of the economy might suggest an eventual 50/50 role between the two sides. The liberalization and deregulation process seen over the last three decades has meant that we have gone far beyond that.

9.3   MYTHS AND REALITIES

On the face of it, this may seem only to confirm the worst fears of those who see currency speculation as an intrinsically malign force, ready to bring down currency systems and governments on a whim. Surely, if currency speculation is such a dominating force within the global currency markets, then it is currency speculation that is responsible for currency crises. Following on with this logic, some may take the view that action should be taken to ensure that currency speculation cannot cause such devastation and damage again! On the face of it, these are understandable conclusions. However, just because they are understandable does not make them right. Indeed, I would suggest that they are at best overly simplistic and at worst flatly wrong for the following reasons:

- Currency speculation does not act or take place in a vacuum. Rather it is a response to changes in fundamental or technical dynamics.
- The essential aim of currency speculation is not to bring down governments, nor to hurt countries economically, nor for that matter to break currency pegs. Simply put, the aim is to make money, pure and simple.

- Currency speculation therefore is neither benign nor malign. Both of these terms have emotional if not moral connotations. Currency speculation is amoral. It aims to make money, whether buying or selling a currency, and it will do that in direct and proportional response to government economic policy.
- In cases such as currency crises where substantial destruction is caused, currency speculation is the symptom rather than the underlying disease. Indeed, in the case of the UK in 1992, currency speculation was the cure to the disease, which was a ridiculously overvalued exchange rate value of sterling within the ERM.
- Currency speculation does indeed provide a valuable service, in giving liquidity to the productive areas of the economy.
- The idea that a speculator is a seller and an investor is a buyer is worse than nonsense. It is propaganda designed to cover policy mistakes.
- In line with this, there are many more kinds of speculation than just currency speculation. Was not the NASDAQ bubble of 1999–2000 speculation? When Alan Greenspan dared to try to temper that irrational exuberance did he not get shouted down by the public and by congress?

This chapter is for both those who seek a clearer understanding of currency speculation, why and how it takes place, and also for the currency speculators themselves. The latter is done with some humility for there are currency speculators who are amongst the most revered and respected — and honourable — participants within the currency markets. In my career, I have met many of these and many are amongst the most brilliant minds out there. Thus it is with care that I have the temerity to suggest that some of these still have a few things to learn about the currency markets! That said, another perspective is always useful. I have certainly found that myself. My experience is as someone who has followed the currency markets for the last decade, first as a journalist, then as an analyst, then as a manager of a currency business and finally as a currency strategist for an investment bank. Perspective is important and being able to look at an issue from several different angles sometimes critical. Thus, I hope I can say that I have gained immeasurably from the wisdom of my economist colleagues. We look at the same question from two completely different perspectives. Equally, it is my hope that even some of the most experienced currency speculators may gain from my no doubt different perspective.

9.4   THE SPECULATORS — WHO THEY ARE

Much has been written about currency speculators in the past, much of it with a few rare exceptions utter nonsense. As noted above, the very term "speculator" can create an emotional reaction. Here, in this section, we seek a dispassionate analysis of just who are the currency speculators, how and why they operate and their function within the overall currency market. The benchmark for this analysis is obviously the definition of currency speculation given earlier; that is someone who trades in currencies without an underlying, attached asset. Trade and investment do not count because of necessity they have attached, underlying assets. What is left — the vast majority — in currency market volume is speculation. So who takes part in this activity? Broadly speaking, currency speculators can be divided into the following main groups.

9.4.1   Interbank Dealers

This group makes up the vast majority of currency speculation and therefore of the currency market as a whole. The primary task of an interbank dealer is to provide liquidity and make markets in currencies for the bank's clients. The principle is that all client positions have to be offset in the market (i.e. if a client sells you Euros against dollars, you the dealer are buying the Euros and therefore have to sell those Euros back to the market to keep a flat exposure).

In theory, the profit you make is the difference between your bid and the market's offer. In practice, as bid–offer spreads have narrowed substantially, there has been a general shift within the currency markets towards keeping some exposures one gains or loses from clients in order to take speculative positions in the market to support the P&L of the dealing desk. In addition, a dealing desk can use the bank's balance sheet to take speculative positions irrespective of client flow. Thus, while the reduction in bid–offer spread has reflected greatly increased information transparency and competition in the market, it has also resulted in a move to increase the "position taking" of an interbank or liquidity dealing desk. Such position taking may be more profitable, and there is no question that it is when a highly experienced and professional chief dealer is in charge. However, this move has also undoubtedly added to the volatility of the dealing desk's P&L. Equally, it may also have added to overall market volatility.

This may seem a contradiction, as narrower spreads should be a reflection of greater volume and liquidity. However, the reality is that as those spreads have narrowed, so position taking has increased. Larger positions are taken on by interbank dealing desks in order to maintain or boost P&L, and therefore as a result larger positions have to be unwound during periods of adverse price action. Equally, those narrow spreads can be an illusion. For instance, the normal spread in spot Euro–dollar may be one pip — i.e. 0.8910/11 — but try transacting USD500 million in that spread when the spot exchange rate is moving two or three "big figures" — 0.89 to 0.90 — a day!

Readers should note that when I say interbank dealers, I mean currency forward and options dealers as well as spot dealers. These also take positions as well as provide liquidity for the bank's clients. Here too, like any market where competition has increased over time, spreads have narrowed and the emphasis to position taking has shifted proportionally. In addition, as the needs of clients have changed and become significantly more specific and sophisticated, so there has also been a move by forward and options interbank dealing desks to meet these needs with more exotic forward and options structures. The advantage for the bank concerned is that the spreads on these products are usually larger than those for plain vanilla forwards or options. However, markets work in real time. Here too, competition has quickly moved to narrow those spreads.

9.4.2 Proprietary Dealers

The second group of currency speculators is that of the "proprietary dealer". This individual is usually among the most experienced currency dealers in the dealing room. He or she plays no part in providing liquidity for client orders, but instead uses a designated amount of the bank's balance sheet for the specific purpose of position taking in the currency markets. A "prop" dealer may take these positions based on any combination of fundamental, technical, flow or quantitative considerations. He or she has the luxury of not having to quote or make markets for others. On the other hand, their value to a bank comes in the form of one number alone, their P&L at the end of the year. They get all the kudos and all the blame depending on what that number is. They are a bit like racing drivers — and many would be happy with that analogy. There are old prop dealers and bold prop dealers, but no old, bold prop dealers! The analogy is meant in light-hearted fashion. Good prop dealers are extremely hard to find. Most that I have met are in complete contrast to the image of a financial market dealer as loud and brash. On the contrary, many are relatively quiet, analytical and extremely bright.

9.4.3 "Hedge" Funds

The very term may for some conjure up the devil incarnate. There is little question that the image of the hedge fund has changed over time. Before we get onto that image, let us first deal with what they do. The first thing to say is that there are hundreds, if not thousands, of different types of hedge fund. The term "hedge fund" is in fact an extremely vague one, encompassing the activity of a very wide variety of funds that trade in currency and asset markets. Certain specific hedge funds may seem particularly synonymous with the term, but while their funds are some of the largest they are in fact the tip of the proverbial iceberg in terms of reflecting this section of the financial community.

For a start, most of them unlike their name do not hedge. Indeed, their aim is to take asset market or currency views, to increase risk albeit selectively rather than to hedge risk. Rather than tie up balance sheet capital through spot positions, they frequently use derivatives to express a view, using leverage. The amount of leverage that hedge funds are allowed to use has decreased significantly since the failure of LTCM in 1998. Hedge funds are still active participants in the currency markets, though their involvement has in fact diminished substantially for a number of reasons. Firstly, the LTCM failure caused the counterparties of hedge funds — the banks they dealt with — to take a broadly more conservative approach with regard to credit and leverage given to the hedge funds. This in turn reduced the ability of hedge funds to take on the large, leveraged positions they had in the past. Secondly, the global equity rally (i.e. bubble) in 1999–2000 represented a competitive threat to this sector of the financial community. Hedge funds achieve popularity with investors precisely because of their outperformance to "the market", that is to the traditional equity and fixed income markets. Thus, when equity markets were exploding higher in 1999, it became extremely difficult for some to achieve that outperformance, particularly when this took place at a time of deterioration in the relationship between hedge funds and the rest of the financial markets in the wake of LTCM. Thirdly, the larger a fund becomes the more unwieldy it can become in terms of its market positioning. Benchmarks have to be outperformed and that can be achieved only with size when traditional markets are performing well. Yet, to do that may lead to market disruption, both on the way in and on the way out, reducing the attractiveness of taking the original position. In the end many hedge funds became trend followers in 1999, buying the NASDAQ and running with the crowd, more with the aim of defending returns than generating greater returns. Currency speculation is generally less attractive during times when traditional asset markets are trending so clearly, given that a fundamental part of currency speculation is to find economic imbalances — positive or negative — that the markets are not pricing in and trade on those in the expectation that the markets will eventually realize such imbalances and trade their way. Several hedge funds reduced their currency speculating operations in 1999.

This decision may have been somewhat premature. The bursting of the equity bubble in 2000 has brought hedge funds the opportunity to add value once more, including doing so by means of currency speculation. Indeed, it would not have been difficult to beat the NASDAQ's return in 2000 and the first half of 2001! Equally, while there may have been a reassessment of hedge funds in the US, both from within and without, the hedge fund community has blossomed and flourished in Europe subsequently, particularly in several countries in continental Europe.

The umbrella term of "hedge funds", even those that focus on the same asset or currency or have the same trading style, can reflect a variety of different types of organization. Recently, a number of total return or leveraged funds have been created. These may have not have a strict mutual fund structure, which helps at least to give some definition to the traditional hedge funds one thinks of, but they do have a very similar trading approach. In addition, banks can have internal hedge funds for specific client products. In sum, there are a very large number of hedge funds that "speculate" in a large number of assets and currencies. The performance of speculative currency funds is measured by a number of organizations, including the MAR (Manager Accounts Report) Trading Adviser data (available at: www.marhedge.com), Parker Global (www.parkerglobal.com) and the Ferrell FX Manager Universe. The irony with regards to their critics is that most base their trades either on inconsistencies in market pricing, which can instantly be arbitraged, or on sound macroeconomic principles. This latter group, known as the "macro" hedge funds, make up by far the largest group of funds that are publicly known. They are speculating according to fundamental principles. Thus, one could argue they are not speculating at all.

While many may seek to make a clear distinction between speculative and non-speculative activity, any such line of distinction is frequently uncomfortably blurred. At its most basic level, there is the idea that corporations take currency positions purely for transactional or hedging purposes, while hedge funds or prop dealers take currency positions for directional gain, with no underlying asset. The idea that there is such a clear distinction between the two sides is a fiction. Over the last decade, several major corporations have experienced painful losses and some have even collapsed as a result of taking on financial market positions that subsequently went sour. In this regard, problems tend to start when financial speculation overtakes the underlying business in importance.

Whatever the case, there are therefore other currency market participants we need to examine, which can at times be considered as currency speculators. Though many would no doubt bristle at the term, that is what they are if the individual transaction they are conducting has no related, underlying asset.

9.4.4   Corporate Treasurers

I realize fully the reaction that may be caused by labelling some corporate Treasurers as speculators, but frankly that is what some of them are *according to my definition of currency speculation*. This is in no way whatsoever a criticism. It is however a reflection of the realization that while most corporate Treasuries see their main goal as management and reduction of risk, a (not small) minority see the Treasury as a profit centre in addition to the underlying business. These deliberately take asset and currency market positions for the specific purpose of adding to the company's bottom line. There is no definitive answer as to whether this is "right" or "wrong" in very simplistic terms. It goes without saying that one had better know what one is doing if conducting such speculative activity. While adding to the company's bottom line is clearly a good thing — both for the company and for the Treasurer — financial markets charge a risk premium for P&L or balance sheet volatility. This should be a consideration when deciding whether or not to allow active speculative activity within the Treasury, using that balance sheet.

The other and decidedly more frequent kind of speculation that corporate Treasurers go in for is in not hedging out currency risk. We looked at this in Chapter 7 in substantially more detail and it is certainly not for here to go through that again. However, within the overall topic of this chapter, it is important to reiterate and make clear the point that not hedging currency speculation equates to taking a currency view, and that in turn equates to currency speculation. Granted, it is a stretch to fit this type of currency "speculation" within the narrow definition chosen for this book. There is after all an underlying asset. That said, not hedging means leaving that underlying asset exposed to financial market volatility. Such a decision would seem to be speculative under most broad definitions of speculation. This is in no way to suggest corporate treasuries should hedge currency risk each and every time they have an underlying exposure. The aim here is not to counter one extreme with another. Rather, it is to seek to challenge an idea, an ideology almost.

The idea and the ideology is that currency hedging represents a cost, while losses due to not hedging are simply the result of unpredictable market volatility. To me, the latter represents an abandoning, a shirking of responsibility. It is part and parcel of the job of a Treasurer or finance director to predict their business needs. Should it not be also to predict the context within which those business needs exist, the context being of course the global financial markets that specifically affect the risk profile of their business? A corporate Treasurer may say that they have to explain the cost of a currency hedge to the company's board, particularly if it had a notable impact on the company's figures. They should equally have to explain when they do not hedge, and subsequently the company's unhedged currency exposure leads to extraordinary losses and balance sheet pain. It is sloppy thinking to just leave it to the market to blame. If markets were completely unpredictable, strategists or analysts would not exist. Granted, some are better than others, but the very existence of the profession suggests that at least some are getting it right part of the time. That in turn suggests that a corporate Treasurer or finance director, who is far more senior in both experience and rank to a bank's strategist, should be at least as well informed as the latter. Companies exist within the market context their businesses operate in. The two cannot be separated. Some need to do a better job of understanding that context.

9.4.5 Currency Overlay

Again, it is probable that most currency overlay managers might not appreciate being labelled as speculators. Here however, the definition we have used in this book for currency speculation appears to work well. After all, the very job of a currency overlay manager is to differentiate currency risk from underlying asset risk within the overall risk profile. Active currency overlay requires that currency risk be managed separately and independently from the underlying. Therefore *de facto*, it falls within our definition of currency speculation. This does not mean that a currency overlay manager is of necessity anything like a prop dealer or a hedge fund. The job of a currency overlay manager may be either to ensure the total return of the portfolio by reducing risk as much as possible, or alternatively it may be to add alpha.

Either way, currency overlay managers use currency hedging benchmarks, as we saw in Chapter 8. They can manage the currency risk passively by maintaining the currency risk according to the benchmark. Alternatively, they can manage the currency risk actively by trading around the currency benchmark to add to the total return of the portfolio. The former are clearly not currency speculators in that they are hedging currency risk related to an underlying asset and moreover they are doing so passively. They are not "taking a view". The latter group, who trade actively around the currency benchmark, are indeed currency speculators in that they are taking positions not specifically related to the underlying asset.

Corporate Treasurers and currency overlay managers may think their world is as far away as one can get from those of the prop dealer or hedge funds, but there are times when the distinction between the two sides becomes decidedly less clear than many might like to think. In turn, this should mean one takes a more balanced and measured view of the very topic of currency speculation.

9.5   THE SPECULATORS — WHY THEY DO IT

The obvious answer is of course simply to make money. At a slightly more sophisticated level, market participants undertake currency speculation for the reason that they think they can earn excess returns by doing so. In turn, the reason they think that is because they or others have done so in the past.

Just as fashions and retail trends change over time, so does the idea of "conventional wisdom" within financial markets. In the 1970s, despite the break-up of the Bretton Woods financial system, the conventional wisdom was to have pegged currency regimes and maintain a significant degree of government control over the economy. In the 1980s, the US and the UK underwent substantial financial reform, opening up their economies and capital markets to the idea of free trade of goods, services and capital. With regards to currency or exchange rate regimes, the conventional wisdom has gone from governments trying to maintain control to allowing freely floating exchange rates. A slight fine tuning of this in the wake of the currency crises of the 1990s is the idea of the "bi-polar" world so eruditely explained by Stanley, former First Deputy Managing Director of the IMF, in speeches and written research notes. This argues that in a world of open capital accounts and free trade, exchange rates have to be managed according to either the hardest of pegs or the freest of free-floating principles, that anything in between these two poles will eventually prove unsustainable. Whatever the merits of this argument, there is little doubt that it has become the conventional exchange rate wisdom of the day, notwithstanding the protests of a few dissident voices.

The conventional exchange rate wisdom of the time of necessity affects the way markets operate, and thus how markets speculate for or against currencies. For instance, market participants who have been used to making good profits by speculating against pegged exchange rates may try to do so again, against a currency peg in a completely different part of the world. To a very large extent this is self-fulfilling. For this reason, a currency board regime that gets attacked in one part of the world can lead to markets attacking other currency boards on the other side of the world. For this very reason, the currency boards of Argentina and Hong Kong are often linked, although that link has been gradually reduced in the market's mind as the Hong Kong authorities have proved time and again their determination to maintain the currency board.

Currency speculators trade currencies to make money, pure and simple. They have a variety of methods, which we will look at subsequently, but the incentive is always the same. The fact that they can do so in the reasonable expectation of achieving their aim causes a problem with standard economic theory, not least because the theory suggests it is impossible over time. According to the theory, currency speculation is zero sum gain, which of necessity cannot result in consistent excess returns given the unpredictability of currency markets. The fact that excess returns can and have been achieved suggests this theory needs to be amended!

9.6   THE SPECULATORS — WHAT THEY DO

As noted previously, there are a wide variety of currency speculators and therefore it is no easy task to explain their methods or techniques since they too vary widely. The techniques of currency speculation vary widely, just as with stock market speculation. Indeed, the analogy is a good one. Just as in equity investment where you have "top down", "bottom up", "value investing", "growth or income" investing, so in currency markets you have speculators or investors — however one likes to term them — who focus on the macroeconomic "big picture", long-term currency valuation, microeconomic factors affecting currencies, money flow and technical analysis. The titles are perhaps different but the guiding principle is the same; what separates and differentiates the framework within which they analyse the market. Below, we attempt to summarize the types of techniques and strategies with which currency speculators approach the currency markets.

9.6.1   Macro

This approach is for the most part identified with the so-called "macro hedge funds". Broadly speaking, "macro" or macroeconomic-based currency speculators look for market pricing inconsistencies between the prevailing economic fundamentals and the long-term currency valuation, with the current market pricing. Their raison d'être and their incentive is that current market pricing is "wrong" relative to those fundamentals and valuation, and they can earn excess returns by trading against that market pricing.

Here again, the line between the currency speculator and the "fundamental" market participant is blurred. After all, where is the difference in terms of incentive and action between the asset manager who invests in a country's equity or fixed income markets and the macro-based currency speculator who invests in a currency because they think it is undervalued relative to fundamentals and valuation?

It is widely assumed that currency speculators only trade against currencies rather than in their favour, but this is very far from the case. Indeed, during the Asian crisis itself, a number of macro hedge funds bought Asian currencies such as the Indonesian rupiah on the view that they had overshot their fundamental value — unwisely and prematurely as it turned out. It has frequently been easier to make excess returns by trading against currencies rather than in their favour during the 1990s, not for any malign reason but simply because it was discovered that semi-pegged exchange rate regimes were incompatible with free and open capital markets. Keeping on the Asian example, to focus on currency speculation for or against Asian currencies is to ignore the fact that the Asian boom became a speculative bubble that was in any case waiting to burst, a bubble which the authorities were seemingly unwilling or unable to stop. Macro currency speculators are a stabilizing force against economic imbalance, an arbiter of government economic policies. The disruption that currency markets might experience is not caused by their activity. Whether they were capable of doing so in the past due to much greater leverage, that is certainly not the case now. They can merely accelerate the process, but they cannot cause it. The real cause is the government policy in the first place, which triggered the economic imbalance.

9.6.2   Momentum (and Fellow Travellers)

Momentum funds have a different trading approach as regards currency speculation. Rather than focusing on apparent disparities between the economics and the price, they use so-called momentum models to trigger buy or sell signals in currency pairs irrespective of the economics. Granted, one could argue that since economics affects the price of the currency, so it also affects their models and therefore their trading approach. However, it is fair to say that economics is not their primary focus. Their aim is to be disciplined to the extent that they rigorously follow the trading signals of their momentum models. As one might expect, the nature of these models varies. For instance, one such momentum model relies on technical analysis indicators to provide short-term moving averages. When a 5-day moving average crosses up through the 15-day moving average they buy and when the opposite happens they sell. Granted, this is a vast oversimplification and there are many significantly more sophisticated momentum models than this. That said, the principle is surely the correct one. Momentum models, however complex and whatever indicators they rely on, focus on changes in market prices as their key determinant for providing signals rather than economic fundamentals. Therefore, it is probably a reasonable generalization to say that they are more short term in their trading approach than macro-based currency speculators might be, depending of course on how long the momentum signal lasts.

9.6.3   Flow

It is debatable whether or not momentum traders are trend-followers. There is no debate when it comes to flow-based currency speculators. The very act of using order flow information for the purpose of trading in the currency markets requires that the user is following the trend suggested by that flow data. Currency speculators who focus on flow, use that information to anticipate the continuation or end of a trend. Clearly, with flow products, both the quality and the relevance of the flow data are crucial elements in deciding whether or not to use such products as one's primary information source for trading. There is no point in using a flow product where the order flow is neither reflective of the currency market as a whole nor has any impact on it. Flow-based currency speculators can certainly earn excess returns, but as with other trading approaches discipline is needed. Unlike in the case of the momentum trader where the model creates the signal irrespective of all other factors and therefore the trader's only job is to execute according to that signal, there is still a significant degree of discretion and interpretation in flow-based currency speculation. For instance, temporary seasonal factors can distort flow. If the flows model were passive, this would mean that a trading signal would be triggered irrespective of this important consideration. That said, the aspect of discretion automatically increases the possibility of misinterpretation and making mistakes. As with most types of trading or currency speculation, experience counts.

9.6.4   Technical

Lastly, we focus on currency speculators who use technical analysis, either primarily or solely in order to determine their trading in the currency markets. Again, I have found that it surprises some economists that such people exist, not least because it flies in the face of the view that markets are efficient and that pricing is therefore irrelevant. My answer and more importantly the answer of the technically-based currency speculators themselves is that markets are not perfectly efficient, though they are predictable to an extent and technical analysis helps with that. As discussed in Chapter 4, there are a number of schools of thought within technical analysis, such as Elliott Wave, Gann and Fibonacci. A good technically-based currency speculator would use a number of types of technical analysis, not least to test their core view before executing the position. As with other types of currency trading, technical traders can be short or long term in their approach. More generally however, all are looking for trading opportunities using existing market pricing, either for or against the existing trend.

9.7   CURRENCY SPECULATION — A GUIDE

Readers who are familiar with most serious works on currency markets, which deal with the issue of currency speculation, will be familiar with the fact that most do so from the perspective of economic theory. That is to say, most look at the act of currency speculation in terms of its role relative to the specific types of exchange rate regimes, within the context of the overall economy. For instance, there have been several works that look at currency speculation relative to "target exchange zones". Optimal currency areas are in this specific sense those which are sufficiently strong and balanced to be able to deter most currency speculation and withstand that which is foolish enough to try.

There is nothing out there — and I have searched — on how to be a better currency speculator. Again, I realize this may cause a reaction within some. I must only reiterate that I see currency speculation neither as a benign nor as a malign force. Currency speculation does provide needed liquidity to those areas seen as productive within the economy. It also acts as a necessary arbiter of economic policy. Governments are answerable to the voters, but they are also answerable to financial markets, just as a board is answerable to its shareholders. Equally, governments must ensure against excess within those markets. The balance between the two is a delicate one, a dynamic one that changes over time. Both sides are cause and effect. There must be regulation and there must also be free markets, not least because all alternatives have been tried and have proved miserable failures. Completely unfettered, unregulated markets may prove chaotic and damaging. Equally, overly regulated markets may stagnate. Currency speculation plays a useful role as regards the overall health and vitality of the financial markets. Granted, this has been a role which has been little understood. Hopefully, this chapter has helped to achieve at least some clarity in this regard.

So, how to be a better currency speculator? As we have seen above, there are many techniques for currency speculation, depending on the framework one uses to analyse the market. I would suggest however that there are some guiding principles in the art of currency speculation, which should help speculators generate consistent excess returns. My perspective is that of an adviser rather than a trader. Having watched the currency markets for over a decade and in the process benefited from the knowledge and experience of the hundreds of currency market contacts that I have made or come into contact with, as an emerging market currency strategist I advise a bank's traders, sales and clients on what are the best trading and hedging strategies within emerging market currencies. The recommendations that I have made are compiled in an EMFX leveraged model portfolio[1] which produced annual cumulative simple returns of 46.3%, 25.9% and 47.1% in 1999, 2000 and 2001, respectively. As a result, I feel reasonably qualified to make some suggestions, which though they may undoubtedly not prove definitive at the very least add to the debate.

(1) **An integrated approach** — The most powerful, consistent form of currency analysis and therefore of currency speculation is that which brings together all the main analytical disciplines to create a combined trading signal. Fundamentals may or may not be enough on their own. However, currency speculators who want to create consistent outperformance and high excess returns do not deal with "maybes". Fundamental, technical, flow and valuation analysis need to be coordinated and integrated to provide the clearest picture of what is going on in the market and how one can profit from it. This is the heart of currency economics that I have tried to impart. A very simple and effective discipline is to create a signal grid for these four types of analysis and stick to it rigorously (see Table 9.1). Only when at least 3 of 4 readings are showing "green" or "red" should one put on a major new position. The advantage of this is that it should greatly reduce the bias created by relying only on one analytical type.

(2) **Risk appetite** — Use a risk appetite indicator as a gauge of overall market sentiment and as a benchmark against which to measure your positions. The one I mentioned in Chapter 2

---

[1] These figures are based on the simple cumulative returns resulting from recommendations and have not been officially audited.

Table 9.1   A currency strategy signal grid

	Currency economics	Flow analysis	Technical analysis	Long-term valuation
Exchange rate	Buy/sell	Buy/sell	Buy/sell	Buy/sell

is an excellent one, the *Instability Index*, but there are others. When your signal grid is showing no clear signal, but the risk appetite indicator is in risk-neutral or risk-seeking mode, go long a basket of higher carry currencies, albeit selectively chosen, in order to boost the total return. When the risk appetite indicator moves from risk-seeking to risk-neutral, take half your profit. When it moves from risk-neutral to risk-averse, cut your position entirely and go short the carry basket of currencies you have used. This strategy, used in a disciplined way, can add significantly and consistently to your total return, particularly during periods when the signal grid is showing mixed signals (which will be most of the time).

(3) **Trading discipline is at least as important as having the right view** — A currency speculator can have the right view but bad trading discipline can reduce or even reverse trading profits. The view should be the unequivocal result of the combined trading signal from the four analytical disciplines, or as a result of the risk appetite indicator. There is nothing else to consider. "Gut feel" can earn excess returns for a period of time if you are a good and experienced currency speculator, but it is not enough on its own. Eventually it will result in you getting burned. The more overconfident you are, the more badly you are likely to get burned. As regards positions, the entry, exit and stop levels should be decided by flow and technical considerations. Run profits, depending on technical and flow developments. Always cut losses. The field of behavioural finance teaches us what we know intuitively, that it is much harder to cut a position, whether it is running a profit or a loss, than to initiate it. Hoping or wishing a position to come back in your favour is a beginner's mistake. Be disciplined and that means at times being ruthless. Not cutting losses is the easiest and the most efficient way of destroying your total return.

(4) **Emotion comes before a fall** — Currency speculation is about making money pure and simple. There should be no emotional aspect to it. It is neither moral nor immoral. Furthermore, try to remain detached from your P&L to the extent that it does not affect your trading approach. Great danger lies in the making of both profit and loss. The more profit you make, the more your view of financial markets appears to be confirmed and the more overconfident you become. Many have produced incredible results speculating against market inconsistencies to the point where they appeared to believe they were the market. That is usually the signal that the good times are about to end. Losses can also be dangerous because they make you loss averse and thus reduce the amount of potentially profitable opportunities you can take advantage of.

(5) **Less is more** — Take fewer trading positions rather than more for two reasons. Firstly, a small number of trading positions is more easily managed than a larger number of positions, and that takes us back to point 3. Secondly, currency speculation is the pursuit of inconsistency in currency market pricing. There are rarely a very large number of inconsistencies at any one time, not least because if it were that easy we would all be doing it. The aim of creating the signal grid and using the discipline of the risk appetite indicator is to trade on sure-fire winners and nothing else. A portfolio that has a very large number of positions suggests a portfolio that is trading on more than sure-fire winners, a portfolio that is increasingly relying on such vague concepts as luck, hope, belief and emotion. Currency speculation is not a game, it is

not betting and there should be no luck involved. If there is, you have the wrong position. Cut it.

(6) **Speculators make predictable mistakes** — Everyone makes mistakes and currency market practitioners are no different. However some mistakes are more predictable than others. In this regard, there are three key themes of behavioural finance that should be considered as a guide to the usual mistakes made, and therefore how to avoid making them in the future. Readers who have well understood the points above will of course note that the mistakes below reflect straying from the signal grid and the risk appetite indicator:

- Heuristic-driven mistakes[2] — Currency speculators frequently rely on "heuristics" or rules of thumb in relation to their approach to trading. For instance, one such heuristic or rule of thumb can be that previous trends will continue. If something has gone up for six weeks it will go up for a seventh and an eighth. Heuristic-driven trading is biased in that the very act of establishing a rule of thumb approach to one's trading reflects one's past experience. Because of their reliance on heuristics, or rules of thumb, currency speculators can hold biased beliefs that make them vulnerable to committing errors, errors which result in painful losses.
- Frame dependence — This idea deals with the distinction between form and substance. Framing is about form. Frame dependence means that the results of one's currency view are dependent on the frame or framework within which one focuses one's view and thoughts. Frame dependence can deal not only with one's fundamental view but also one's approach to trading generally. One can be loss averse, meaning that one is far more reluctant to make a certain-sized loss rather than put on the risk necessary to make that level of profit. Losses result in emotion, which results in regret, which in turn alters the frame one uses to look at markets.
- Markets are inherently inefficient — The idea of financial markets being perfectly efficient is an elegant nonsense, which clearly deals with a perfect rather than a human being. Market mispricing happens all the time. Heuristic and frame dependence create consistent errors and therefore consistent losses. Learning how to distinguish such behavioural patterns means one can reduce such losses.

Heuristics, frame dependence and any belief in the supposed efficiency of financial markets are all aspects that lie outside of the rigorous trading discipline of the four analysis signal grid and the risk appetite indicator. For those currency speculators who use the rigorous, disciplined approach, there are no such things as "rules of thumb". In addition, the very act of using four types of analysis rather than just one should eliminate the risk of frame dependence.

9.8 SUMMARY

This chapter has sought to delve into the world of the currency speculator in greater detail than has hitherto been tried, both for the purpose of shedding light on them and their methods and also to attempt some ideas on how to be better at currency speculation. There can be no doubt that the issue of currency speculation will remain controversial. The aim here has been to take out some of the emotional aspects of the issue and try to look at it coolly and dispassionately. Speculators can accelerate change but they cannot cause it in the first place. To

---

[2]For more on the field of behavioural finance, readers should consult the excellent work by Hersh Sheffrin, *Beyond Greed and Fear: Understanding Behavioural Finance and the Psychology of Investing*, Harvard Business School Press, 2000.

forbid speculation is to forbid the market's evaluation of risk and thus to leave the market blind to policy error. If anything, that would be the real speculation. Having looked at the real world of corporations, real money investors and currency speculators, we turn in the last chapter to bringing together the ideas that have been presented in this book into an integrated analytical framework for the purpose of making corporate executives or investors better currency analysts and thus boosting their bottom line.

10
Applying the Framework

So far in this book, we have looked at the various key components that go into currency strategy. The aim in this last chapter is therefore simple — to pull together all these components into a single, integrated framework of analysis. To this end, it is important first to *crystallize* (rather than repeat) the main points we have learned to date, both to further clarify their importance and to make them more easily remembered. Having done that, we then need to apply this currency strategy framework to the practical world of corporations, investors and speculators, showing how they may use it to boost their bottom line.

First, briefly we recap and crystallize the main points made to date. Thus, currency strategy is the analytical discipline that consists of the following:

1. Currency economics
2. Flow analysis
3. Technical analysis
4. Long-term valuation

10.1 CURRENCY ECONOMICS

Classical economics has sought and failed to explain short-term exchange rate moves on a consistent basis. Currency economics is an attempt to fine tune economic theory to the practical relevance of the currency market. Broadly speaking, it seeks to analyse those aspects of the economy that are relevant to the exchange rate value, such as:

- Trends within the balance of payments, including the current and capital accounts;
- The accounting identity for economic adjustment $(S - I = X - M)$;
- The Real Effective Exchange Rate (REER) and the external balance;
- Relative productivity measures.

Naturally, all other aspects of the economy should be considered such as growth, inflation and so forth, but the ones mentioned above are the key indicators relevant for our purpose of currency analysis and strategy. Growth *per se* does not make a currency rise or fall on a consistent basis. Currency market practitioners, while keeping an eye on other parts of the economy as well, should seek to focus primarily on those specific aspects of the economy that affect the exchange rate.

10.2 FLOW ANALYSIS

As barriers to trade and capital have broken down in the last two decades, so capital flows have become increasingly important, both in terms of their impact on the economy and in turn on the exchange rate. At USD1.2 trillion in daily volume, the currency markets trade the equivalent of annual global merchandise trade every day of the year. Like any market, the currency market is affected by demand and supply, which in this case is reflected by order flow. It has been found that tracking order flow can provide both a useful explanation of past price activity in currency markets and — more importantly — can be used as a predictor of future price action. The basic premise behind this is that changes in order flow, if sufficiently large, can have predictable and sustainable impact in the currency markets in terms of price action. There are several short- and medium-term flow indicators which the reader should be aware of.

Short-term flow data:

• The IMM Commitments of Traders report

Medium-term flow data:

• US Treasury "TIC" capital flow report
• Euro-zone portfolio report
• IMF quarterly report on emerging market financing
• IIF capital flows report

In addition to flow data provided by the trading exchanges as in the case of the IMM and by official sources as with the TIC and Euro-zone reports, there are also proprietary flow models created by commercial and investment banks to analyse client flows going through the bank's currency dealing rooms.

• Order flow/sentiment models

Flow data and models provide direct evidence of the effect of order flow on market pricing. A more indirect but no less useful to way to do that is to look at market sentiment indicators such as:

• Option risk reversals

These are a very useful gauge of the market's "skew" or bias towards an exchange rate. Analysing risk reversal trends over time relative to the spot rate may allow one to make predictions as to future spot rates based on the risk reversal.

10.3 TECHNICAL ANALYSIS

Crucial to both flow and technical analysis is the idea that financial markets are not in fact inherently efficient and that the past can in fact impact the future. With flow analysis, one is dealing with trends in order flow. With technical analysis, one is analysing past pricing to make predictions about the future. At its most basic, technical analysis uses such concepts as "support" and "resistance" to denote points of dynamic market tension between supply and demand for an exchange rate, equity, bond or commodity. At a more sophisticated level, technical analysis relies on patterns in mathematics to suggest they may be reproduced in market pricing. Fibonacci, Elliott Wave and Gann analysis are examples of these.

"Charting" remains a controversial subject for some within the financial and academic communities who appear to regard it as little more than voodoo. In the real world of trading, hedging and investing however, nothing counts except results. Unlike in the economic world where the quality of the story is seen as important, almost irrespective of its accuracy, for traders, investors and corporations the bottom line *is* the bottom line. To that end, while classical economics has failed to explain short-term exchange rate moves on a sustained basis, flow and technical analysis have stepped into the void. Just as in economics, there are "good" and "bad" chartists or technical analysts. The profession of technical analysis however has consistently outperformed the returns generated by random walk theory and frequently also those by economists. In analysing exchange rates, currency market practitioners who do not use technical analysis in addition to fundamental analysis are hampering their own ability to produce consistently high returns.

10.4   LONG-TERM VALUATION

The dividing line between currency economics and long-term valuation analysis is somewhat blurred. There is a difference however and it concerns the time span involved in one's analysis. The aim of currency economics is to look at the parts of the economy that affect and are affected by the exchange rate, such as the balance of payments and inflation differentials, in order to give an idea about that exchange rate's *current* valuation and direction. Long-term valuation models, such as those that focus on REER or FEER, are trying to give a multi-month or more likely a multi-year view of exchange rate valuation. In line with this, the main exchange rate models that focus on long-term valuation are the following:

- Purchasing Power Parity
- The Monetary Approach
- The Interest Rate Approach
- The Balance of Payments Approach
- The Portfolio Balance Approach

Most of these models focus on the relative price of an asset or good which should over time cause an exchange rate adjustment to restore "equilibrium".

10.5   THE SIGNAL GRID

The four analytical disciplines of currency economics, flow analysis, technical analysis and long-term valuation which come together to make a currency strategy decision can be expressed in the form of a signal grid, as shown in Table 9.1. To be sure, this is a very simple model. However, what is important here is having the discipline to create it. Only when all four analytical indicators are reading buy or sell together should one put out an official currency strategy recommendation. Granted, this is still no guarantee of success. It should however have a number of positive effects on one's trading or analytical performance:

- It should eliminate the bias created by relying only on one analytical type
- By nature, four buy signals make up a more powerful buy signal than just one
- The bottom line — it should improve one's performance and total returns

10.6   RISK APPETITE INDICATORS

When there is no clear, unequivocal signal from the signal grid, that is when not all four signals are pointing in the same direction, currency traders and investors can still boost their total return by using a risk appetite indicator to gauge overall market sentiment in terms of "risky" or "safe" assets, both in terms of putting on new positions and in terms of measuring their existing positions. Risk sentiment can be divided up into three levels:

- Risk-seeking/stable
- Risk-neutral
- Risk-aversion/unstable

When the indicator is in risk-seeking or risk-neutral mode, be long a basket of higher carry currencies, either in the developed or emerging markets. Conversely, when it is in risk-aversion mode, obviously having moved there from risk-neutral, cut and reverse the position, going short the carry basket of currencies. Risk appetite has become an increasingly important concept not just because of the need to create more accurate models for forecasting short-term currency moves, but also because the last few years have shown a marked pick-up in cross-asset market volatility. There are several risk appetite indicators created by the private sector for this purpose. Not just currency traders or speculators can use this. A risk appetite indicator can be a crucial tool for corporate Treasurers and institutional investors, not least in providing them with an informed context within which their exposure exists.

10.7   EXCHANGE RATE REGIMES

The signal grid and the risk appetite indicator should be the two main tools of the currency strategist. There are however other aspects of the currency markets that still have to be considered. For instance, the type of exchange rate regime is an important consideration as it can have a significantly different impact on the economy depending on what type of regime is being used. The latest fashion within the official community in Washington DC is to advocate the so-called "bi-polar" world of exchange rates, supporting the idea that in a world of free capital markets only the hardest currency peg or a completely free-floating currency are appropriate, and that anything else is unsustainable. It seems likely that this will ultimately give way to a new trend, whereby there are significantly less currencies, all of which are freely floating. As far as currency market practitioners are concerned, key questions that a corporate executive or an investor must ask if they are exposed to a currency peg regime are:

- Does the currency peg itself contribute to macroeconomic stability?
- What is the degree of participation in global capital flows of the country concerned?
- Is the currency peg at the right value?

Most soft or semi-pegged exchange rate regimes have gone, voluntarily or otherwise. If you have currency exposure to a pegged exchange rate regime and you are concerned about currency risk, the rule to remember is that you should hedge when the market has no interest in hedging and thus when risk premiums are low. By the time the market is keen to hedge currency risk, liquidity and price conditions will have deteriorated and it will be too late to obtain anything but the most expensive of currency protection.

The beauty of freely floating exchange rates is that they act as a self-adjusting mechanism, transmitting changes in fundamental dynamics across the economy. In that sense, a freely floating exchange rate regime cannot be defeated, unlike a pegged exchange rate regime. That said, they can still be highly volatile at times.

10.8   CURRENCY CRISES AND MODELS

10.8.1   CEMC

Most of the currency crises of the 1990s happened against soft currency pegs. In the wake of the Asian currency crisis, I made a stab at creating a model which focused on how exchange rates typically performed in the run to and after the break down of a pegged exchange rate regime. For good or ill, the Classic Emerging Market Currency Crisis (CEMC) model was the result. To be sure, the title is a mouthful, but for the most part it tells the story of most emerging market currency crises during the 1990s and thus may serve as a useful barometer should any such crises be experienced going forward. This can be broken down into five phases during which the currency crisis takes place:

1. Capital inflows and real currency appreciation
2. Fundamental deterioration and inevitable currency collapse
3. A positive current account swing and a liquidity-based rally
4. The economy hits bottom; a period of consolidation
5. The fundamental rally

A key aspect of these crises was the relationship between the real exchange rate and the external balance. In floating exchange rate regimes, economic imbalances are usually smoothed out over time. In pegged exchange rate regimes, they can build up to unsustainable levels, thus forcing the collapse of the exchange rate peg, if not checked by changes in macroeconomic policy.

10.8.2   The Speculative Cycle

While CEMC focuses specifically on pegged exchange rates, the "speculative cycle" model focuses instead on freely floating exchanges. This model consists of four phases, describing the relationship between "fundamental" and "speculative" forces within the markets and the effect they have on the economy:

1. Capital flows are attracted and the local currency rallies
2. Speculators join the crowd and the local currency continues to rally
3. This causes fundamental deterioration, causing increased price volatility
4. Fundamental selling overwhelms speculative buying and the currency collapses

The basic idea behind this is that freely floating exchange rates are not random, but instead tend to trade in cycles, though the length of those cycles can vary from weeks to years depending on other factors such as capital flows.

10.9   MANAGING CURRENCY RISK I — THE CORPORATION

10.9.1   Types of Currency Risk

For corporations, there are three key kinds of currency risk they have to manage. They are:

1. Transactional risk (receivables, dividends, etc.)
2. Translational risk (balance sheet)
3. Economic risk (present value of future operating cash flows)

Transactional risk or exposure is essentially cash flow risk. Translational risk, for its part, results from the consolidation of group and subsidiary balance sheets, and deals with the exposure represented by foreign investment and debt structure. Economic risk is an overall measure of the currency risk of the corporation, focusing on the present value of future operating cash flows and how this present value in the base currency changes as a result of changes in exchange rates. Over the long term, however, exchange rates adjust through the concept of PPP, depending on relative inflation and domestic price levels. Thus, theoretically, a corporation whose foreign subsidiaries experience price inflation in line with the general level of inflation should be returned to its original value through an adjustment in the exchange rate exactly according to the PPP concept. In such circumstances, one might argue that economic risk or exposure is irrelevant. However, corporations rarely experience cost inflation exactly in line with the general level of inflation. Therefore, economic risk does matter. The best way of dealing with this is to finance operations in the currency to which the firm's value is sensitive.

10.9.2   Internal Hedging

There are of course well-known methods of hedging internally, such as:

- Netting (debt, receivables and payables are netted out between group companies)
- Matching (intragroup foreign currency inflows and outflows)
- Leading and lagging (adjustment of credit terms before and after due date)
- Price adjustment (raising/lowering selling prices to counter exchange rate moves)
- Invoicing in foreign currency (thus reducing transaction risk)
- Asset and liability management (to manage balance sheet, income, cash flow risk)

10.9.3   Key Operational Controls for Treasury

Assuming that the corporation has accepted in principle that it needs to manage its currency risk, it then has several choices to make with regard to how it will go about achieving this — the instruments it will allow itself to use, the type of currency hedging carried out, positional and credit limits and so forth. All of these matters need to be dealt with in a systematic and rigorous way *at the start, before the currency hedging programme begins*. Performance measurement standards, accountability and limits of some form must be part of a Treasury foreign currency hedging programme. Management must elucidate specifically the goals and the operational limits of such a programme.

10.9.4   Optimization

For a given exchange rate view, an optimization model can create an "efficient frontier" of hedging strategies to manage currency risk. The most efficient hedging strategy is that which is the cheapest for the most risk hedged. This is a very efficient and useful tool for hedging currency risk in a more sophisticated way than just buying a vanilla hedge and "hoping" that it is the appropriate strategy. Hedging optimizers frequently compare the following strategies to find the optimal one for the given currency view and exposure:

- 100% hedged using vanilla forwards
- 100% unhedged
- Option risk reversal

- Option call spread
- Option low-delta call

10.9.5   Budget Rates

The budget exchange rate can drive both the corporation's hedging strategy and its pricing strategy as well, and can be set in a number of ways. It can simply be the spot exchange rate at the end of the previous fiscal period. This is often referred to as the accounting rate. Alternatively, when dealing with forecasted cash flows, the issue becomes slightly more complex. Theoretically, the budget exchange rate should be derived from the domestic sales price and the foreign subsidiary sales price. Thus, if the parent sales price for a good is USD10 and the Euro area sales price for argument's sake is EUR15, the theoretical budget rate would be 0.67. The Euro–dollar exchange may be different from that, so the corporation needs to evaluate whether there is room to change its Euro-denominated pricing without reducing margin substantially in order to set a budget rate that is closer to the spot exchange rate. If there is a major difference between the spot exchange rate and the budget rate, the corporation may have to reassess its currency risk management policy. Once the budget rate is set, the Treasury has to secure an appropriate hedge rate and ensure minimal slippage relative to that hedge rate. Timing and the instruments used are key to achieving that. Finally, it is important to note that the budget rate comes from relative price differentials. This however is also at the heart of PPP, which states that exchange rates should adjust for relative price differentials of the same good between two countries. Thus, a corporation could use PPP as a benchmark for setting budget rates.

10.10   MANAGING CURRENCY RISK II — THE INVESTOR

Managing currency risk remains a controversial issue for institutional investors. At one end of the spectrum, you have many international equity funds who either do not hedge their currency risk or use an unhedged currency benchmark. At the other end, you have fixed income funds that use a currency overlay manager to manage their currency risk actively. To be sure, this is a gross generalization. There are equity funds that do manage their currency risk, whether on a passive or an active basis, and equally there are fixed income funds that make a deliberate choice not to hedge their currency risk. That said, it is the case that fixed income funds are generally more responsive to the idea of managing their currency risk separately and independently from the underlying than their equity fund counterparts, because currency risk empirically makes up a substantially higher portion of the average return volatility of a fixed income portfolio than for an equity portfolio. The figures are roughly 70% and 30% respectively, not least because equities are generally more volatile than bonds. When investing abroad however, there are two core principles concerning currency risk:

1. Investing in a country is not the same as investing in that country's currency.
2. Currency is not the same as cash; the incentive for currency investment is primarily capital gain rather than income.

Like corporations, institutional investors face transaction risk when they make investments in a foreign currency. They also face translation risk on net assets if they spread their operations overseas. Whether or not it is done by the same individual, it is a core view of this book that currency risk and underlying asset risk should be managed separately and independently from each other. The way currencies and underlying assets are analysed and the way they trade are both different from each other. Consequently, the way they should be managed should also be different.

Having decided to manage a portfolio's currency risk, one then has to decide whether the aim is to achieve total returns or relative returns.

10.10.1   Absolute Returns: Risk Reduction

Just as a corporation has to decide whether to run their Treasury operation as a profit or as a loss reducing centre, so a portfolio manager has to make the same choice in the approach they take to managing currency risk. If a portfolio manager is focused on maximizing absolute returns, the emphasis in managing their currency risk is likely to be on *risk reduction*. In order to achieve this, they will most likely adopt a strategy of *passive currency management*. This involves adopting and sticking religiously to a currency hedging strategy, rolling those hedges during the lifetime of the underlying investment. The two obvious ways of establishing a passive hedging strategy are:

- Three-month forward (rolled continuously)
- Three-month at-the-money forward call (rolled continuously)

The advantage of passive currency management is that it reduces or eliminates the currency risk (depending on whether the benchmark is fully or partially hedged). The disadvantage is that it does not incorporate any flexibility and therefore cannot respond to changes in market dynamics and conditions. The emphasis on risk reduction within a passive currency management style deals with the basic idea that the portfolio's return in the base currency is equal to:

The return of foreign assets invested in + the return of the foreign currency

This is a simple, but hopefully effective way of expressing the view that there are two separate and distinct risks present within the decision to invest outside of the base currency. The motive of risk reduction is therefore to hedge to whatever extent decided upon the return of the foreign currency.

10.10.2   Selecting the Currency Hedging Benchmark

The most disciplined way of managing currency risk from a hedging perspective is to use a currency hedging benchmark. There are four main ones:

- 100% hedged benchmark
- 100% unhedged benchmark
- Partially hedged benchmark
- Option hedged benchmark

Being 100% hedged is usually not the optimal strategy, apart from in exceptional cases. Equally, using a currency hedging benchmark of 100% unhedged would seem to defeat the object. Many funds are not allowed to use options, thus in most cases the best hedging benchmark to use is partially hedged.

10.10.3   Relative Returns: Adding Alpha

Portfolio or asset managers who are on the other hand looking to maximize relative returns compared to an unhedged position will most likely adopt a strategy of *active currency management* whether the emphasis is on adding alpha or relative return. Either the portfolio manager or a professional currency overlay manager will "trade" the currency around a selected currency hedging benchmark for the explicit purpose of adding alpha. In most cases, this alpha is measured against a 100% unhedged position, although it could theoretically be measured against the return of the currency hedging benchmark. With active currency management, the emphasis should be on flexibility, both in terms of the availability of financial instruments one can use to add alpha and also in terms of the currency hedging benchmark itself. On the first of these, an active currency manager should have access to a broad spectrum of currency instruments in order to boost their chance of adding value. Similarly, their ability to add value is significantly increased by the adoption of a 50% or symmetrical currency hedging benchmark rather than by a 100% hedged or 100% unhedged benchmark.

10.10.4 Tracking Error

Just as corporations have to deal with "forecasting error" in terms of the deviation of forecast exchange rates relative to the actual future rate, so investors have to deal with *tracking error* within their portfolios, which is the return of the portfolio relative to the investment benchmark index being used. A portfolio manager can significantly affect the tracking error of their portfolio by the selection of the currency hedging benchmark. Empirically, it has been found that a 50% or symmetrical currency hedging benchmark generates around 70% of the tracking error of that generated by using a polar of 100% currency hedging benchmark. Put another way, the tracking error of a polar currency hedging benchmark is around 1.41 times that of a 50% hedged benchmark. The advantage of a symmetrical or 50% currency hedged benchmark for a portfolio manager is that it reduces tracking error and it also enables them to participate in both bull and bear currency markets.

Two popular types of active currency management strategy are the differential forward strategy and the trend-following strategy. Both of these strategies have consistently added alpha to a portfolio if followed rigorously and interestingly have also proven to be risk reducing compared to unhedged benchmarks. Thus, they also help to boost significantly the portfolio's Sharpe ratio.

10.10.5 Differential Forward Strategy

Forward exchange rates are very poor predictors of future spot exchange rates, in contrast to the theories of covered interest rate parity and unbiased forward parity. As a result, one can take advantage of these apparent market "inefficiencies" by hedging the currency 100% when the forward rate pays you to do it and hedging 0% when the forward rate is against you. The differential forward strategy has generated consistently good results over a long time and over a broad set of currency pairs.

10.10.6 Trend-Following Strategy

The idea behind this strategy is to go long the currency pair when the price is above a moving average of a given length and to go short the currency pair when it is below. Currency managers can choose different moving averages depending on their trading approach to the benchmark. Lequeux and Acar (1998) showed that to be representative of the various durations followed by investors, an equally weighted portfolio based on three moving averages of length 32, 61 and 117 days may be appropriate. If the spot exchange rate is above all three moving averages, hedge the foreign currency exposure 100%. If above two out of the three, hedge one-third of the position. In all other cases, leaves the position unhedged. Trend-following strategies have shown consistent excess returns over sustained periods of time.

10.10.7   Optimization of the Carry Trade

As with corporations, institutional investors can use optimization techniques. With corporations, the aim is to achieve the cheapest hedge for the most risk hedged. In the case of the investor, the aim here is to add alpha by improving on the simple carry trade. The idea behind the carry trade itself is that, using a risk appetite indicator, the currency manager goes long a basket of high carry currencies, when risk appetite readings are either strong or neutral, and conversely goes short that basket of currencies when risk appetite readings go into negative territory.

It is possible to fine tune or optimize this strategy to take account of the volatility and correlation of currencies in addition to their yield differentials. This should produce better returns than the simple carry trade strategy. The optimized carry trade hedges the currency pairs according to the weights provided by the mean–variance optimization rather than simply hedging the currency pairs exhibiting an attractive carry. The returns generated by the optimized carry trade strategy are actually better than those generated by the differential forward strategy on a risk-adjusted basis.

10.11   MANAGING CURRENCY RISK III — THE SPECULATOR

If the idea of currency hedging is controversial to some, then that of currency speculation is even more so. Currency speculation — that is the trading of currencies with no underlying, attached asset — makes up the vast majority of currency market flow. Given that the currency market provides the liquidity for global trade and investment, it is therefore currency speculation that is providing this liquidity. When looking at the issue of currency speculation, one should immediately dispense with such descriptions of it being a "good" or a "bad" influence and instead focus on what it provides. It is neither a benign nor a malign force. Rather, its sole purpose is to make money. Furthermore, it does not act in a vacuum, but instead represents the market's response to perceived *fundamental* changes. Thus, it is a symptom rather than the disease itself, which is usually bad economic policy.

Currency speculators are usually made up of one of three groups — interbank dealers, proprietary dealers, or hedge or total return funds. However, at times, currency overlay managers or corporate Treasurers can also be termed currency speculators if they take positions in the currency markets which have no underlying attached asset.

10.12   CURRENCY STRATEGY FOR CURRENCY MARKET PRACTITIONERS

Having gone through the main points that we have covered in this book so that they are clear, it is now time to put them into practice. Currency market practitioners can use currency strategy techniques for basically two activities:

- Currency trading
- Currency hedging

10.12.1   Currency Trading

This section includes currency speculators and active currency managers. Some corporate Treasuries are run as a profit centre and thus this part will also be of interest to them. For the purpose of dividing currency activity into trading and hedging, we assume the generalization that corporate Treasury for the most part uses the currency market for hedging purposes. The aim here is to show how a currency market practitioner can combine the strategy techniques described in this book for the practical use of trading or investing in currencies. Given that I focus primarily on the emerging market currencies, we will keep the focus to that sector of the currency market, though clearly these strategy techniques can and should be used for currency exposure generally. The example we use here is that of a recommendation I put out on January 10, 2002. The key point here is not just that the recommendation made or lost money, but also how the strategy was arrived at. The aim is not to copy this specific recommendation, but to be able to repeat the strategy method. Note that these types of currency strategies should be attempted solely by professional and qualified institutional investors or corporations.

Example

On January 10, 2002, I released a strategy note, recommending clients to sell the US dollar against the Turkish lira, via a one-month forward outright contract. For the past couple of months, we had been taking a more positive and constructive view on the Turkish lira, in line with the price action and more positive fundamental and technical developments. Thus, we came to the conclusion that while the Turkish lira remained a volatile currency, it was trending positively and was likely to continue to do so near term. Hence, we recommended clients to:

- Sell USD–TRL one-month forward outright at 1.460 million
- Spot reference: 1.395 million
- Target: 1.350 million
- Targeted return excluding carry: +3.2%
- Stop: 1.460 million

From a fundamental perspective, we at the time took a constructive view on Turkey's 2002 economic outlook. While recognizing persistent risks to that outlook, the prospects for a virtuous circle of investor confidence appeared to have improved significantly. To recap, the Turkish lira had devalued and de-pegged in February of 2001 and since then had fallen substantially from around 600,000 to the US dollar before the peg broke to a low of 1.65 million. That decline in the lira's value had severe consequences for the economy, triggering a dramatic spike in inflation. Indeed, in the third quarter of 2001, currency weakness and rising inflation appeared to have created a vicious circle, whereby each fed off the other.

The CEMC model tells us however that the low in a currency's value after de-pegging and the high in inflation are highly related, and that Phase II of the model is related to a liquidity-driven rally in the value of the currency after inflation has peaked. By the end of 2001, inflation had clearly peaked on a month-on-month basis and was close to peaking on a year-on-year basis at just over 70%. Thus, from the perspective of the CEMC model, the signs were positive as regards prospects for a continuation of the rally in the Turkish lira, which had begun somewhat tentatively in November 2001. A further positive sign, also in line with Phase II of the CEMC model, was a massive and positive swing in the current account balance, from a deficit of around 6% of GDP in 2000 to a surplus of around 1% in 2001. This was largely due to the collapse of import demand in the wake of the pegged exchange rate's collapse, just as the CEMC model suggests. In January 2002, what we were witnessing was a classic liquidity-driven rally in a currency which had hit its low after breaking its peg the previous year. This phenomenon was far from unique to the Turkish lira. Exactly the same phenomenon was seen in the Asian currencies after their crisis in 1997–1998, and to some extent also in the Russian rouble and Brazilian real.

In addition to such economic considerations, favourable political considerations were also an important factor, keeping Turkey financially well supported, particularly in the wake of the successful passage of such important legislation as the tobacco and public procurement laws. Strong official support for Turkey at the end of 2001 appeared to make 2002 financing and rollovers look manageable. Finally, "dollarization" levels — that is the degree to which Turkish deposit holders were changing out of lira and into US dollars — appeared to have peaked in November 2001, after soaring initially in the wake of the lira's devaluation in February 2001. In our view, if the 1994 devaluation was any guide, this process of de-dollarization may have been only in its early stages. Granted, any positive view on the Turkish lira still had to be tempered with some degree of caution about the underlying risks. Any proliferation of the anti-terrorism campaign to Iraq and/or renewed domestic political squabbling would clearly have the potential to upset markets, as would any hint of delay in global recovery prospects.

There was also the "technical" angle to consider. Despite the fact that the Turkish lira had been a floating currency for only a relatively small period of time, the dollar–Turkish lira exchange rate appeared to trade increasingly technically, in line with such technical indicators as moving averages through September and October of 2001. Indeed, in November of 2001, dollar–Turkish lira broke down through the 55-day moving average at 1.479 million for the first time since the lira's devaluation, and then formed a perfect head and shoulders pattern (see Figure 10.1). The neckline of that head and shoulders pattern came in around 1.350 million, which was why we put out target there. Such technical indicators as RSI and slow stochastics were also pointing lower for dollar–Turkish lira.

In sum, both fundamentals, technicals and the CEMC model all seemed aligned at the time for further Turkish lira outperformance. Looking at the dollar–Turkish lira exchange rate through the signal grid, we would have come up with the results in Table 10.1. While recommendations can be made on the basis of only one out of the four signals, they are clearly more powerful — and more likely to be right — if all four signals are in line.

So what happened to our recommendation? To repeat, the aim here is not to focus overly on the results of this specific recommendation, but rather on how a currency strategist puts a recommendation together, using the currency strategy techniques we have discussed throughout this book. This example is used only for the general purpose of showing how a recommendation might be put together. As for this specific recommendation, the dollar–Turkish lira exchange rate hit our initial target of 1.35 million spot, but we decided to keep it on. Subsequently, it traded as low as 1.296 million, before trading back above 1.3 million. With a week left to go

Table 10.1   USD–TRL signal grid

	Currency economics	Flow analysis	Technical analysis	Long-term valuation	Combined signal
Buy/sell	Sell	Sell	Sell	Sell	**Sell**

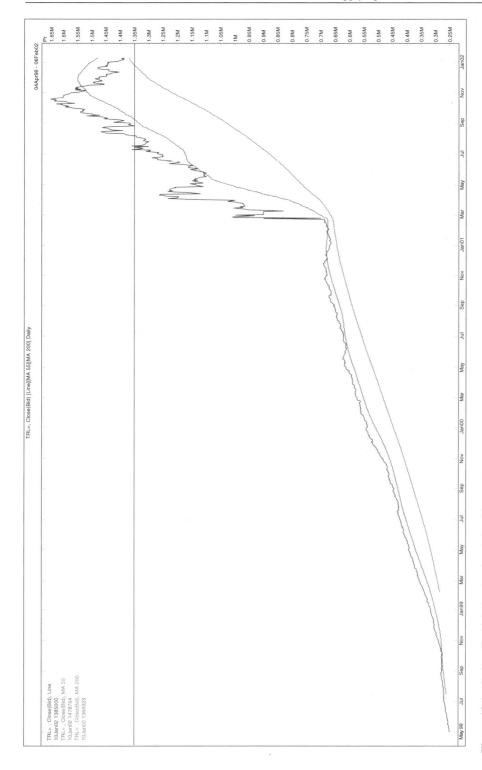

Figure 10.1 Dollar–Turkish lira: head and shoulders pattern
Source: Reuters.

before the forward contract matured, we decided to take profit on the recommendation for a return, including carry, of +8.4%.

What is important to remember from this example is not that the recommendation made such a return — I freely admit that I have put out recommendations that have lost money. Rather, the important thing to remember is the discipline that was involved in putting the recommendation together.

10.12.2   Currency Hedging

For its part, this section should be the focus of passive currency managers and corporations. Here too, the discipline of how one puts together a currency strategy is the same, though the purpose is different. The currency market practitioner has to form a currency view. That view can come from the bank counterparties that the corporation or asset manager uses, but the currency market practitioner should also have a currency view themselves, with which to compare against such external views. The view itself is created from the signal grid, incorporating currency economics, technicals, flow analysis and long-term valuation. The currency market practitioner should be aware of all these aspects of the currency to which they are exposed. Not being aware is the equivalent of not knowing the business you are in. In the example I have chosen, we keep the focus on emerging market currencies, this time looking at the risk posed by exposure to currency risk in the countries of Central and Eastern Europe.

Example

The Euro has flattered to deceive on many occasions. Countless times, currency strategists in the US, the UK and Europe have forecast a major and sustained Euro rally, and for the most part they have been wrong. This is not to say the Euro has not staged brief recoveries, notably from its October 26, 2000 record low of 0.8228 against the US dollar, reaching at one point as high as 0.9595. However, such recoveries have ultimately proved unsustainable, not least with respect to both hopes and expectations.

This has been extremely important for UK, US and European corporations with factories or operations in Central and Eastern Europe. The reasons for this are simple — just as the Euro has been weak against the US dollar over the past two to three years, so it has also been simultaneously weak against the currencies of Central and Eastern Europe. Indeed, there is a close correlation between the two, not least because the Euro area receives around 70% of total CEE exports. Equally, the Euro area is by some way the largest direct investor in CEE countries, ahead of EU accession and ultimately adopting the Euro. The pull for convergence has been irresistible. Substantial portfolio and direct investment inflows to CEE countries, combined with broad Euro weakness, has meant that the Euro has weakened substantially against the likes of the Czech koruna, Polish zloty, Slovak koruna and also the Hungarian forint, after Hungary's de-pegging in May 2001, in the period 2000–2002.

For corporations that invested in the CEE region, this has been excellent news. As the Euro has weakened against CEE currencies, so the value of their investment has appreciated when translated back into Euros. More specifically, consolidation of subsidiary balance sheets within the group balance sheet has been favourable as the value of the Euro has declined.

This raises an obvious question — what happens if it goes up? As we saw when looking at translation risk in Chapter 7, corporations face translation risk on the group balance sheet on the net assets (gross assets − liabilities) of their foreign subsidiary. Usually, corporations do not hedge translation risk given the cost, the potential for "regret" and the view that balance sheet hedging to a certain extent negates the purpose of the original investment. However, as I have tried to show, sustained exchange rate moves can have a significant impact on the balance sheet if not hedged. Equally, the initial investment does not negate the need to manage the balance sheet dynamically.

The threat in question is that of the Euro strengthening against CEE currencies. Readers should note that once more that is a theoretical example and I do not mean to suggest that this is in fact a threat. Rather, readers should be considering what they might have to do were it a real threat. Consider then the possibility that the Euro might appreciate, perhaps significantly against CEE currencies. For a corporation, this represents a balance sheet risk when translating the value of foreign subsidiaries' net assets back onto the group balance sheet. It might also represent transaction and economic risk as well, in terms of the threat to dividend streams and to the present value of future operating cash flows.

Thus, supposing there were a real threat of significant Euro appreciation against CEE currencies, that threat would according to our signal grid have to be quantified in terms of currency economics, flows, technical analysis and long-term valuation. When — and only when — all four are aligned in the form of a BUY signal should the corporation consider strategic hedging, that is hedging more than just immediate receivables. For the purpose of this exercise, assume that all four are indeed aligned. Our corporation therefore has to think seriously about hedging the various types of currency risk associated with their investments in the CEE region.

How to go about hedging? Having first decided to carry out a hedge, using the combined signal from a currency strategy signal grid, there are two further steps in this process. The first is to quantify the specific type and amount of risk involved. For a corporation, this means whether we are talking about transaction, translation or economic currency risk. The type of currency risk may have a significant bearing on what type of currency hedging instruments will be used. The second step in this process is to focus on the specific types of instruments involved. For this purpose, I have provided a shortened version of the menu of possible structures available in Chapter 7 (see Tables 10.2 and 10.3). The corporate Treasury should get its counterparty bank to price up a menu of possible hedging strategies, which are in line with their currency view, in order to be able to compare the costs and benefits of each strategy and arrive at the cheapest hedging strategy for the most risk hedged.

The investor or asset manager will look at currency risk in a slightly different way, but for that should still adopt the same degree of rigour in seeking to manage it. Passive currency managers will presumably buy the same tenor of forward or option and continue to roll that

Table 10.2 Traditional hedging structures

Type	Advantages	Disadvantages
Unhedged	Maintains possible yield on underlying investment	Speculative, *reflecting a view* that there is no or little FX risk
Vanilla EUR forward	Covered against FX risk	No flexibility, high cost if interest rate differentials are large, vulnerable to unfavourable FX moves
Vanilla EUR call option	Covered against FX risk, flexibility (does not have to be exercised)	Premium cost

Table 10.3   Enhanced (option) hedging structures

Type	Advantages	Disadvantages
Seagull	Partly covered against FX risk, can be structured as zero cost	Not covered against a major FX move
Risk reversal	Directional and vol play	Cost of the RR given interest rate differentials, though could be structured to be zero cost
Convertible forward	Converts to a forward at an agreed rate during the tenor of the contract, customer can take advantage of a contrarian move in spot up to but not including the KI	The strike is more expensive than the forward and this has to be paid if the structure is knocked-in
Enhanced forward	If the currency stays within an agreed range, the rate is significantly improved relative to the vanilla forward	If spot goes outside of the range, the forward rate to be paid becomes more expensive

position, though as the value of the underlying changes so they may have to adjust their hedges in order to avoid slippage.

The line between currency trading and currency hedging blurs when it comes to active currency managers who trade around a currency hedging benchmark. The difference between the two clearly comes down to incentive, and also to whether one is targeting absolute or relative returns. Active currency managers also hedge currency risk, either on a rigorous basis relative to a currency hedging benchmark or on a purely discretionary basis. Within the emerging markets, dedicated emerging market funds may have a currency overlay manager who hedges/trades relative to a currency hedging benchmark. On the other hand, G7 funds that allocate 2–3% of their portfolio to the emerging markets are unlikely to have a specific currency hedging benchmark for such a small allocation, and are only likely to hedge currency risk on a discretionary basis. The suggestion here is that both could do so more effectively and more rigorously through the use of a signal grid and by comparing a menu of hedging structure costs, assuming that their fund allows them to use more than just forwards.

10.13   SUMMARY

The aim of this chapter has been to bring together the core principles of currency strategy into a coherent framework and then to apply them through practical examples to the real world of the currency market practitioner. There are no doubt aspects of currency strategy that I have missed out. For instance, I did not have a chapter specifically dedicated to the emerging markets and how emerging market currency dynamics are specific and different from their developed market counterparts. Rather than separate the book in that way, I did attempt to outline the emerging market angle in each chapter as a more practical way of demonstrating how the emerging markets are different in a number of important ways. Equally, some currency strategists run their forecasts in the form of a model currency portfolio. For leveraged funds, this is a particularly useful benchmark of performance. It would have been useful and interesting to look at the trend in the currency market towards fewer currencies, and whether or not that is a positive trend. Finally, it might have been instructive to look at structured products for the purpose of hedging currency risk. Space and time have unfortunately meant that such issues will have to wait until a second edition of this book. That said, such constraints notwithstanding, I hope the reader feels that the book has examined the topic of currency strategy, if not exhaustively, then certainly in sufficient scope and detail to be able to make a measurable difference to their bottom line. Talk is cheap. The point of this book is to make a difference to the total or relative returns of investors and speculators, and in terms of reducing hedging costs and boosting the profitability of corporate Treasury operations. It is my sincere hope that it has gone some way to achieving this aim.

Conclusion

There is no getting away from it — currency forecasting let alone hedging, investing or trading remains a tricky business. To the uninformed, such activity represents little more than tossing a coin. If I have succeeded at all in this book, then I hope to have shown that it is significantly more complex and sophisticated a process than that.

Economic theory, despite the intellectual weight of many of the great theorists of our time, has struggled in its ability to model and successfully predict short- or medium-term currency moves on a consistent basis. In reaction, some have taken the easy way out by relapsing into the excuse that short-term exchange rate moves obey a random walk and therefore cannot be predicted. To me, this is nothing more than the reaction of those who do not actually know the answer to the puzzle of predicting exchange rates, but are afraid to admit it. Indeed, the very success of such analytical disciplines as flow and technical analysis suggests serious flaws, both in the idea of exchange rates obeying a random walk and in the idea of markets being perfectly efficient. Both capital flow analysis and "charting" have added significantly to the profession of currency strategy, not least in its ability to deliver results — and herein lies the key. The arguments against the likes of flow and technical analysis are usually emotionally — or ideologically — rather than empirically based. No-one has actually proven that flow or technical analysis do not work, and what empirical evidence we have in fact suggests that they do work and frequently on a more consistent basis than traditional exchange rate models.

The focus of the currency strategist, and in turn the currency market practitioner, should be purely practical. This is a business and a business has to achieve measurable results. If that business is to succeed, its results have to outperform consistently. While there are no guarantees — and certainly not with regard to exchange rates — adopting an integrated approach to currency analysis, incorporating currency economics, flow analysis, technical analysis and long-term valuation based on traditional exchange rate models, gives you the best chance of achieving that outperformance. At the end of the day, currency strategists do not have the luxury of just giving a view. Your "P&L" is measured in terms of your reputation, and that in turn is a direct function of the performance of your views over time. That is exactly how it should be. For corporate Treasurers or for asset managers or currency speculators, they are not putting theoretical money on the line. On the very first day I joined the bank in 1998 as the Asian crisis continued to flare, I was asked by the Finance Director of a multinational corporation whether they should hedge their exposure to the Hong Kong dollar and would the peg "go"? My answer was equivocal, not because I am the sort to usually give equivocal answers but rather because there were two questions involved! On the first, I said that the competitive depreciation of Asian currencies against the Hong Kong dollar meant that the risk premium embedded in Hong Kong dollar forward prices would most likely rise and potentially substantially. On the second, I said that the peg would remain in place because of the solid foundations of Hong Kong's currency board system and the determination of the Hong Kong Monetary Authority to keep it in place. Nowadays, this might seem like stating the obvious, but at the time there was real fear in the market that Hong Kong's "peg" might break, as was the case for Asian currency pegs during the Asian currency crisis. I mention this example neither for the purpose of 20/20 hindsight nor to "look good". Rather, I have included it to show the stakes involved. Of course, the Finance Director will have had his own informed view of the risks involved in the corporation's specific exposure to the Hong Kong dollar. At the time, he most likely wanted an outsider's view, either to confirm or to question his own view. That outsider's view of the currency strategist makes a difference to the end result. If it didn't, professional currency market practitioners would not waste their valuable time.

For both corporations and investors, the exchange rate remains a crucial consideration within foreign or overseas investment. At some point, when the world has but one currency, this will not be the case, but until that happy(?) day, it remains so. The techniques used today, not just to give an exchange rate view but more specifically to analyse and hedge a corporation's balance sheet risk or for that matter to help a currency overlay manager to add alpha, have grown significantly in terms of complexity and sophistication in the past few years. Furthermore, what currency instruments were only recently deemed as complex within the developed markets are now seen as plain vanilla relative to the increasingly tailored needs of currency market practitioners — and moreover are increasingly being demanded by local market participants within the emerging markets.

It was said at the outset and it has to be repeated here that there is no such thing as objectivity, certainly not where human beings are concerned. This book is the result of my knowledge and experience, for good or ill, and therefore it is naturally skewed in a particular direction. That direction, that bias has stemmed from the view that there has been a gaping hole in the analysis of the currency markets, a hole which this book attempts to fill. More specifically, having long been fascinated by the subject of the currency markets, I have wanted to read a book which went beyond the traditional exchange rate models, both for the purpose of examining how the currency market practitioners themselves deal with currency risk and moreover to have the temerity to suggest to currency market practitioners a more integrated and rigorous way of doing so. In short, I could not find anything out there that was actually aimed at currency market practitioners themselves, so I decided to write such a book myself.

This is not to say the book is complete. Frankly, practically any book that is focused on financial market analysis, however seemingly exhaustive, is likely in practice to be incomplete. Space and time simply do not allow for all aspects to be covered. For instance, I would have liked to have dealt in more detail with such issues as how corporations can use investor-based tools such as a risk appetite indicator or such techniques as the differential or trend-following strategies to time tactical and strategic hedging. Equally, it might have been instructive to look at how currency speculators take advantage of perceived inefficiencies in options markets through non-directional or "non-linear" trading strategies. Finally, ahead of EU accession in 2004 or 2005 by a number of countries within Central and Eastern Europe, it might have been interesting to look at the issue of asset manager hedging of currency risk. Assuming that the magnetic pull relating to EU convergence continues to increase, should asset managers consider hedging currency risk at all? As the reader can see, when you enter a field such as currency analysis and strategy, there is no discernible end in sight. Subjects such as these must, given the practical considerations of space and time, be left to the prospect of a second edition of this book.

To conclude, the "problem" with trying to analyse, forecast, hedge, trade and invest in the currency markets is that currencies are affected by so many factors simultaneously — and to complicate matters further the importance of those factors may change over time — so it is difficult to tell the combined impact of the sum of these factors. To date, none of the traditional exchange rate models have been able to incorporate all of the possible factors that might impact exchange rates to the extent that they are then able to predict exchange rates on a consistent basis over a short-term time horizon. Given the number of possible factors involved, this is hardly surprising. The changeability of the importance of these factors is a further complication. For instance, in 2001 a key factor affecting exchange rates was foreign direct investment or FDI. Indeed, in 2001 the top three currencies in the world against the US dollar — the Mexican peso, Peruvian sol and Polish zloty — were all the recipient of major FDI inflows which offset their current account deficits and thus gave them a basic balance surplus. Within the developed markets, FDI inflows have played an important though changing role in the performance of the US dollar. In 2000, the US was the recipient of huge FDI inflows, which in turn was seen as a major contributing factor for US dollar strength. FDI inflows slowed sharply in 2001, causing the market to anticipate that the US dollar would fall sharply. It did not happen. While admittedly it did not hit new highs against its major counterparts, the US dollar remained relatively strong as the shortfall in FDI inflows was made up for by portfolio inflows, which in turn helped finance the current account deficit. The danger in setting rules about how capital should flow to countries with the highest nominal or real interest rates was also apparent in 2001. In that year, the Federal Reserve cut interest rates 11 times, bringing the Federal funds' target rate down from 6.50% to 1.75%, while the European Central Bank only cut its refinancing rate from 4.50% to 3.25%. In other words, the difference between the Fed funds rate and the ECB's refinancing rate went from +200 to −150 bp. Despite that, the Euro was still unable to rally on a sustained basis. Relative growth patterns, which at times have been a key driver of the Euro–dollar exchange rate, were also not the main answer. In late 2000 and 2001, US industrial production contracted for the longest consecutive period since July 1932, or the Great Depression. In the end, the market came to the view that financial markets rewarded aggressive growth-oriented monetary policy, such as that adopted by the Federal Reserve, in the form of portfolio inflows. All that one can say about this is that such market favouritism has not always been the case in the past and is unlikely to always be the case going forward. Indeed, in the future, there may well be other factors that surpass this in terms of their impact on the exchange rate.

The discipline of trying to analyse and forecast exchange rates continues to require great flexibility. If any exchange rate model were able to successfully incorporate all major factors to produce consistently accurate exchange rate forecasts, it would surely be worthy of the Nobel Prize for Economics. For now, the best answer for currency market practitioners remains to adopt an integrated approach to currency analysis and strategy, involving the four disciplines of currency economics, flow analysis, technical analysis and long-term valuation based on the traditional exchange rate models.

Finally, it should not be forgotten that, despite the increase in global trade flows and the even greater increase in portfolio capital flows over the last two decades, the currency market is essentially speculative in nature, that is to say a majority of currency market practitioners are "speculators", trading currencies without any underlying, attached asset. In trying to forecast exchange rates, the forecaster is effectively trying to predict the sum of the intentions, views and trading styles of all such currency market practitioners, which is why such disciplines as flow analysis, technical analysis and behavioural finance — or the psychology of the market — come in particularly handy. Newspapers and newswires frequently describe market movement in emotionally laden terms such as "panic", "sentiment" and "market psychology". At the end of the day, currency market participants are human beings. They act or react according to their own views, their own biases, and their own "skews". Just as information is not perfect, so the way information is interpreted is often skewed one way or another. The field of behavioural finance has done much generally to illuminate the psychological aspects of financial market activity and more specifically to demonstrate the kinds of mistakes that market participants tend to make on a consistent basis. Active currency market participants would do well to learn and remember these for the purpose of avoiding them in future. Market "sentiment" can be a powerful thing. It can continue and extend far beyond any fundamental valuation, and of course the longer it does that the more powerful the snap back when it eventually comes.

In the end, it comes down to that most economic of concepts, incentive. Speculators, who make up the majority of the currency market, trade for the most part for the purpose of capital or directional gain rather than income. The incentive of the interbank dealer is that of a surfer, to ride the waves of liquidity that ebb and flow in the market, for the most part offsetting client flows, sometimes taking positions either in their favour or against them. Split-second timing and reactions are needed, and mistakes are punished. Equally, traders need to trade in order to make a living, even in the absence of fundamental changes in the economy. *De facto*, at those times when there is no fundamental change, they have to rely on other types of analysis to explain and forecast price action. It is no coincidence that technical analysis has so deeply penetrated the interbank dealing community. That is not to say interbank dealers ignore fundamentals. Rather, it is to say that their job requires they look at more than just fundamentals and specifically those types of analysis that might be better suited to short-term exchange rate movement. In short, the people who devise these exchange rate models should spend time on a dealing floor before they finish their work.

Lastly, a key aspect of this book is that I have attempted to be much more user friendly than the works on currency markets that I have been used to. These days, it is not enough to trot out theory and leave it to the client to extrapolate some practical meaning. Anyone can do that. It does not add value. Instead, as noted above, through this book I have tried to bridge the gap between economic theory and market practice. It is my hope therefore that the people who really matter, the practitioners of the currency markets, be they corporate Treasurers, investors or speculators, will have benefited in a measurable and practical way by the experience in managing their own respective currency risks. It is this aspect in particular which I hope has differentiated this book from the vast majority of books and research papers on the subject of exchange rates.

Index